Power and responsibility in health care

The National Health Service as a political institution

W.J.M. MACKENZIE

Published by the Oxford University Press
for the Nuffield Provincial Hospitals Trust

Published for the Nuffield Provincial Hospitals Trust
3 Prince Albert Road, London NW1 7SP by the
Oxford University Press, Walton Street, Oxford OX2 6DP

Oxford London Glasgow
New York Toronto Melbourne Wellington
Ibadan Nairobi Dar es Salaam Lusaka Cape Town
Kuala Lumpur Singapore Jakarta Hong Kong Tokyo
Delhi Bombay Calcutta Madras Karachi

ISBN 0 19 721222 0

© The Nuffield Provincial Hospitals Trust 1979

Designed by Bernard Crossland
Printed in Great Britain by
Burgess & Son (Abingdon) Ltd,
Station Road, Abingdon, Oxfordshire

Medicine is a social science
and politics nothing else but
medicine on a large scale.

RUDOLF VIRCHOW (1821–1902)

(Quoted by the late Henry Miller,
Medicine and Society, 1953)

CONTENTS

FOREWORD

GORDON McLACHLAN

The nature of illness and its consequential effects are such that some aspect of health care is never far away from the thoughts and experience of most people. This is especially the case today, when recent events have raised concern about the apparent drift of the NHS from the idealistic goals of thirty years ago. The subject is a sensitive one, likely to be for special debate after the Royal Commission on the NHS has reported, for there is a disposition on the part of many of the multitude of interests involved in the realities of that imaginative concept to await that event before taking their several stances about future directions.

Professor Mackenzie's book is an important contribution, possibly unique to the general debate, for despite the author's diffidence in describing it as 'primarily a conceptual and analytical study rather than a practical one', by discussing certain key questions from the point of view of a political scientist, he illuminates as never before the contradictions and mythologies of an institution which has a special niche in British social history and in which there is an almost inordinate pride among the population at large.

The fact that the NHS as a great social institution seems to be at an important crossroads makes it appropriate now for scholars to examine coolly the assumptions on which it was founded and shaped as part of the political process. Professor Mackenzie illustrates the essential complexity of the simple concept of the NHS, and raises fundamental questions about the realities of power and accountability which one hopes the Royal Commission has deliberated upon. Indeed, without such consideration there is bound to be some blurring of issues affecting the recommendations the Commissioners are likely to make, for the analysis shows the almost insuperable difficulties involved in the relationships between the political (in the widest sense), professional, and supportive groupings within the existing pattern of a Service, about which public and individual expectations are perhaps higher than is sensible. That the NHS has a special character and is not analogous to any large-scale organization in either the public or the private sectors is beyond doubt and the series of compromises on which it was founded and has developed to meet the aspirations of the diverse elements of society who need it—and who operate it—ought to be reassessed. It was the first public institution of any size concerned with a welfare service universally available in which a different kind of democracy from that traditionally understood was introduced by a form of direct delegation from a Minister to chosen individuals representing a wide sweep of special and professional interests, but because of an intricate consultation process, where several interrelating responsibilities were left vague. What this departure from traditional democratic modes means and how it has fared is but part of the problem as we see it now of integrating power and responsibility. In this respect it is interesting to relate Professor Mackenzie's observations to the political agonies about the implications of this change in democratic practice suffered by the founders of the NHS in more idealistic but less sophisticated times.

ACKNOWLEDGEMENTS

My thanks are due to all those at the Nuffield Provincial Hospitals Trust, and in Glasgow University who instigated and promoted this enterprise; and in particular to Fanny Mitchell and Barbara Stocking who helped to sustain my often flagging morale.

But I alone am responsible for prejudices, errors, and omissions.

W.J.M.M.

Glasgow
December 1978

CHAPTER 1 INTRODUCTION

The present study involves two related projects. It is concerned on the one hand with the elucidation of two basic concepts in political science, the concepts of power and of responsibility. These are both what Professor Gallie has called 'essentially contested concepts' (1); that is to say, we are all occupied with them and concerned about them, even in simple matters of everyday life, yet they are hard to pin down and apply accurately, and they remain ambiguous and debatable, rhetorical rather than scientific, even after centuries of intellectual analysis. Their usage and definitions cannot be finally settled; at best they can be classified and illuminated by application in different contexts.

One traditional example is that of the power and responsibility of doctors and of others concerned with health care.

On the other hand, one must ask whether these concepts cast any light on the special problems of the field to which they are applied. A great deal of important work has been done in the fields of health care economics and health care sociology and this book owes much to it. But I know of only one book which deals with *health care politics* in the present sense, and that is by an American (2). It is true that much has been written about the management of the National Health Service by distinguished students of public administration, who are well aware of its public character and of the special problems which this entails. But there has been no attempt to place these in the context of political science as a tradition and as a discipline.

This is therefore primarily a conceptual and analytical study, rather than a practical one. It is directed towards the

Notes and references for this chapter begin on page 189.

understanding of the NHS as seen from one point of view, not towards recommendations for change, nor towards comprehensive description. It does not attempt to do the work of a Royal Commission, as proposer of improvements; nor does it do the work of a text-book writer. It is to be hoped that I have got the facts right, with no more than the usual proportion of human error and ignorance, but I have not tried to produce either a text-book or a work of reference. Some very good ones are already available.

But I was aware from the outset of the dangers of this kind of exercise. One of them is that one may become locked into one's own conceptual framework, bored by it and in the end disillusioned; if one thinks too much about a word it loses all meaning. Another danger is that one may lose the sense of close relationship between word and thing at the level of the common everyday experience of ordinary people.

Therefore, at an early stage I discussed with my Glasgow colleague Mrs Fanny Mitchell and with various advisers the possibility of running a minor empirical study in parallel with my conceptual study; and in the end we settled for a small piece of research on decisions and communication in dermatology (3)—from patient to GP, from GP to consultant, from consultant to hospital bed—based on sample studies in Glasgow and in Oxford. This is Mrs Mitchell's project, conducted independently and not (I hope) influenced by my work in progress. But it has undoubtedly influenced me (partly because I have been a skin patient myself) more than can be justified by strict canons of method, in that my working models of health and ill-health, patient and doctor, have been tested partly against the experience of 'skins'—and skins are peculiar.

They are peculiar in at least five respects.

1. 'Skin troubles' seem to be as universal as the common cold, from infancy to old age, and (like a cold) they continually pose the question 'What should I do about it?'

2. As with the common cold, there is a strong impulse towards self-care, and this supports a large industry with a wide spectrum graded from respectable old remedies, through traditional 'patent medicines', to the disreputable fringes of the cosmetic trade. I have not found any reference to this by economists, but clearly 'care of the skin' is big business.

3. A consequence of this situation is that sufferers do not think of troubling a doctor except in the last resort. But doctors can do more for skin trouble than they can for the common cold. There are drugs available only on prescription which clear up familiar ailments quickly; and there are dangerous possibilities implicit in ailments that do not cure themselves. The only killer, it seems, is malignant melanoma, which is said to be on the increase, perhaps because of ultra-violet light on the fair skins of northern sun-bathers. But there are disastrous chronic conditions, such as rodent ulcer and psoriasis, and there are tormenting conditions such as various forms of pruritic itch. Skins can turn nasty.

4. They pose in an awkward way two questions about the limits of medical care. One of them is that of the relation between medical and psychological; some conditions have to be defined as 'psychosomatic' or 'due to stress', words which give very little useful information. The other is that social consequences may be more important to the sufferer than are the physical symptoms in themselves. The commonest example is that of acne and the self-consciousness of young people; but there are many other examples relevant to the situations which the sociologist Erving Goffman has described in his books on *Stigma* (4), and on *The Presentation of Self in Everyday Life* (5). To take an example to which I return later, one of the main concerns of the Psoriasis Association (there are said to be about one million sufferers in the UK) is to educate the general public about the condition, which is unsightly but not infectious. But there are very few of us who are not in some way blemished or stigmatized.

5. Finally, the case of dermatology illustrates in an extreme way some of the difficulties of measuring costs and benefits in the health service. It is possible, at least conceptually, to measure the cost of the dermatology services provided by consultants, hospitals, and GPs. It is also possible to find out by sample survey and from aggregate data the number of working days lost through absence due to skin disease. But there is no means of putting value on the discomforts of young and old, who are not wage-earners in the community. Nor is it possible to see how to place a value on the physical discomfort and the social stigma which reduce the quality of life for sufferers.

Will I therefore distort the argument in so far as I use models based on dermatology? I hope not. Skins are indeed peculiar, but so are most other fields of medical specialization, each of which has its own special 'mix' of the five elements described: delay in consultation, the scope for self-care, a wide range of possible outcomes, a psychological and social element, and an ambiguity about real costs and real benefits. I hope I have used the case of skins (along with much other material) to illustrate the complexity and range of differences rather than to impose a pattern.

Another factor which may distort the image is that I have lived for the last twelve years in Scotland where things are the same, and yet not the same. The statutes and regulations of the NHS in Scotland do not differ very much from those in the rest of the UK; but the geographical and social setting is quite distinct from those in England and in Wales. In particular, there is nothing comparable to the concentration in London of teaching hospitals, of students, of professional private practice, of pay-beds, of private hospitals. But much less research has been published about the NHS in Scotland than about the NHS in England; and in consequence my printed sources are largely English, though my recent experience is Scottish. But I had thirty years in England and throughout that period I maintained an interest in the NHS, both as student and as patient. So I hope this mixture of experience has done no serious harm (6).

CHAPTER 2 POWER AND RESPONSIBILITY

Thereafter he launched into a philosophical discussion on the nature of political power. If there was to be a national health service at all, power to administer it must reside somewhere. No Parliament could surrender that power to the profession. It might be dispersed among many bodies, notably the local authorities. Did the doctors want that? It was better in their interests, no less than in the nation's, that everyone should know and see who wielded the authority. . . . The open exercise of power, the banishment of all surreptitious manipulations, was what he meant by democracy.

NYE BEVAN to the BMA Negotiating Committee, December 1946
MICHAEL FOOT (1973), *Aneurin Bevan: A Biography,* vol. ii
(London: Davis-Poynter)

The problems raised by these two words are complex, and cannot be discussed at length here. But readers not formally trained as students of politics deserve some brief explanation.

The word 'power', as used in this context, means the capability to affect people, to change the paths of their lives. No one doubts that such power exists, and that some people are more powerful than others. Likewise, no one doubts that pure power, exercised for its own sake, is bad. In a sense, we should all like to be more powerful than we are, so that we can (as it were) clear a space around ourselves in which we can move freely and without dependence on others. Others feel the same, and therefore the boundaries of our power conflict. How are such conflicts to be resolved without leading to mutual destruction, such as threatened Vietnam and now threatens Rhodesia and Lebanon?

One answer would be to amass overwhelming force and to eliminate all competitors. This is not practicable, and if it were practicable it would be wicked. It is not practicable because such overwhelming power can in practice be exercised only by raising a 'force' or 'posse' of adherents. One can perhaps postulate a science fiction model of the man who has his finger on the trigger of the ultimate weapon and can demonstrate its

Notes and references for this chapter begin on page 189.

effects, single-handed and without scruple. But even an H-bomb silo requires many participants; those who built it, those who maintain it, and those who police the surrounding countryside. There is a quotation well known to political scientists:

> The Soldan of Egypt, or the Emperor of Rome, might drive his harmless subjects, like brute beasts, against their sentiments and inclination. But he must at least have led his *mamelukes* or *praetorian bands*, like men by their opinion ... It is therefore on opinion only that government is founded (1).

One can think of exceptions only by postulating small enclosed societies; the drunken father ruling by his fists, the shrewish mother ruling by her tongue. Even they must sleep, and they take the risk that in the end they will be murdered or will be deserted. But for all ordinary situations power rests not only on force but also on opinion. To apply another famous old quotation: 'Will not force is the basis of the State' (2).

To put it almost as succinctly, 'power to be effective must be legitimated within a system'. This introduces two further concepts, 'legitimation' and 'system'.

'Legitimate power' would, I think, generally be described by the word 'authority', though that also may be ambiguous. Authority may be legal authority, conveyed formally by the laws of the state; or it may be customary or moral authority conferred by a consensus of opinion within the sphere of action of the power in question. 'Opinion' may grow out of debate at any level of the system, and talk at various levels varies greatly in range, rigour, and sophistication. Perhaps, in the present state of the language, the contrast most frequently is that between responsible and irresponsible exercise of power.

The word 'responsible' meant at first no more than 'answerable', but it has acquired quite a wide range of ambiguities in the course of usage. One can begin with the simple usage: 'answerable to someone, for something'. A is required to answer to enquiries made by B, under threat of penalties for silence, for false answers, and for answers that contradict B's policy and instructions. The simplest form of organization theory, for instance, that embodied in the NHS Grey Book of 1973 (3), postulates that the efforts of many people can be harnessed and unified by a hierarchical system of division of labour. Each individual is given a prescribed field of activity corresponding to his (or her) known and certified capabilities, and for that field he is responsible to a defined and known superior, who is similarly placed in a hierarchy of functions. As the centurion says in St Matthew's gospel (expressing the self-image of the Roman Imperial Army):

I am a man under authority, having soldiers under me: and I say to this man, Go, and he goeth; and to another, Come, and he cometh; and to my servant, Do this, and he doeth it (4).

Power is legitimated by responsibility; 'this is my job, I am doing it under authority' (5).

But the word 'responsible' is so favourable a word that people use it rhetorically to recommend various other forms of 'responsibility' which are not the same.

One of these is political and constitutional. Our system of government would be described formally as 'representative and responsible' government, not merely as 'democratic' government; and it would include both the 'collective responsibility' of the Cabinet and the 'individual responsibility' of each Minister for his department. Political scientists attempt to disentangle what these words mean (6). They do not seem to be meaningless (by comparison we can disentangle differences between, say, US President and British Cabinet in the scope and form of 'responsibility'), but it is very hard to define their meaning except in terms of specific historical happenings, such as the fall of Nixon in 1974, the responsibility of Chamberlain for Munich in 1938, of Eden for Suez in 1956.

Luckily we do not have to face these issues here. But the language of health care continually uses the words 'responsible' and 'irresponsible' in a different and difficult sense. 'Professional people act in a responsible way'; 'young people are often irresponsible'. Doctors and nurses are annoyed if patients act 'irresponsibly'. Similarly, at the national level, in the autumn of 1978, we are involved in a period of mutual abuse about wage settlements and the control of inflation. Who is acting 'irresponsibly'—government, trade unions, employers, unofficial strikers?

Are the words to be construed simply as expressions of emotion, 'hurrah-words' and 'boo-words'? There is some evidence for that view; professionals use them against those not bound by professional solidarity and a professional ethic. Tired GPs use them against exasperating patients; the old use them against the young, as a term of abuse rather milder than the term 'vandal'.

And in general a 'responsible person' is a good sort of person; 'mature' might be an equally vague synonym.

The original sense of 'answerable' seems to survive only in that a 'mature and responsible' person is answerable primarily to himself/herself, to a conscience or identity or self-image, to all that constitutes a person.

This overlaps with the sense of professional identity; that a responsible person does not let colleagues down and does not let clients or patients down. He/she acts out the norms of the profession to which he/she 'belongs', to which he/she owes all or much of his/her social being.

And perhaps there is also a time dimension; the irresponsible person lives and acts discontinuously from moment to moment, blown to and fro by whims and fancies. The responsible person looks ahead, thinks out implications and acts with reasonable consistency towards a goal not immediately present.

And perhaps also the responsible person is guided by an image of the world which contains other real people besides himself. He/she is not responsible primarily to any institutional boss, but responsibility is mutual; we are interdependent, the responsible person is aware of mutuality and makes it a guiding principle (7) (8) (9).

These are not problems that I hope to resolve; but I hope the point is made, that there is a language of debate about power and responsibility which is common to the health service and to the larger political system in which it is encapsulated.

That raises my last conceptual point, the notion of 'system'. It is a valuable word, and also a treacherous one, in that it allows us to invoke metaphors and analogies from 'systems', which are studied more rigorously than we can hope to study the political system; biological, cybernetic, ecological, meteorological, atomic, and so on. It is doubtful whether science could maintain its grip on the world without the concept of open system, of interaction between parts within a boundary which is permeable. We are committed to the study of the economic system, of social systems; surely political systems have equal rights to recognition?

There are two snags. One of them is that one can visualize a system most easily in terms of physical boundaries on the ground, or within a skin or membrane, or in terms of enumerated individual members. Whereas one must define the health care system including all of us within the boundaries of the UK in so far as we are motivated and act from a concern for health and health care. That 'in so far as' is difficult, and I have no idea how it could be measured or 'operationalized'.

The other difficulty is that the whole thing rests on law, in particular on the statutes of the Parliament of the UK. Law defines membership of the UK political system for each of us, and that includes permanent immigrants and resident aliens. It also defines a great deal (by no means all) of the network of rights and obligations which constitute the NHS.

These are both formidable difficulties conceptually; but it has become a tradition that one can make progress by assuming that a distinguishable system exists and by framing hypotheses on that basis. My major hypothesis is that much can be learnt about the NHS if one treats it as a political system, a system of power and responsibility; a system within a greater system, that of the politics of the UK.

In the next chapter, therefore, I attempt to face the problem of defining the boundaries of the system for the purpose of further exploration. It would be very convenient if we could get agreement about this, and the chapter owes a great deal to parallel discussions among health economists and sociologists of medicine. But in the last resort we must each define boundaries for ourselves, in relation to our own explorations.

For my purpose I accept the argument of some health economists, that the boundary must be defined in terms of care by qualified persons, a precise legal specification, and not in terms of health and ill-health, words that live on the lips of men, in ordinary speech, but baffle exact definition.

There then follow three chapters concerned with actors within the system of medical care; the patient, the doctor, and the nurse. In each category I try to adopt an action schema, not merely a behavioural one. That is to say, I try to report on the actors as very diverse and strongly-marked individuals, who can speak and be understood. Such is the character of human speech and writing that they are a prime source of understanding and of misunderstanding too. I have no desire to pick a quarrel here with Professor B. F. Skinner and others, who stake everything on rigorous observations of behaviour; and I am quite well aware of the risks involved in taking seriously the actors' explanations of their own actions. But this is that sort of book (10).

Then there are two chapters (7 and 9) which deal with arenas of action, rather than with actors; the hospital and the government. But these chapters serve also to introduce other actors who have speaking parts, such as the para-medics, the domestic staff, the technicians, the craftsmen, the union officials, the administrators.

Also, I introduce here, in Chapter 8, the necessary concept of a human system as a store of information and a network of communications. This introduces yet another slippery metaphor, that of *the nerves of government* (11); the model is difficult to use accurately, but without it the concept of a purposive human system must collapse.

The last chapter does not include reasoned conclusions and recommendations. I have simply tried to stand back from the NHS and to understand it, in terms of my own training and experience. By limiting my scope I feel that I have gained understanding. I am less certain that this understanding can be shared.

CHAPTER 3 HEALTH, CARE, DEMAND, NEED

In the last few years there has been much discussion of the semantics of health care, caused partly by the entry of trained social scientists into the debate about the NHS.

The service at the time of its creation was dedicated to the concept of need; 'to each according to his need'. A human being *qua* human being has a right to equal treatment of his or her needs, irrespective of his or her resources. It was realized in the 1950s that needs were in principle inexhaustible, and that the concept of need could not be separated from the concept of cost. Cost has two aspects: costs to the nation, and costs to the individual. The cost to the nation might be mitigated by the fact that

> The National Health Service is a wealth producing as well as a health producing service. In so far as it improves the health and efficiency of the working population, money spent on the National Health Service may properly be regarded as productive (1) even in the narrowly economic sense of the term.

The implied accounting for profit and loss is very hard to work out, but at least it adds a pragmatic justification for public spending to the ideological justification on the basis of human needs and rights.

The cost to the individual patient requires even more sophisticated analysis. In economic theory, need is expressed by demand, but it is also constricted, in that demand is related to supply by the mediation of price. Since the 1950s and later there has been a series of complex devices for controlling, or at least mitigating, demand by imposing prices, as for instance on prescriptions, dental work, spectacles. The cash value to the service is relatively low (about $3\frac{1}{2}$ per cent in 1976–7) (2), and the effect of these prices on demand has never been convincingly measured. But money costs are not the only sort of costs imposed by the service in individual patients. One of the costs is the cost of queuing (3); an exact match of provision and demand is impossible in any large-scale operation, and in consequence there arise waiting lists for health services just as they arise (for instance) for local authority housing. As with housing, the length of queue varies for different services in different areas of the country, but the total national waiting list for hospital in-patient services has remained pretty constant at about 500,000 in relation to an annual turnover of about $5\frac{1}{4}$ million in-patient cases. Not a very long queue in the circumstances? But queuing is itself a cost for a patient suffering from an operable condition, such as hernia or varicose veins: queuing is a deterrent, and some customers look at the length of the queue and then drop out; others pay the cost in cash by leaving the public sector for the private sector.

In addition, each consultant or group of consultants applies priority rules (not always explicit) based on an individual assessment of medical and social need: that is to say the doctors in the end settle priorities for their own services—an example of the power and responsibility of doctors. There is no reason to believe that such power is enjoyable: and certainly there is no one who would like to take it over by introducing lay judges or by centralizing the system.

These paragraphs illustrate the difficulties faced by the Guillebaud Committee in defining a standard of 'adequacy' for the NHS.

> We conclude that in the absence of an objective and attainable standard of adequacy the aim must be, as in the field of education, to provide the best service possible within the limits of the available resources. . . . The development of the National Health Service is one among many public tasks in which objectives and standards must be realistically set and adjusted as time goes on both to means and to needs (para 98).

Twenty years later the position has not changed. The allocation of resources is still determined pragmatically, within the

NHS and between the NHS and other services within the sphere of action of 'the government'. It is an open question whether the academic debate about semantics has improved practice; but it has at least cleared our minds and defined the points at issue.

Let us start then with Health with a big H, *mens sana in corpore sano* (4), that great maxim of the Victorian public schools.

Most discussions begin with the famous WHO definition 'A state of complete physical and mental and social well-being' (5). I have not enquired about the history of its drafting, and I do not myself wish to argue against Utopias in general. But this one is universally condemned because it gives no hold on reality: to seek perfect health is to seek to be like gods. Compare Katharine Mansfield's definition (6):

> By health I mean the power to live a full, adult, living, breathing life in close contact with what I love—the earth and the wonders thereof—the sea—the sun. . . . *I want to be all that I am capable of becoming*, so that I may be—there's only one phrase that will do—*a child of the sun* (author's punctuation and italics).

Both definitions remind me of Aristotle's comprehensive definition of 'The Good of Man' as 'a working of the Soul in the way of the best and most perfect Excellence, in a complete life' (7).

If, to follow a very different trend in philosophy, we seek not the meaning but the use—if we try naive semantics with the help of the big dictionaries we can risk various findings. Health is one of a family of words—well, ill, illness, sickness, strength, weakness, normal, out of order, out of sorts, and so on—and I am inclined to say that all or most of them function socially in three ways which are at first sight quite distinct.

First, they are universally a basis for quite formal social greetings, presumably because they open up (like English weather) a topic in which it is assumed that we all share an interest.

Secondly, there is a very widespread philosophical use, perhaps Pythagorean and Platonic in origin, involved in the debate about what is the right way to live; sometimes by metaphor as between soul and body, sometimes by asserting the absolute identity of soul and body.

Thirdly, there is the practical use, in which there is a specific reference to the question of 'what is wrong with me?', a sentiment of unease. The question still asks for a subjective answer; but it is feeling its way towards interpersonal statement about what is wrong and what must be done to correct it.

I do not criticize these ambiguities; on the contrary, I appreciate their importance in the complex tissue of human thought and language. But they make it hard to use this family of words with clarity in specific enquiry, as distinct from social intercourse.

There is a *prima facie* case for excluding entirely from our discourse the idea of positive health.

Nevertheless, the whole western world is publicly committed to the public provision of a commodity called 'health'. We cannot be left without a measure of success or failure, a measure of comparison. We can relegate positive health to the realm of mythology or Utopia; yet we act publicly in the name of health—we spend public money on it—and we cannot choose to remain in a state of Socratic ignorance and enquiry. There seem to be at present two routes of escape; that via negative definitions of health, and that via pluralistic or opportunistic health indicators. I do not wish to spend much time on this step in the argument, which is fairly obvious.

The *negative concept* is at its best when it is dealing with specific injuries externally inflicted, and perhaps Army doctors were the first to perform specific services recognized, honoured, and effective (8), like the physicians Machaon and Podaleirios with the Greek army before Troy some 3,000 years ago. Fine, but of course a wounded man may be either healthy or unhealthy in his general bodily state or *hexis*. It is not quite so happy when it is dealing with intruders invisible to the naked eye or the magnifying glass—invaders of the healthy human body. It is really in trouble when it seeks to operate in terms of these invisible conceptual intruders called diseases; there is no doubt that western man, like pre-literate Africans, conceptualizes ill-defined troubles in terms of unknown entities, and of their expulsion by something called cure. Diseases by definition exist to be cured, whereas wounds and fractures if kept clean and quiet heal themselves. But this is no place to digress into the argument between Hygiea and Asclepius (9), the harmony of man and environment, against the intervention of sophisticated technology. For my point it is enough to note that there are eloquent and persuasive arguments on both sides. Hygiea is at present fashionable among intellectuals; but Asclepius gets the cash.

The concept of *operational indicator* is closer to the ground, in that our choice of indicators is governed not only by conceptual insight but also by the availability of data. Let us measure what we *can* measure and let the rest go by. Hence the rag-bag character of the indicators that can be used and are used. I am only vaguely familiar with the area, but I have at hand no. 3 of the *OECD Social Indicator Development Programme* and I summarize some pages to suggest the relation between a 'plain language' statement and the indicators judged to be feasible statistically (the (1)–(8) headings) (10).

Development and proposals for indicators

Length of life

Indicator

1. Life expectancy at age 1 (20, 40, 60).
2. Perinatal mortality.

Healthfulness of life

3. Proportion of predicted future life to be spent in a state of disability. . . .

4. Proportion of persons disabled as a result of permanent impairment. . . .

Quality of health care

5. Maternal mortality.

Delivery of health care: physical accessibility

6. Average delay between emergency and treatment.

7. Average delay between awareness of functional disturbance (non-emergency) and treatment.

Economic accessibility

8. Disposable income of households in relation to full cost of health services, in relation to health insurance.

Finally, there is Talcott Parsons' concept of 'the sick role', a bold attempt to substitute for 'scientific' concepts of health and disease a sociological concept of sickness and the sick person. The point is that to define someone as sick expresses no medical opinion about disease or cure, what it does is to define a social role (or status?) which releases the sick person from old obligations (for instance to struggle to do a normal day's work) but imposes new ones on the sick person (for instance, to do his best to get well) and on those immediately concerned (11).

This is an important topic in medical sociology; to my mind it concerns the politics of medical care only to the extent that official medicine is licensed to legitimate the sick role, in so far as it has legal consequences in such spheres as pension rights, sickness benefit, civil claims for damages.

I apologise for these abstract arguments, but now I come to the point I need as a ground for closing my political system for purposes of analysis.

There are thus great difficulties about all general definitions of health—positive, negative, and operational; the word seems to be too vague as a foundation for a system or for systematic analysis. The health economists (or some of them) have found a way round by offering a definition not of health but of health care. In A. J. Culyer's phrase, 'the commodity "health care" defined generically as the kinds of service provided by surgeons, physicians, nurses, hospitals, etc.' (12).

This is an institutional definition with which we are fairly safe. It might be safer to drop the weasel word 'health' and just call the system medical care or 'medicare' (without a specific US reference). What commodity it produces is obscure: but it is at least perfectly clear that this is an institution provided by law and staffed primarily by persons licensed to do certain actions. The law is difficult in detail: but the principles are simple. There are things which constitute a punishable offence if done by persons not licensed or in premises not officially inspected and approved. This is a minimum legal framework: in many countries there will be more detailed specification of people and places, as in National Health Service Acts, and usually there will also be provisions which on certain conditions give these licensed persons specific powers to make regulations for what the Germans (see Dubos, p. 16) call Sanitary Police (13).

But as with other formal institutions, the law of medicare is glossed by social structure and ideological structure; and it is at least partially closed in on itself, in that the licensed persons make the law that licenses them and have almost complete licence to admit new licensees to their body.

If we are converging towards that sort of definition, it suits me as political scientist very well, and from this I can develop the sort of analysis set out in Chapter 2. Medical care constitutes a system defined by law and encapsulated in the law of a state, the UK, which has relations with the law of other states, and also to an international institution, the World Health Organization. But this system or sub-system is not merely juridical; it is also a political, social, economic, and ideological system of a very complex kind.

But I require one further step. One of the earliest 'systemic' books on business management, *The Functions of the Executive* by Chester Barnard (14), insisted that the customers of a business should be treated for purposes of analysis as being within the system of the business. (Barnard was much influenced by discussions of biological systems at Harvard in the 1930s.) Similarly, as regards the system of medical care; I prefer to use the word 'constituents' rather than 'customers', but the principle is the same. Medical care has a constituency or perhaps two constituencies. One constituency consists of the public, as consumers and as financial providers; in them reside the demand and need for medical care, they are its representatives, towards them medical care has a relation of power and responsibility.

About the other constituency I am less certain; that of the (not necessarily unskilled) employees of the licensed persons and institutions. Recent events show us that we have stupidly neglected this aspect of the matter, particularly in hospitals. But there has not been much work done on the economic and social experience of ancillary workers in the health service, and on the growth of consciousness and organization among them. I simply do not know enough to risk generalization.

I therefore go straight to the problem of specifying demand and need for medical care.

One difficulty here is that of the difference between ordinary usage and the professional language of economists. One could pile up examples and images of the way people talk and think. 'Demand' is a rather ugly word; the fist thumping the table, the mob threatening violence, the angry workers on strike. 'We demand our rights' (after a week spent with two grandsons, I would now vary the language to include the 'demands' made by very young children). In the case of medicare one must qualify the image: one cannot get medicare, as one might get food, by looting the food stores. It is not a commodity that can be taken by force except in rather extravagant scenarios—kidnapping a doctor in order to attend the wounds of the chief bandit, with a gun at his head or with threats to his wife and family. So we substitute for the image of mob the image of a queue, or of a crowded surgery.

The concept of need is more complex. 'Demand' is subjective; one can demand something imaginary or unattainable, or superfluous, or even deadly to oneself (15). Such things one cannot 'need'; in easy cases one may get away with it—'I need a drink of water.' But in more serious cases, and especially in medicare, it is relevant to answer, 'Oh, no, you don't.' I am reminded of a naive young man of my acquaintance who had a very bad wrist and walked into a X-ray clinic saying 'I need an X-ray': to which the medical answer was, 'No, you don't; go away and get a note from your GP', 'But I have no GP', 'Then get one'. A need requires independent verification; in the present context that means verification by a licensed person; a need must be for something which is feasible, even if not immediately available; it involves adjudication on priorities—which is the greatest need?: and it raises questions of justice, fairness and rights.

In all this the health economists have been deeply involved because the word 'demand' has for them a fixed technical sense. That is stated very simply in two sentences by Alan Williams.

> In its simplest form demand constitutes one individual's ordering of his own priorities as he sees them, this ordering being constrained by the resources at his command. In the ordinary discourse of economics, the demand for medical

care would be taken to mean the amount that individuals are willing and able to pay for at some going price (16).

That in turn postulates a market, with certain defined characteristics, and effective demand or 'revealed preference' is known objectively not by asking the supposed demander but by observing his behaviour in the market.

But (as Alan Williams goes on to note) this does not work for a free health service such as the NHS; and in any event medicare is an odd sort of commodity, even when it must be bought. Health economics (indeed the whole economics of welfare) can only be reckoned as economics if it lives within the bounds of the demand concept; and it can only do so by complex re-definition.

Perhaps the concept of need can be adapted to fill the gap? Williams wrote in 1973 of the confusions of what he then dubbed 'needology', and he quotes what he and his colleagues wrote in 1972:

> . . . the word 'need' ought to be banished from discussion of public policy, partly because of its ambiguity but also because . . . the word is frequently used in . . . 'arbitrary' senses. . . . Indeed . . . in many public discussions it is difficult to tell, when someone says that 'society needs . . .', whether he means that *he* needs it, whether he means society ought to get it in *his* opinion, whether a *majority* of the members of society want it, or *all* of them want it. Nor is it clear whether it is 'needed' regardless of the cost to society (17).

But by 1976 Culyer had registered disagreement:

> Economists will be surprised at my conversion to the language of 'need'. At one time, indeed, I had quite convinced myself that the word was an incubus on the back of any serious student of the NHS or of health problems in general. I am now, however, equally convinced that, accepting the definition given it in this book, it is an indispensable and profoundly useful tool of both analysis and policy (18).

Curiously—perhaps rightly—he gives no single succinct definition of need, but instead marks off its characteristics.

> First, '. . . the need for health care is defined by reference to some third party's view as to what a particular individual or class of individuals *ought* to receive' (19).

> 'At the most general level, the shadow in the wings is you and me' (20).

> 'At more specific levels, the "shadow in the wings" may be a health service minister, or administrator, or a doctor, nurse, etc.' (21).

> And this specification raises two sets of questions.

> (1) '. . . which third parties should have their judgements legitimised in the health care system—the public, experts, economists, social workers, doctors, administrators, politicians? If each is to have a legitimate role in the defining of need, what is that role to be?' (22).

> (2) Secondly, need for health care is not absolute:

> '. . . the technical concept of need as the selection of an appropriate means towards a given end is not absolute' (23).

Nor is the need for health care ethically or normatively absolute. Man has many needs (thus defined) and all cannot be satisfied at once.

> Of necessity, this requires us to trade off one need against the other. Not only, therefore, *do* we do this trading off, but it is also logically inescapable and, ethically, completely legitimate (24).

Broadly I accept that argument: and I note that it enables Culyer to get into his stride as an economist operating as professional expert in the logic of choice. But he blanks off the fact that he is dealing with *social* choice not *individual* choice.

The argument also points the way towards political analysis of choice. The words 'responsibility' and 'power' are not stated, but are surely implied; and I like to equate them with the dual character of political analysis (25), stealing the words *praxis* and *process* from a very different author, Aaron Esterson, who in his turn borrows from Sartre:

> I am using the terms praxis and process after Sartre. Praxis refers to events that are the deeds of doers or groups of doers, or to the intended outcome of such deeds. It refers to the acts of an agent. Process refers to events as a pattern of events of which no doer or agent is the author. Thus, praxis expresses the intention of a person or group of persons, while process does not. Process in a system may be initiated by praxis, e.g. a blow to the head; but the pattern of events that follows the blow, the pattern of trauma or physiological change within the organism, is determined mechanistically. This pattern of change is one of process.
>
> The ordinary medical concept of illness is a concept of process. It refers to events occurring within the person, and affecting his organism according to the laws of natural science (26).

In this terminology my topic is praxis and process in the politics of the NHS; and I find a perfectly satisfactory launching pad in Culyer's exercise in needology.

Nevertheless, I do not propose to become a 'needologist', and (rather apologetically) I choose a different word to label the driving force of this particular system. The word is 'concern', and I want to start with the quite colloquial phrase, 'a concern about the health of some individual or individuals, self or others'. I do not wholly agree with the rest of David Robinson's book, *The Process of Becoming Ill* (27), but I found that the diaries kept for him by a few mothers gave exactly the picture I needed; I select one case, rather an extreme one, but the pattern is typical (Figure 1).

Concern, of course, is a Quaker word as well as a colloquial one; and if I understand it right, personal feelings of concern are within the Quaker system built up through Committees of Concern into some important forms of political action. I am glad that that implication is present in the word: but I am not trying, at least at this stage, to convert the word into a technical term. Nor do I want to break with those following A. F. Bentley, who understand politics as a system of interests. It is

Day	Symptom	Action taken	Comment
1	Nothing today		
2	Nothing today		
3	Nothing today		
4	J (girl 18 months) very cross teething K (girl 6) has a cold	Gave J. Aspirin bought some Woodward's teething medicine to try	H (Husband) and I very weary listening to J crying all day
5	J still cross		Getting on our nerves
6	I think I'm catching cold, chest very tight has a cough so have children	Rubbed children's chests with Vick, took some cough mixture	
7	Children have got bad colds, so have I J still cross		J's constant grizzling getting on our nerves think I'll see doctor
8	J must have had abscess in ear, found dry crustiness in her hair and over face. Knew she was cross for a reason. A (girl 4) has started passing watery liquid from bowels again. Cried for a solid 2 hours	Sent for Dr for A. Didn't come so am taking her to clinic tomorrow	Very tired from cleaning A's bottom all day. Something will have to be done about A. Would like to see specialist
9	A still same	Took A to clinic. Dr says it's all in her mind. Don't believe him	Think Dr should give A thorough exam to find out what's wrong
10	A still same K's cough worse	Kept changing A all day. She's very sore around back passage	Nerves on edge listening to A crying
11	Think K has touch of bronchitis, chest seems congested	Sent for medicine from Dr for baby K	A still crying all day getting on everybody's nerves
12	A seems worse today Baby still chesty might be teething	Sent for Dr again for A. He suggested specialist and X-ray on bowel. I am very GLAD	Very satisfied that application has been sent for appointment for specialist. Only wait now

Figure 1. *Extract from the J family health diary (build up to 'doing something')*

simply that the word 'interest' does not seem at home in the present context.

Three things then follow at this colloquial level:

First, there is a network of concern. The diaries quoted by David Robinson are written from the point of view of one person only, the wife and mother, and he rightly says somewhere that she is still the nodal point of our society, at least in families with young children. But she has some slighter concern for others outside the family; her own mother and father if they are alive; siblings and friends who have been close to her; even, perhaps, rather remotely, for others whom she imagines as experiencing the same problems. Conversely, others have concerns which overlap with hers; above all the husband and father; and then the reciprocals of her own lesser concerns. Theories of social networks are relevant here, but I have not explored this further than Elizabeth Bott's original presentation (28).

Second, I am postulating quite naively a transition from concern to action. I find the word 'threshold' (29) to be appropriate here and elsewhere (it is for instance very relevant in regard to consultation about skins). The image conveyed is one of a dam or barrier of inhibitions, and the water of concern washes against it. Concern may be dissipated without action; or it may rise above the barrier and flood over into channels of action.

Such pictorial images of action are notoriously treacherous, but this one perhaps justifies three further steps.

The concern may not be identified as a health concern, it may be no more than a feeling that things are in some way wrong. The vagueness is by no means always a matter of muddle and ignorance; there are areas of real ambiguity, particularly in the early stages of 'mental illness', such as depression, schizophrenia, and paranoia. It is perfectly good sense to treat these as traits of character, as mistakes in social behaviour, to be assimilated and made endurable not by 'treatment' but by 'social learning'—there do exist (as they say in the jargon of football) '50/50 balls'.

In the second place, even though the concern is identified as one related to bodily health, it does not always or at once home in on the official or legitimated system of medical care.

There is quite a wide range of choice; 'wise' (30) persons of one's acquaintance; popular sources such as advertisements and women's magazines; often (and not only in transitional societies) some form of alternative medicine. I am indebted here to Ronny Frankenberg and Joyce Leeson for their studies of the relation between scientific and traditional medicine in Lusaka (31), but here at home also we are in darkest Africa— the young man I mentioned went first to the local manipulator ten miles over the hill before he went to ask for an X-ray, and a friend of his (more sophisticated) is now setting out on a four-year course of training in acupuncture. Homeopathic medicine has a long history; so in a sense has osteopathy. Finally, there are the healing sects (Christian Science, Scientology) which figure largely in Bryan Wilson's book on *Religious Sects* (32).

Our legitimated system of scientific medicine is set in a milieu of self-help approved socially in other ways, and it catches only a tiny proportion of the action arising from concern over bodily lesions and ambiguous states. I think this is now generally realized, in a vague way; but I have found very little about the threshold between concern and action, or about the weighting of choice between alternative policies (33).

There are some obvious things: For instance, that official persons sweep up helpless casualties as they find them and feed them into the machinery of official medicine; that official medicine certifies officially; and that the public (on the whole) have recourse instantly to official medicine in cases of serious mechanical repair to the body as a machine—breaks, cuts, sprains, burns, and so on. It is also probable that the load on medicare is increasing, that a larger proportion of concerns impinge on official medicine than was the case in its earlier days. There is talk of the waning prestige of doctors, and there certainly is a strong reaction against official medicine diffused through all classes of society—keep out of the doctor's hands, keep out of hospitals, and live according to nature. This whole area remains vague: it is at least certain that enough concern homes in on medicine to drive that great engine.

Thirdly, one cannot contemplate medicare for long without realizing that much concern for persons is not friendly but hostile. One scarcely needs Esterson's complex theory of scapegoating, the Azazel: it is enough to take a tiny story from *New*

Society (35), about the tenants in a decayed tenement petition-
ing 'the authorities' and all and sundry to get rid of a violent
schizophrenic downstairs—to have her 'put away'. We may
stipulate for 'tender loving care' (36) but there are a great
many cases for which we refuse responsibility and demand a
custodial service. The demand is in many cases sad, helpless,
unspoken, and there is no means of estimating its weight except
by observing results. But this kind of analysis prompts me to
see the problem of custodial services versus community care
as one of balance between the personal concerns of the public
and those of the professionals. The balance of public concern
is to push them in, that of professional concern is to push them
out, since medicine can do nothing for them and has other
'concerns' of its own.

Indeed, the concerns and standards of public and professionals may conspire to spend resources on keeping alive those
who have not much concern for themselves. I was rather
cheered to see a fact that Cooper (37) reports with gloom:
'The increase in life expectancy at 70 since 1901 is only eleven
months for males, whilst the corresponding increase at birth
is twenty years and four months!' Good!

And in this area also one must place the now tedious contrast of Hygiea and Asclepius. The most intense of concerns is
for cure; the expulsion from an individual (myself or a supre-
mely significant other) of the bad invader. And it is probable
that in our scientific and bureaucratic culture this supreme
concern turns always, at some point, to scientific and official
medicine. But there is ample evidence even now that this is
rarely the first resource, rarely the last resource. The Healer is
a necessary public official, but healers also 'grow wild'.

But one may contrast the wide and impersonal view, that of
Hygiea; disease is the enemy, aggregate data are the battlefield. A rather small band of professionals develop a specific
concern for global statistics and for all mankind, past, future,
and to come. Individuals have perhaps a faint concern for
posterity, which they imagine to be themselves reborn; the
Asclepian professionals also have a faint concern, product of
their scientific culture and dedication. But the pressures on the
latter demand personal care—my son, my wife, my baby—
responsibility for people who are alive now.

In this chapter the argument, in spite of concrete illustrations, is necessarily abstract, and 1 am not wholly at ease with it. So I recapitulate here, as succinctly as I can.

The concept of health

(*a*) Common usage; its confusions.

(*b*) Positive health; its Utopian and transcendental character.

(*c*) Negative health: 'freedom from . . .'. Strong in relation to physical repair. Troubled by the difficult concept of 'disease'.

(*d*) Operational indicators: statistically meritorious, qualitatively weak.

Health care systems

(*a*) Specification in terms of official systems of medical care

(*b*) The constituencies of medical care.

(i) the public

(ii) the subordinates.

(*c*) Demand and need for medical care; Their legitimation.

(*d*) Legitimation of 'the sick role'.

Public concerns

Networks of concern.

Thresholds; from concern to action.

Alternatives to medical care:

(*a*) Confusion and ignorance.

(*b*) '50/50 balls'.

(*c*) Self-care, in all its variety.

(*d*) The concern to 'put away' what is humanly inconvenient.

Hygiea and Asclepius

CHAPTER 4   WHAT IS A PATIENT?

> 'A doctor', Lord Moran explained to me with sly self-mockery,
> 'prescribes his pills and potions and expects the patient to
> take them, if necessary three times a day, without demur and
> in perfect assurance. That the patient, particularly a poli-
> tician, should cavil and tell the doctor what to do is an
> insufferable presumption'.
> MICHAEL FOOT (1973), *Aneurin Bevan: A Biography*, vol. ii,
> p.104 (London: Davis-Poynter)

The upshot of Chapter 3 is that a system of 'health care' can
usefully be defined in terms of (on the one hand) a cry for help,
(on the other hand) a body of practitioners who have some
recognition by public authorities, some privileges, some special
training and experience.

The traditional relationship

On this relation between the patient's concern and the doctor's
response is founded the mythology of a special commitment on
each side, a social institution with a documented history of at
least 3,000 years. It certainly existed in ancient Egypt, in
Greece it was recognized in the Homeric poems, perhaps
800–700 BC, and the structure of a profession emerged during
the next 300 years, so that the tradition became associated with
the medical school on the island of Cos, and its most famous
alumnus, Hippocrates (1). 'Hippocrates' has been handed
down to us as a style and a method rather than as an individual
man. There is a large body of work of similar style, of various
dates, which has a 'Hippocratic' character. On the one hand,
the doctor must be a good scientist, one who pursues reason
according to the intellectual standards of his time. On the other
hand, though he is not priest or magician, he is a good man,
scrupulous in respect to the gods and to common humanity.

More than any other profession, doctors have searched their
own consciences in order to set down clearly the ethical
principles involved in the relationships between doctor and

Notes and references for this chapter begin on page 192.

patient and between doctors. As I write, eight of these statements are on my table; the old Hippocratic oath, the Declaration of Geneva (1948, amended 1968), the Declaration of
Helsinki (1964), the Declaration of Sydney (1968), the Declaration of Oslo (1970) (2), Thomas Percival's *'Code' of Medical
Ethics* (1794, published 1803), the Warning Notice of the Disciplinary Committee of the General Medical Council, the Ethical
Code of the British Medical Association (3). These are far too
lengthy to quote here; the most helpful perhaps in the present
context is the first of the medical aphorisms attributed to
Hippocrates:

> Life is short, science is long; opportunity is elusive, judge-
> ment is difficult. It is not enough for the physician to do
> what is necessary; the patient and the attendants must do
> their part as well, and circumstances must be favourable (4).

There is a dangerous situation, and a complex pattern of
participants; but the primary axis is between the doctor's
knowledge and the patient's concern.

This axis is not detached from its social and economic setting. Money, power, and status are part of the system within
which medical care is given, and they affect both the character
of the system and the priorities assigned by doctors in assessing
patients' needs. But the setting cannot distort the two roles
radically without destroying the system. The rich, the powerful, and those deemed socially valuable (a fabulous athlete
perhaps?) may command priorities: but the patient is still face
to face with a person to whom he has conceded authority to
inflict pain because of his faith in cure. The poor and weak may
be condemned to great discomfort and interminable delay;
nevertheless, the doctor *qua* doctor must give treatment to the
limit of his time and skill, within the resources available to him.
Indeed the structuring of medical training in England was
built upon treatment of the poor in charitable hospitals, and
even in the strictest period of Chadwick's Poor Law the mere
existence of the sick and helpless paupers slowly compelled the
establishment of poor law infirmaries, ancestors of the modern
general hospital (5).

The relationship is essentially one between consenting adults,
in a social setting given historically. However sublime the

patient, king, or prime minister, or great in intellect or skill, he or she has 'put himself in the hands of' the doctor. The patient assumes an attitude of helplessness and submission to a superior; acceptance of 'doctor's orders'.

The patient's consent

In fact, the postulate of consent is still honoured, legally and politically, and there is much bureaucratic and legal debate about the drafting of consent forms and their acceptance by the patient or the patient's guardians. Indeed, there is also philosophical debate about intellectual understanding as a pre-condition of effective individual consent; and perhaps there is some agreement that full understanding between doctor and patient is not in a practical sense possible. The patient's consent is in the last resort an act of individual faith, socially conditioned.

It must be added that our system postulates that some patients are not capable of valid individual consent, or that their consent is irrelevant to the public interest. There is the case of a victim seriously damaged in an accident, and brought to hospital unconscious. Medical aid must not be held back till the patient can 'consent' to treatment, though it is perfectly possible that he or she may have conscientious objections (for instance, for religious reasons), which would be respected if he were conscious and could be clearly warned. There is the possible case of a baby or young child; the consent of the parents is required—what if they disagree with one another? There is the case of mental incapacity; a branch of the law greatly eased in the last twenty years, but still very difficult, perhaps most difficult in terms of the relationship between families and 'confused' old people (6). Similarly, problems arising out of old fears of infectious disease have been eased by medical victory over plague (at least in the west), but the public health authorities (essentially medical) still have very wide powers. Here for instance is one taken almost at random from a textbook (7):

> Section 85 (of the Public Health Act, 1936) provides for the compulsory cleansing of a verminous person on the report of the medical officer of health to the local authority,

and if the person refuses consent, an order of the court may be obtained. The cleansing of females may be carried out only by a registered medical practitioner or only by a woman authorized by the medical officer of health.

This is in the true spirit of nineteenth-century public health reform—Sanitary Police. *The Times* wrote in 1854:

Aesculapius and Chiron, in the form of Mr Chadwick and Dr Southwood Smith, have been deposed and we prefer to take our chance of cholera and the rest, than to be bullied into health (8).

Both action and reaction now seem archaic, but similar provisions for the enforcement of public health would come into effect very quickly, with full public support, if there were for instance a major smallpox scare, as in South Wales in 1962 (9).

All these examples and others (e.g., medical practice in prisons and in forces under military discipline) illustrate how far the principle of consent must be eroded in practice. On the face of it the power of the patient is small, that of the 'registered medical practitioner' is tremendous. The patient entrusts responsibility to him, and the 'practitioner' is responsible only to his peers and to his conscience. The law of consent is remote, complex, and ambiguous, and it is not very much emphasized in recent reports on medical education (10) and on the role of the General Medical Council (11). Yet the patient, his kindred, and the general public are not passive, and they have for centuries sought safeguards stronger than those of the doctor's conscience and his professional code. The quest has left us with a complex set of institutions, some legal, some extra-legal, which occupy the rest of this chapter.

Patient power, patient responsibility

I divide the argument into three parts.

First, there is the exercise of choice by potential patients: 'I think most people only go to the doctor when they've failed to make themselves better' (12).

Secondly, there are many channels open for individual complaints, redress and even vengeance.

Thirdly, the concern of individual patients has in recent years been absorbed to some extent into voluntary organizations for 'self-help', a movement first systematically described for the UK in the book by Robinson and Henry, which has excellent references to previous studies of experience in the USA.

THE SOVEREIGN CONSUMER

The first option can perhaps be described in terms of consumer sovereignty; the 'market for health' is more diverse than it may seem at first sight, even in a country like the UK, in which consumers are sophisticated and 'state medicine' is highly organized. Private medicine survives and can be bought; but it is not substantially different from state medicine which is free. The interesting aspects of the market relate to the other possibilities.

Alternative medicine

I find it helps to begin from the work done by Ronny Frankenberg and Joyce Leeson on the options open to African sufferers in Zambia (13).

Zambia as a whole is poised between traditional and modern patterns of living, and this is particularly conspicuous in the mining towns of the Copper Belt, and in Lusaka, the capital. Those developed areas are not (by African standards) badly off for public clinics practising Western medicine, free of charge and at low cost. But there exist also traditional practitioners of various kinds, covered by the word *nganga* (14), and the patient will choose on the basis of family connections, social network, and the nature of his concern. The authors were able to be present at consultations with one practitioner, who (helped by an audience of concerned relatives) provided rituals of drumming and dance which tended to involve the patient strongly; herbal remedies likely to be innocuous in themselves; and much talk with bystanders from which the practitioner gained insight into the patient's social *milieu* and its stresses. All these things have a legitimate place in the practice of healing, but western medicine does not offer them, partly on principle, as not being 'scientific', partly because it is simply not organized to do so. But it can and does offer drugs and surgery which are for the most part technically efficacious, and the authors' view is that urbanized Africans are pretty shrewd in deciding whether to join an endless queue for medication at a clinic or to seek social comfort in a family confrontation with a traditional healer. They are cautious in generalizing about a complex situation, but one gains the impression that there is recourse to healers particularly in matters of fertility (which has very strong social significance) and in puzzling cases of disturbed behaviour.

The western situation is not of course closely parallel, but the study offers a simple analytical model for the study of 'unofficial' healing in western societies. I have not found any methodical discussion of this, but perhaps one can perceive a spectrum. At one end, there are what might be called alternative technologies: osteopaths, homeopaths, chiropractors, and perhaps acupuncture. In these cases there is no doubt that a healing art exists, and that physical benefit is possible. But so are physical disasters, and scientific medicine refuses recognition because healing skill is not placed in the context of medical science.

There have been many well-publicized battles between outsiders and orthodoxy. An early case was that of Herbert Barker, a bone-setter or osteopath without medical qualifications, who was extremely successful in the years before 1914. Not being a member of the profession, he was out of its disciplinary reach; but it was able to strike at him indirectly in 1911 when his anaesthetist Frederick Askham, was struck off the medical register for 'infamous conduct'—giving anaesthetics for an unqualified practitioner (15).

Most recently, there has been the case of Dr Issels and his clinic for terminal cancer patients in Bavaria, which became widely known because Lilian Board, one of the best middle distance runners of her time, died there of leukaemia in her early 20s. There was no doubt that a few remarkable remissions had taken place at Dr Issels clinic; there was also no doubt that he had inter-personal skill and could give hope and encouragement to dying patients in a way not possible in an orthodox hospital; but a fair-minded body of doctors could find no scientific merit in his treatment (16). Professional recognition was withheld. In the USA at present there is violent controversy over a supposed cancer cure called laetrile, supported by a minority of doctors, denounced by the medical establishment as a whole; legal in some states, banned in others. There is a large factory (laetrile is made of apricot kernels) and a large clinic over the border in Mexico, and smuggling laetrile is an organized and profitable trade (17).

Healing sects

Then there is a sector in which deviant healing is associated with a deviant religious sect, and a good deal about these is to be found in Bryan Wilson's (18) books on religious sects. Perhaps one would place the scientologists here; certainly the Christian Scientists, perhaps the Mormons, perhaps some of the ecstatic sects which have been carefully researched in Africa, but are by no means peculiar to 'blacks'.

Then there is the Maharishi, the Ananda Marga, and the legion of gurus, astrologers, and transcendental meditators. And, most exotic of all, the Church of England, belief, austere and orthodox, that the Christian priesthood includes a Mission of Healing and that some priests can sustain the tradition of miraculous cures achieved by prayer and the laying on of hands.

All these things exist strongly in the western world, and many are guided to them by concern. We all know, anecdotally, the cases of worried people who have gone to them, and are grateful. But there has been no attempt at measurement, and perhaps none is feasible.

Self-medication

Then there is the very large sector concerned with self-medication, 'non-ethical' preparations (i.e. those advertised directly to the public), and cosmetics. There have been many recent surveys of the pharmaceutical industry in relation to modern medicine (19); but I have met no similar survey of the 'non-ethical' industry, the descendants of 'snake-oil' and 'tiger-balm', of the itinerant fairground salesman (the visual image of W. C. Fields at work) the old Victorian 'patent medicines' and their slogans: Beecham's Pills 'worth a guinea a box', (20) Veno's Lightning Cough Cure, 'Pink Pills for Pale People', 'Sloan's Liniment', Dr. J. Collis Brown's Chlorodyne, and so on. In the

UK at least, the old preparations have been caught in a dilemma; if they contain active elements they may be dangerous, and are driven off the open shelves by 'safer drugs' legislation, if they are inert then they are a matter for the advertising industry rather than for the health industry.

'Skins' offer perhaps the strongest case. The working textbooks on dermatology advise that the GP must do all he can to find out what preparations a patient has already been using. It is a fair guess that most people troubled with painful or unsightly skin conditions try first to find a remedy themselves, from advice sought personally, or from the claims of advertisements, or both. Advertisements about skins and about hair are clearly the work of highly skilled and highly paid professionals, and clearly they earn profits for their masters. Perhaps their skills and their techniques of measuring success are described in their own text-books. No one, so far as I know, has studied them as a social scientist, but one can venture a few hypotheses. The market is for all ages and both sexes, but with special emphasis on adolescents, boys as well as girls. The official organs of control now have a pretty firm grip on preparations with active ingredients, and the advertisers make promises more by pictures than by words. But the pictures imply that 'you too can be beautiful'. These claims are guarded, in that beauty is partly a matter of fashion, of styles and colours, partly a matter of health: and the women's magazines have columns of advice about skins, often good sense. But it is hard for them to say bluntly: 'in such and such cases do not buy the goods here advertised; go to a doctor'.

No one now expects to buy a miracle drug across the counter; established medicine and established drug firms have combined effectively to narrow the scope of market choice to one official channel. But of course they do so at the risk of creating black markets and fraudulent organizations, especially in the hard drugs and in the theme stated thirty years ago in *The Third Man,* that of grave local shortages of antibiotics.

The herbalists
Perhaps a fourth section should be reserved for the modern herbalists, supporters of a much smaller market and of a

thriving Do It Yourself industry. But this also is territory which has been little explored by medical and social science (21).

INSTITUTIONS FOR COMPLAINT BY INDIVIDUALS

It costs effort, and some stress, to cross the 'threshold' which separates 'medical care' from 'normal life'. For most people (there are exceptions) 'the sick role' (22) is one to be avoided, and so is the role of the 'patient'. Even when it costs nothing but time and trouble (and perhaps strength to overcome the fear of future pain) to step across the threshold in search of a cure, it is done (by most people) with reluctance and suspicion. There is a 'double bind'. On the one hand, a burden is eased if one can cast it upon 'the doctor'; on the other hand, we have then lost our autonomy and our self-confidence. And yet, complaints after the event are not numerous as a percentage of cases; one can be pretty sure that gratitude greatly outweighs them. They can, however, be rancorous and persistent; political pressure has in the UK given a store of weapons to patients with which to attack the citadel of medicine.

These can be classified very roughly into institutions for individual action and institutions for collective action. Much of this area has been well researched and is covered by good text-books, so that I can be relatively brief.

The courts of law

First, action by process of law. There are three aspects. A doctor is subject to the ordinary law of the land in relation to ordinary criminal offences. But he is in a sense doubly subject to it, because any conviction involving a doctor must be reported (this is the second aspect) to the General Medical Council, the governing body of the profession, which will take note of the conviction and will consider whether the record suggests that the doctor should be deemed unfit to continue professional work. As the Merrison Committee explains (23), the procedure is like that of a court, but the GMC acts not to punish the doctor but to assert 'the responsibility of the medical profession to the public'. 'While the general welfare of the public is not at risk from an habitually drunken poet, it is from an habitually drunken doctor.' Cases that come to them are not numerous, but they involve questions of professional life and death.

The third aspect of judicial control lies in civil suits raised by individual plaintiffs, after the event, against the doctor or his employer—what the Americans call 'malpractice suits'. The legal possibilities are complex; but in the vast majority of cases they arise under the common law of tort.

The elements of liability are

(i) an act or omission by the defendant;
(ii) intention, or negligence, or breach of strict duty; and
(iii) damage to the plaintiff, with not too remote consequences (24).

This is still the only procedure by which a doctor can be formally called to account for failure in professional skill; and it has potentially far-reaching effects on the whole character of the relationship between doctor and patient.

There are certainly no disastrous consequences in the UK. All practising doctors belong to one of the Medical Defence societies (two in England and Wales, one in Scotland) which insure doctors against the costs of legal action and the risk of damages, for a comparatively modest fee. There are no statistics for actions raised and for the outcome, but it is clear from the modest insurance fees that the risk is not very high.

The position is very different in the USA. Since the 1960s there have been recurrent panics about the future of health care, based on a very elegant model of the effects of malpractice suits. In the USA (but not in the UK) it is professionally acceptable for a lawyer to act for a client on a profit-sharing basis. If the case is won he accepts a share of the damages in lieu of fees. This (it is said) stimulates legal action and increases the risk of practising medicine. This in turn pushes up the level of insurance which a doctor must carry; in rich states insurance for top doctors reached $19,000 a year in 1976 (25). This in turn, it is said, promotes defensive medicine; that is to say, the doctor takes every precaution, applies every biological and chemical test, that a hostile witness could imagine, thus putting up the cost to the patient and perhaps also the risks. A fairly high (but disputed) proportion of American patients are now covered by insurance, which is quite substantially backed by public funds. Thus there is a built-in escalation of the costs of medical care; worse treatment (medicine which goes beyond 'reasonable' precautions) adds higher costs beyond the increases already involved in the growth of high technology medicine.

Professor Somers treats this tempting argument with scepticism, and raises doubts about the validity of the facts postulated at each stage of the cycle. But he of course also has his bias, a bias in favour of commonsense and against hysteria. Whatever the facts, the argument has mythological power, turns up regularly in debates about the 'free enterprise system', and goes along with discontent (and avoidance) all round the cycle in patients, doctors, hospitals, and insurance agencies. It serves to symbolize what might happen if 'patient power' in the law courts grew too fast.

Procedure for complaints against doctors

In the UK this has not happened. Indeed, the British fear law-courts at least as much as they fear hospitals, and there has been a rather strange build-up of compromise institutions, partly administrative, partly judicial, quite typical of the way in which political instinct in the UK finds ways to evade academic categories.

There are at least four strands, each of them pretty well documented.

Complaints made by patients. First, there is the procedure for patients who have complaints against their GPs, the old 'panel doctors' under the National Health Insurance Act of 1911 (26). This system survives, without break in tradition, in the NHS of 1978, because GPs (even if they work from publicly sponsored health centres) are still 'independent contractors', and not salaried employers of any public body.

'The number of complainants who persist to the point where their complaint is included in the official statistics . . . is around 800 or 900 a year' of which about half are complaints about GPs (Klein, p. 16). The number, as a percentage of patients, is tiny, but an immense flow diagram (Klein, Fig. 1, p. 20) is necessary to show the paths which may lead to the NHS Tribunal and to the Secretary of State. The whole structure was debated in 1911 and again in 1946, and has become a set-piece in academic argument about adjudication by courts of law, by administrative tribunals, and by administrative bodies. Its importance is merely that it exists; it is a symbol of the special status of GPs, and cannot be changed unless there is a revolutionary change in that status.

NHS disciplinary procedure. Given these antecedents, it is therefore logical that there should be a separate procedure for doctors employed directly by the NHS and its various agencies (the question of 'who is the employer?' in each case is itself complex). These procedures are conducted largely in confidence, and there is no study comparable to that by Rudolf Klein, but a long formal statement is included as Appendix 4 to the Merrison Report (Cmnd 6078 of 1975) (26). There are two main cases:

(a) Procedure to be followed in serious disciplinary cases involving hospital doctors or dentists (p. 29).

(b) Machinery to assist in preventing harm to patients resulting from physical or mental disability, including addition, of hospital medical or dental staff (p. 30).

Dangerous drugs. There is also (and this applies to *all* doctors, GPs as well as hospital doctors) a special procedure under various Dangerous Drugs Acts since 1920.

To quote the Appendix to the Merrison Report (p. 42), 'The corollary to giving exemptions from the general law' (about possession of dangerous drugs) 'to doctors and certain other groups is that there are, and have been in the past, controls on practitioners who abuse their privileged position'. This is often a police matter and may lead via a conviction in court to withdrawal of registration by the GMC. There is, however, also the possible case of 'irresponsible prescribing', abuses 'which primarily concern professional judgement and conduct'; and for these there is a special Tribunal, proceeding formally, with one lawyer presiding over four doctors. In fact, says 'Merrison', it has never been invoked—but perhaps it will be, if anxiety about over-prescribing of barbiturates is not allayed (27).

Sick doctors. In all these procedures there is a certain implication that the position of a professional man must be protected
by careful procedures against unfounded complaints. The
Merrison Committee do not react against this, but they state
very forcibly, citing some gruesome examples (p. 329), that
'there *are* very sick doctors, and by no means all of them have
enough insight into their condition to retire from practice
before they endanger their patients' (p. 322); and they go on
to explain why the existing machinery is inadequate. Most of
their proposals have been incorporated in the Medical Act of
1978.

But at various points in the argument they refer to the unpleasant fact that the procedure is useless unless set in motion,
and that it can only be set in motion by colleagues who see the
inadequate doctor at close quarters (e.g. para. 261, para. 340).
Their first impulse may be to 'carry' him by judicious rearrange-
ment of duties and toleration of his absence. The second impulse will be to talk privately to him and try to persuade him to
resign. This may be a slow process, and unsuccessful in the
end. What it comes to, in the end, is a matter of ethical decision
as between men and women, professional decision as between
doctors.

And the patient has little say.

On the other hand, there have in the last ten years been
effective complaints against the living (and dying) conditions
of helpless patients in a number of geriatric, psychiatric, and
mental deficiency hospitals (28). These have in the main,
affected confused, disabled, and lonely people, in 'custodial'
institutions scarcely worth the name 'hospitals'. Their outside
connections have been few and weak; and it reflects a great
deal of credit on various young people working in the ghettos
of the NHS that they have stood up against bullying and
victimization and have set complaints in motion effectively.
There was also a slow but positive reaction from central government. A powerful Committee on Hospital Complaints Procedure was approved early in 1971 and reported in 1973 (29).
Their substantive contribution was to draft 'The Code of
Practice' (pp. 121–59), substantially a codification of existing practice, but with significant improvements and with
emphasis on telling patients and their relatives that a complaints

procedure exists (between 85 and 95 per cent of patients were not aware of this at the time of the enquiry (p. 117)).

The Committee's own survey of patients produced a pretty uniform pattern of response; between 70 and 80 per cent of patients were tolerably satisfied, rather less than 20 per cent were prepared to grumble. Many of the grumbles were about the frustrations endemic in large complex organizations: and among these (of course) is the 'nobody ever tells me anything' syndrome, to which I hope to recur in the chapter on information flows in the system of medical care.

However, to quote one of the Committee's witnesses,

> There is a very real problem in that many patients are unable to use a complaints procedure (p. 81). There are about 720 hospitals which cater wholly or mainly for mental illness, mental handicap, chronic sick or geriatric patients, and more than one-half of the beds in all types of hospital (235,000 out of 420,000) are occupied by these patients (p. 82).

One consequence of the series of 'scandals' and of the Davies Report was to force these figures on the notice of 'policy-makers' and to encourage a slight shift of resources in favour of the under-privileged patients. The Davies Committee also emphasized the external machinery for handling complaints—the Health Service Commissioner and the Community Health Councils (discussed below) the Hospital Advisory Service (Chapter 9 below), and the formal machinery for local enquiries. The procedure for pursuing complaints is now pretty good; the remaining problem, perhaps not soluble, is that of generating complaints—not so many as to destroy morale, not so few as to restore apathy.

THE HEALTH SERVICE OMBUDSMAN

The last institution relevant to this section is the office of Health Service Commissioner. In the 1960s there spread across the world a wave of interest in an obscure Swedish institution, that of the Ombudsman, in origin an independent official appointed by the King to probe weaknesses in the centralized royal administration: a role not unlike that of the administrative courts in France and elsewhere in Europe, but less formal

in jurisdiction and procedure. For some fifty years now there
has been in the UK an undercurrent of complaint about the
evils of 'bureaucracy', and for most of that period, Professor
W. A. Robson has been arguing cogently that the right remedy
is to create a coherent system of English administrative law,
which would necessarily include health service law. Some progress has been made in that direction, but there has never been
much enthusiasm among English lawyers, English politicians,
and English administrators for thoroughgoing rationalization
of the law. And one of many piecemeal reforms was the institution in 1967 of the anomalous office of Parliamentary Commissioner for Administration. The office is anomalous in that
the House of Commons insisted on its own supremacy as channel
for redress of individual grievances, and has made the 'PCA'
essentially an officer of the House of Commons, who deals
with complaints channelled to him through MPs. Another
anomaly is that the PCA can deal only with matters of administration, not with matters of policy; this in spite of the familiar
maxim that 'policy is secreted in the interstices of administration'.

The first holders of the office proceeded discreetly and con-
servatively, with very few revelations of scandal; there were no
complaints of abuse of jurisdiction, a good deal of complaint
about lack of publicity for this potential remedy for maladmini-
stration. Hence there was not much expression of feeling, for or
against, when the Heath government announced in February
1972, that the post of Health Service Commissioner was to be
created in forthcoming legislation. The then PCA, Sir Alan
Marre, was asked to double as Health Service Commissioner,
in the first instance, and this practice continues. The HSC is
however unlike the PCA, in that complaints can come to him
direct from the public; like him in that his scope is limited to
'action taken by the health service authority' (30), with the
further gloss that this excludes not only 'policy' but matters of
'clinical judgement'. This latter limitation was discussed at
length by the Select Committee on the PCA (31) and they
strongly recommend that it be abolished. Meantime, the DHSS
has watered down its proposals for action on the Davies Committee Report (32) in the face of objections from the professions;
and it is likely that (in the words of the Select Committee,

para. 16) complaints procedure will remain 'complicated, fragmented and slow'.

There are other restrictions, and in fact in 1976–7, 413 out of 582 complaints made were rejected as outside jurisdiction (33). The number of complaints pursued was therefore quite tiny (169), in relation to a service which (in hospitals alone) has well over 20 million patients a year (34). But this amounts to the publication of 424 pages of reports, 102 of them; succinct, but specific and hard-hitting. A fair number of the complaints reported reflect what might be called (metaphorically) 'endogenous depression'; they originate primarily in the distress of patient or complainant in a very painful situation, and no one is 'to blame'. But no complaint is dismissed as frivolous, and no excuses are found for muddle and bad manners on the part of NHS staff. These are good reports, reflecting able and sympathetic investigation. The problem is—who reads them? It is scarcely possible for them to be read widely in the service itself. One hopes that journals concerned with NHS administration pick out and publish specially bad cases; the daily press pays some attention to each volume on its appearance, but no major scandals have been revealed, and the column inches allowed have been tiny. The time is coming when a thorough retrospective study will be worth while, and it may be possible to organize this mass of detailed investigation and to distil some general principles about what goes wrong. At first sight the new institution adds little to other channels of complaint, in so far as the latter are now properly organized, and yet the sequence of cases illustrates vividly the ways in which a big complex organization can be at fault. One is reminded of the title of Katherine Whitehorn's book, to which the Davies Committee refer—*How to Survive in Hospital* (35).

COLLECTIVE ACTION

Elected persons

The NHS in its present form is a highly centralized service, organized hierarchically from national headquarters. Centralization is mitigated a little by the fact there are four distinguishable centres, in London, Edinburgh, Cardiff, and Belfast; and at various lower levels of the hierarchy appointed local worthies sit with doctors, nurses, administrators, and finance officers, to execute national policy. This has become so familiar that it blots from our minds the history of the service, created largely by locally elected persons acting in concert with aggressive and reforming doctors, the Medical Officers of Health. These two elements created a more or less liveable urban environment, hunted down infectious diseases, built what were once the poor law hospitals; and they were still, after the First World War, moving forward in the creation of specialist clinics of various kinds, notably those for mothers and young children.

And yet the majority of the medical profession have always been hostile to management by elected local authorities. Even in the 'provinces' (and of course much more strongly in London) the doctors aligned themselves with local elites and with the management of the voluntary hospitals. They did not like councillors, nor did they much like their managerial colleagues, the MOHs and the medical superintendents. Battle was joined at the time of Lloyd George's National Health Insurance Bill of 1911; the local authorities were outmanoeuvred and defeated then, and they have never recovered. It seems quite vain to imagine now the reorganization of the NHS on the same lines as those of the 'National Education Service', in which much the largest part is played by local Education Committees and their chief officers.

The inheritance has been divided up in a complex way, with unpredictable effects. Environmental health must continue to be an essential part of the reorganized health service. The MOHs have been reborn as specialists in community medicine, and are still primarily concerned with areas coinciding (so far as possible) with hospital areas, general practice areas, and local government areas. What they are asked to do is to practise (or indeed to invent) community medicine, to be focal points in the study of the health of a community as a whole, in face of increasing specialization and 'ad-hoccery'. We wish them well, but they seem to have lost some of their old strengths; for instance, their effective field force of sanitary inspectors and health visitors, and their power to mobilize public opinion by 'waving the bloody shirt' (some call it 'waving the shroud') at an influential elected body whose decisions and policies commanded all the available local publicity (36).

Community Health Councils

Instead, we have Community Health Councils, excellently described in a recent book by Rudolf Klein and Janet Lewis (37).

> The political problem, therefore, was how best to square the circle of elitism and populism: how to reconcile the emphasis on centralized planning with the currently fashionable rhetoric of local participation . . . to add, as it were, a Gothic folly to the Palladian Mansion (p. 13). But while CHCs may have started out as a symbolic nod in the general direction of democracy and participation, their development suggests that substitutes for action may paradoxically turn into a practical commitment to action (p. 16).

Their terms of reference are vague: 'to represent the interests in the health service of the public in its district '(1973 Act, 9 (3) (a)), and *perhaps* other functions. Their areas are to be defined by the Secretary of State; there are in fact 225 of them in England and Wales. The rules for membership are left to be defined, except that at least half are to be appointed by elected local authorities, at least one-third from voluntary bodies. They will have no staff of their own except a secretary and his assistants. (Apparently the relevant community physicians are not expected to act with them so as to maintain continuity with the old role of the MOH. But a community physician from 'the district team' will usually be nominated by the elected local authority to act as its 'Medical Officer for Environmental Health', a medical adviser with some executive functions.) None of their members are to be lay or professional members of the NHS hierarchy. And there is to be some sort of central body (9 (6)(a)) 'to advise the Councils with respect to the performance of their functions and to assist Councils in the performance of their functions' (a provision which perhaps reflects the success of the National Council of Social Service in fostering the Association of Parish Councils, as a support for 'local democracy' in the countryside).

And after the Bill was passed, the Department issued a sort of Agenda for CHCs which swings from sparsity to overabundance (38):

the effectiveness of services being provided; the planning
of services; collaboration between health services and local
authorities; assessing the extent to which district health
facilities conform with the published departmental policies;
the share of available resources devoted to the care of
patients unable to protect their own interests, especially
those living in hospital for long periods or indefinitely;
facilities for patients; waiting periods; quality of catering;
and monitoring the volume and type of complaints re-
ceived about a service or institutions.

'There's glory for you' said Humpty-Dumpty; in this case a
promise of much paper and little action? Personally I believe
more has been done, and can be done, by a voluntary movement
of quite a different kind, which has no statutory basis and has
only recently attracted attention both in the UK and in the
USA (39).

Associations of patients and their kin

The study of interest groups, pressure groups, 'the lobby', has
a central position in modern political analysis but no one has
ever contrived an adequate definition and classification (40).
This is because the field is almost coterminous with the organization of modern life; a kaleidoscope, but one in which the
units are continuously in process of transformation and adapta-
tion, and which seems to change as the viewer's position changes.

In their study of self-help groups Robinson and Henry found
91 such groups active in the UK, but at least 26 of these raise
problems about definition. Using an even looser definition
than theirs, I found over 160 potential candidates in that
remarkable volume, *The Directory of British Associations and
Associations in Ireland* (41) and this includes almost all those in
the Robinson and Henry list.

Perhaps one can proceed cautiously on the basis of type-
cases and of historical sequence. In the last ten years or so there
have appeared a large number of 'patient organizations' associated with specific diseases, many of them rather rare; here are
a few: Anorexic Aid (1974), Association to Combat Hunting-
ton's Chorea (no date), Association of Parents of Vaccine-
Damaged Children (1973), Association for Spina Bifida and

Hydrocephalus (1966), Coeliac Society (1968) and so through the alphabet down to 'U and I Club', Urinary Infection in Your Home (Cystitis) (1971), and Vasectomy Advancement Society of Great Britain (1972). Many of them are small, and there must be a certain mortality among them, unrecorded.

Some of them are groups specifically organized to make demands (the thalidomide cases and the 'vaccine-damaged children'), at the other extreme are associations primarily created for 'togetherness', where at least one primary objective is to recognize and meet fellow sufferers. 'Togetherness' may be primarily a method of strengthening one another psychologically in face of a shared misfortune; it may be regarded as a tool of healing, as in the case of Alcoholics Anonymous, which took much of its practice from the Buchmanite technique of 'the Oxford Groups' the 'life-changers' (42). But short of this, the group may be a practical instrument for 'learning to live with it' by exchanging information about experience (Coeliac Society (1968), Colostomy Welfare Group (1967), Mastectomy Association (1974)). Some consultants are rather suspicious of patients who try to know too much for their own good. But in general these societies have good relations with relevant specialists, are well briefed by them, and are concerned to help research, though not able to contribute much financially.

There are two rather different phenomena, which should be distinguished. In the USA there is a general movement towards 'medical self-care' (43), quite distinct from 'alternative medicines' or 'fringe medicine'. Especially in small towns and country places, the American 'health system' has virtually eliminated the GP, and specialist medicine is remote and expensive. It is simply good sense to form groups (largely of well-educated women) primarily for self-education and mutual education in medical matters. There is perhaps a germ of this here in the familiar First Aid classes of the WRI; but on the whole we are still remarkably well looked after by the country doctor and the district nurse, and we are not being forced to go further along the American road.

A totally different phenomenon can be illustrated from Robinson and Henry's book: The Beaumont Society (Transvestites), The Campaign for Homosexual Equality, Icebreakers (Gay Lib), The Paedophile Information Exchange, Paedophile

Awareness for Liberation, the Scottish Minorities Group, and so on, under various slightly obscure titles and acronyms. The case is that of sexual deviations, which may be variously labelled as diseases or as vices, or as harmless forms of sexual pleasure.

The whole area is full of test cases for phenomenological sociology: Berger and Schutz (44) on 'the social construction of reality', Goffman on 'stigma'. Recently the paedophiles made a rather tentative move towards publicity; one of the PR men at the Open University was involved and was in consequence sacked from his job: a job that he was doing perfectly well— except for the publicity attracted by his private life. Rather similarly (but with less disastrous effects) a popular paper tried to get up a cry against a doctor who was prepared to organize A.I.D. for stable lesbian couples, so that one of them might have a child.

I have no intention of following up this topic here; except to say that if your conditions is labelled 'disease' and that label is endorsed by establishment medicine, then your status is that of patient and your organization is clearly within the law.

But the concept of stigma has a much wider reference. I am myself a member of the Psoriasis Association (1968) because I am (in a very minor way) a patient. Psoriasis is unlucky in its name, which most people cannot spell nor remember, and I was astonished to find that it affects about 1 in 50 in the population, say a million people in the UK. Until I joined the association I had never consciously met another psoriatic in my life, except for one chance conversation in an aeroplane. Psoriasis is a skin disease arising because patches of skin become over-active, and replace themselves much too fast, with regular shedding of whiteish scales. It is not infectious, contagious, or cancerous; it is not lethal, and causes itch rather than pain. But it is at present deemed incurable, and it raises rather fundamental and difficult questions about the regulation of cell growth, regulation, and replacement.

It also raises problems about stigma. In our cold climate the stigma is severe only on the rare occasions when one strips in public: in swimming baths and on seaside holidays; in the course of athletics and team games (45). But if there is psoriasis on the face or scalp, the sufferer is in trouble, partly because the disease is so unfamiliar to the public and even to hairdressers and the other 'skin trades' (46): The Association membership card carries (by way of introduction to such strangers) a sentence in six languages—'Psoriasis is a skin condition that is neither infectious nor contagious'.

In fact, by the nature of the disease, the main enemy is stigma—what the public make you out to be. I was present at a meeting called to found a Glasgow branch: 350 turned up for a meeting in a hall that had seats for about 250, and many had to stand patiently through a session of over 2 hours. It was a troubling experience; all ages, all classes, and both sexes, with very little visible sign of disease, yet united in a single concern. It was one of those occasions, so rare except perhaps at football matches (or in the days of the blitz), when embarassment drops away and you can open conversation with strangers easily because you already share an experience.

Of course 'togetherness' is not a cure for psoriasis (though the latter is a condition responsive to stress), and it will only be rather special people who want to chat regularly to other psoriatics. Nor are sufferers a demand group; there are scientific disputes about the best palliative treatments, but no miracles are expected and (within the resources of the NHS) what can be done is already being done. Given the social and medical specification of this disease, the Association is above all an information group; the inner circle, that of the consultant dermatologists, has its own communication network; the Association can spread the network wider through patients, through their parents, friends, and kin, and ultimately to 'the public'.

This must serve as a brief example of how a patient association is moulded by the specific characters of the disease in defining its possible field of activity. The necessities of organization produce common factors in organization—the lay president or chairman, the friendly consultants, the director or secretary, salaried, and full-time once the point of take-off is reached, the structure of committees, the regional, and local groups. But the conditions of activity are as diverse as the different worlds of different diseases.

Two final points in this section:
1. I have concentrated here on recently formed specific

groups. Working backwards through history, I think one can see three stages. In the 1950s there was the rise of groups concerned with parents living with damaged children: Muscular Dystrophy Group (1955), Mentally Handicapped Children (1946); Epilepsy (1950 and 1954), Spastics (1952), Haemophilia (1950), and Polio (no date). Some of these at least followed the example of the previous phase and sought to raise money from the public. That earlier phase, if I understand it rightly, was dominated by great research foundations (notably for cancer and heart disease). These drew subscriptions and legacies from sufferers and their kin, but were not in any other sense patients' associations. And still further back lie the great Victorian 'charities'; Invalid Children's Aid (1888), London Association for the Blind (1857) the National Library for the Blind (1882), Royal Association in Aid of the Deaf and Dumb (1840), Royal National Institution for the Blind (1868), and so on. One may hazard a guess that these two earlier phases can be associated with the growth of special hospitals and with the growth of 'Harley Street' specialists, rather usefully described in chapter 2 of Brian Abel-Smith's book on the history of hospitals (47). Similarly, the latest phase is clearly entangled with the growth of an educated public, the development of medical science and the institution of the NHS.

To my mind, this is the strongest evidence that the patient is escaping from traditional passivity and seeking to be an equal collaborator with the doctors. But it is far too early to talk of revolutionary change.

2. Indeed, my second point is that the patients' associations have hardly recognized themselves yet as fragments of a single movement. Mr Wyatt of the Psoriasis Association has talked to me of possible collaboration in the field of skins with the National Eczema Society (1976) and the Society for Skin Camouflage and Disfigurement Therapy; and other such 'local' groupings are possible. But a very gallant attempt to found a general Patients Association (1963) has not been much heard of recently (though it gave both written and oral evidence to the Morrison Committee on the Medical Profession (1973 to 1975). Robinson and Henry mention very briefly (p. 174) the formation in 1977 of an 'Association for Self-Help and Community Groups', and I have found in *New Society* (9 March

1978) a reference to 'the new National Association for Patient Participation in General Practice', with a brief description. But these seem to represent something analogous but rather different, the emergence of local groups for self-help in the community.

Retrospect

The balance of this chapter may seem to suggest that 'the patient', once humble in the face of medicine, is now armed with so many weapons of offence and defence that the balance of power has changed, and medicine has been weakened so far that it operates under impossible conditions.

This is partly an optical illusion. It has taken only four pages to explain the weakness of the patient, in particular regarding procedure for consent; some twenty pages to explain the patient's responsibility for the choice of treatment and the institutions available for his or her protection. But if it were possible to quantify (which it is not) the balance would look very different. Williamson and Danaher (p. 35) reckon that 'for every person who sees a doctor because of illness there are three others suffering who do not'. But of those who do enter the medical system, an overwhelming majority (75–80 per cent in most studies) report satisfaction and gratitude. Correspondingly, the number of patients who seek to take action against doctors is tiny in relation to the turnover of the system; and many of the institutions for protection are very little used.

In fact, they may be regarded as an expression not of patient power but of patient anxiety. We are all at heart frightened at the combined strength of doctor, nurse, and hospital, of the surrender and indeed the humiliation involved. The situation is one of stress, and it is natural to tinker about with it looking for safeguards. The proposer of new controls can always find a few appalling examples of malpractice, and few patients positively object to safeguards. Most of the opposition therefore comes from the professions (as in the case of the Davies Report) and this gives the impression that patients and professions are drawn up in dialectical opposition, like embattled armies.

This is much too simple a view.

Earlier in this chapter I used the metaphor of a complex

moving kaleidoscope to describe the interplay of factors affecting the power and weakness of that abstract figure, the patient in general. Rudolf Klein chooses the metaphor of a ballet:

> Instead of looking at their relationship [that of the producers and consumers of health] in terms of a Cowboys and Indians conflict, it is therefore much more accurate to picture it as an elaborately choreographed ballet—with the dancers constantly changing partners and adopting new formations as the setting of the drama changes (48).

Others may use other metaphors, but there is at least consensus that any simple summary is wrong. In some respects the patient (and his kin) are no more than helpless suppliants before the throne of medicine, in other respects the patient's needs and their consciousness of them constitute the foundation on which is built the whole edifice of public and private medicine. In some respects the structure is held together by two general factors: the pattern of communications within which a climate of opinion grows and changes; and a hierarchy of decision which makes demands and attempts to allocate priorities. I try to deal with these in Chapters 8 and 9.

CHAPTER 5 WHAT IS A DOCTOR?

> And Asa in the thirty and ninth year of his reign was
> diseased in his feet, until his disease was exceeding great:
> yet in his disease he sought not to the Lord, but to the
> physicians.
> 2 Chronicles 16:12.

Mythologies about power

The doctors (1) look very strong. Individually, each has the
power and responsibility of clinical decision. Collectively, they
can face the power of Whitehall; the doctors and the State are
(as Rosemary Stevens put it) 'interdependent'. 'When the
State is a monopoly employer and the employee is a monopoly
profession, pay negotiations may, if not subtly directed, de-
generate into a trial of strength between two forces' (2).

This is a moderate and acceptable statement of the position,
and Rosemary Stevens can support it by judicious quotations
from leading doctors. Here is one from the *British Medical
Journal* dated 1935, written to cool the potential hysteria of the
American Medical Association (3): 'the much greater experiences [sic] of the British Medical Association in collective
negotiation and bargaining indicates that the power of the
organized medical profession, reasonably exercised, is very
effective' (4). A similar point is made by a distinguished
pathologist who gave advice to a high official before the Second
World War on the organization of a national blood transfusion
service, in expectation of universal destruction by bombing.

> I made out a scheme for him there and then . . . I learned
> that the medical man is in an immensely strong position
> when advising the administrative side on a vital matter
> affecting public health and safety, and the corollary that
> one must be very sure of being right before advising (5).

Much American writing about the medical profession gives
a different and more terrifying impression; partly because the

situation is not the same, partly because American sociologists and political scientists are more addicted than we are to grand theoretical generalizations. Perhaps their starting point lay in the domination of non-medical opinion by two monstrous bogeys; one of them the overbearing tactics of the American Medical Association in the days of its great (but paranoid) General Secretary, Dr Abraham Fishbein: the other the Parsonian 'grand theory' of the place of professions (medicine at their head) in modern society. This is not the place to discuss Parsonian theory at length, but here is one useful paraphrase:

> Parsons defines the professional as someone who is supposed to be recruited and licensed on the basis of his technical competence rather than his ascribed social characteristics, to use generally accepted rather than particularistic scientific standards in his work, to restrict his work activity to areas in which he is technically competent, to avoid emotional involvement and to cultivate objectivity in his work, and to put his client's interests before his own (6).

These are not Parsons' own words, and indeed Parsons is not necessarily self-consistent. But they indicate his general line of thought: modern society is dominated by rational scientific knowledge as expressed in the predominance of the professionals, those who possess a scientific culture and have internalized its norms. The theory derives from Max Weber, and from Prussian society as it was in the days of its greatness, before the First World War. Weber expressed the theory primarily in the context of a hierarchical, 'rational-legal', 'bureaucratic' structure (and we shall meet this again in Chapter 7 below); Parsons (as was natural in the mood of 'Wasp' America, 'middle America', in his time) put more emphasis on the profession as being in some sense a band of brothers who prosper in society because they have 'internalized' professional norms. The Hippocratic oath is still the seal of an effective social bargain.

The Parsonian model was in its day by no means contemptible intellectually, but it could not stand up to the battering of social reality in the 1960s. A whole generation turned away from functional models in sociology and towards conflict models. A rather moderate critic, Eliot Freidson, sees 'the relation of the physician to his clientele as inherently problematic. Indeed, the relation of any service occupation to its clientele is inherently problematic' (7), because the professionals are bound to develop a perspective different from that of their clients. Berlant seems to me to push this point rather further.

> The organized medical profession has sought domination over others as well as the freedom to carry out its own will . . . Even the technical goals of the profession are dominative . . . The physician as a professional, unlike the free labourer, is in a position to command his employer (8).

And so on, to the conclusion that the relationship between doctors and patients is essentially one of confrontation rather than co-operation.

Berlant's arguments are ideological rather than empirical; he has, for instance, an excellent chapter on the history of medical ethics in the UK and the USA, bringing back into the debate the almost forgotten classics of John Gregory (1772) (9) and Thomas Percival (1797) (10), and showing how much more concern there was for the complex relations between doctor and doctor than for those between doctors and patients. To the left of Berlant stand those who rely primarily on observation and on radical (but not Marxist) models of American society. R. R. Alford (11) seeks an answer to the question 'Why does the New York region have so many excellent schemes for rational distribution of hospitals—on which no action is ever taken?' In response he points to the continuance of oligarchic conflict at 'the grass roots'; the management of individual hospitals by groups of businessmen and medical administrators, relying on support from splintered community groupings within a huge metropolitan area. This pattern of interaction (he implies) cannot be transformed except by radical action.

Push this trend of analysis one stage further, and one is almost in the realm of conspiracy theory. The Ehrenreichs' book on *The American Health Empire* (12) can produce plenty of evidence for the interdependence of hospital medicine, the great pharmaceutical companies, the great insurance companies, and the local business leaders—subject to the difficulty always faced by this type of theory, that interdependence does not prove conspiracy. And at the end of the day they see the situation in terms of class conflict and of revolt—student revolt, health workers' revolt, and community revolt.

I do not know how to handle such visions except in pedestrian terms. Hence the pseudo-naive title of this chapter—'What is a Doctor?' It turns out to be a complex and difficult question.

The legal basis of the profession

The formal answer is easy: a doctor is a person endowed by the law of a sovereign state with certain rights, privileges, and duties, not conferred on others within the jurisdiction of that state. In the UK the fundamental law is the Medical Act of 1858: an example of Victorian radical legislation, which was intended to bring order into a period of confused conflict between professional bodies. The earliest claimants were the medical faculties of the universities, one of the three most prestigious medieval faculties, those of theology, law, and medicine. It is odd that in England medical training has been from the outset more strongly based in hospitals than in universities, yet it is only in the English language that 'medical practitioners' have almost wholly appropriated the word 'doctor' as reference to a university degree which relatively few of our doctors have earned.

The position in Scotland is rather different; in England the historical dates are:

1518. The foundation of the College of Physicians, whose earliest statutes were framed in 1555.

1800. The Charter which created the Royal College of Surgeons, culmination of the long struggle of the Barber-Surgeons for parity of esteem with the Physicians.

1815. Between these dates another profession, that of the Apothecaries, had grown up to serve the provincial middle class—never sanctified by Royalty, but firmly established by the Apothecaries Act of 1815.

These were by no means the only bodies involved in England; Scotland and Ireland had separate institutions. The Act of 1858 was the result of some thirty years of agitation and compromise, and left intact the pre-existing qualifications, most of which survive to this day. But it superimposed on them the Benthamite institutions of public examination and legal register of qualifications; essential components of the modern world, conferring the status of 'gentleman' rather than of 'artisan'. I hesitate to write 'bourgeois' because the professional risks no capital except that involved in the time and cost of a long period of unremunerated training and experience. That investment, however, often depended not so much on capital in cash as on family tradition and on a network of friendly interchange between medical families.

The UK system was from the outset (and still is) relatively generous to the unqualified, and states its aim modestly: 'whereas it is expedient that persons requiring medical aid should be enabled to distinguish qualified from unqualified practitioners . . .'

It is not an offence to offer medical advice without being a 'registered medical practitioner', and the UK has been as rich as any culture, past or present, in self-appointed medical advisers. But it is an offence to pass oneself off as a 'registered practitioner', and such practitioners of *Fringe Medicine* (13) are placed in the same category as bookmakers—they cannot sue their clients for their fees. Nor can they legally perform any of the immense list of functions monopolized by doctors by law; some of them remunerative, but all hedged by onerous restrictions which must be observed. Familiar cases are death certificates, cremation certificates, certificates authorizing detention in a mental hospital, 'sick notes' under the National Insurance Acts and in relation to education. The list is in fact enormous, and I have not found any text-book that claims to give it in full. The doctor must, in return for professional status, perform many of the functions generally characterized as 'bureaucratic'—the endless production of pieces of paper duly authenticated, which authorize or refuse official action.

The legal principle remains; a citizen is free to choose his own advisers in matters of his own health, but he will from birth to death require, quite frequently, the signature of a 'registered medical practitioner'. For some of the certificates the patient or his relatives must pay the doctor; others are provided at no cost to the patient because they are essential to the working of very large and complex bureaucratic systems; the health system, of course, and also the education system, the social security system, the long series of Factory Acts, and Public Health Acts. One of the most ingenious proposals for a doctors' strike is that they should treat patients but sign no certificates; but it is very hard even to treat patients without the support of that little NHS pad of prescription forms, the magic which makes us better.

Naturally doctors are often rather too kindly or rather too careless in adding their signatures; and naturally there are heavy professional penalties if certificates are given improperly. But the signing of a form is not a matter that can be policed effectively and it would require a rather special confidential study to map out what actually happens in real-life situations. One can guess that death certificates and certificates relating to mental illness are not given without grave thought; and that most doctors are humane and rather lax about signing a man off work or a child off school. Indeed, a work-to-rule in treating each certificate as requiring a specific personal examination might block the system as effectively as a general strike against all certificates. Perhaps, therefore, it is best not to enquire too closely into the practice rather than the law of certification.

Knowledge and skills

This then is the first point, that in a formal sense a doctor is a 'public servant' (14), an official necessary to the operation of the State. The second point is also a formal one; that a complex programme of book examinations and clinical tests must be completed in order to satisfy the General Medical Council that a medical student is fit to be included in the Register. The syllabuses prescribed used to be extremely rigorous and formal; the practice now recommended is that more should be left to the discretion of universities and other examining bodies, subject to informal discussion about teaching methods and standards (15). Even now, programmes are constructed not in terms of aspirations for liberal education but in terms of a necessary minimum for the protection of the public. 'No country has produced so many wise reports on the improvements of medical education as Great Britain, and no country has done so little about it' (16). 'In 1963 most medical schools, including all the

London schools, retained a basic educational structure little different from that of one or even two generations earlier' (17). There have been two linked traditions. The first is that of pre-clinical work largely in anatomy, physiology, and pathology, taught by lectures and massive text-books, simply as facts to be known; including work in dissection which is essentially factual and not experimental. The second is that of clinical work, partly factual, but also based on 'walking the wards' and acquiring skills by imitation; traditional self-education, finding a good teacher (as distinct from a good doctor) only by accident. This now culminates in the pre-registration year as 'houseman', still much at the mercy of luck. 'Some claim that house officers often revelled in their work: "They love being up to their elbows in blood, sweat, and tears, their own and other people's"' (18).

These two traditions have very long histories, and make their mark on each new generation of students. There are strong liberal movements; on the one hand towards shifting the pre-clinical emphasis so as to create a three-year degree in human biology as a field of scientific exploration; on the other hand towards better planning and better teaching techniques in clinical studies.

But there is still a vast weight of professional opinion which wants to train 'a good practical doctor', rather than a member of the great community of science. The tradition puts students through a pretty rough apprenticeship, not intellectually enjoyable except to a few. Some 50 per cent of the entrants, after five years, express doubts as to whether they were right to choose medicine. But they are tough, and minimum pass standard is not strikingly high; the final 'drop-out' over the five years is only about 10 per cent—though many passed only after frequent re-sits (19).

Student solidarity

So much for the formal structure of medical education; the commodity bought by the public in exchange for its formal grant of specified privileges.

But this education is also a formative experience, coming at the decisive years of late adolescence and early maturity. I have encountered few research reports on the psychological and social experiences that go along with the system of training, and I have only the evidence of my own contemporaries and of more than a century of 'funny' books from Dickens to Richard Gordon—and a few serious ones (20). This scanty evidence confirms theoretical expectations. Medical students are taught together in relatively small groups; annual intakes to medical schools are now increasing, but have in the past been in the range of 50 to 100 students in each school. A group of this size is diverse enough to be self-contained for many purposes, but is also small enough for mutual recognition to grow out of five years of close association and intense experience. Such a group also develops ranking orders, not necessarily all in one dimension, and certainly not in the shape of a dominance hierarchy. The best examinee does not necessarily excel in manual dexterity or in laboratory work. And individuals will also be known temperamentally as stable, friendly, excitable, withdrawn, and so on. The group also builds up experience about 'self and others'; it learns to see itself as one of a number of similar groups and to grade them also on various dimensions. The analogy in my mind is that of similar 'cohorts' of students in boarding schools or in Oxford and Cambridge colleges, or in military academies; situations in some ways more open, and in some ways more strictly enclosed, than those of medical schools.

In all these examples group identity may be reinforced by class affiliation and by kinship. The numbers drawn from social classes IV and V are quite trivial. In England some 30 per cent come from the 'public' schools; in Oxford and Cambridge over half the medical students are drawn from social class I, which is defined largely in terms of managerial and professional occupations. Doctors are reckoned to be members of that class; and about 20 per cent of all medical students are children of doctors —in Oxford and Cambridge the proportion reaches 30 per cent. These percentages vary significantly between England and Scotland and between different medical schools, but patterns remain pretty stable and are recognizable to 'insiders', though not perhaps to the general public (21).

I know of no published data about 'health service marriages'. One notes among one's own acquaintances the relative frequency of marriage between doctor and nurse, and of course

this is a stock theme of hospital 'soap operas'. As the percentage of women in medical schools increases (it is now
climbing beyond 30 per cent, from very small beginnings) one
can guess that marriages between doctors will become more
frequent.

The impression one gets is one of social and professional
solidarity, but not of unthinking solidarity. The Todd Committee's figures (p. 363) indicate a reasonable incidence of doubt
and introspection about careers in medicine, and indeed about
the structure of the medical profession. But choice of career
within medicine is, at the stage of graduation, concentrated on
the scope for being 'a good practical doctor'. The topics of
'greatest interest' to final-year students (p. 356) are physical
medicine (over 40 per cent) and 'responsibility for patients' (35
per cent); to me this suggests an old-fashioned desire to 'take
clinical decisions', and to 'cure people'. There is inevitably a
strong bent towards hospital medicine, but a strong minority
(some 30 per cent) give positive preference to general practice.

Up to this point all the evidence points to a profession
strongly integrated, self-perpetuating, and oriented towards
power and responsibility. They are reared to be decision-
makers, and primarily they look towards the relationship between doctor and patient as I have described it in the previous
chapter. One can readily envisage such a group in the role of
'professional dominance' (Freidson) and 'professional monopoly' (Berlant). In the UK at least, it would be fair to talk of a
'professional elite' (22): but not to press the theme so far as to
assert dominance or monopoly.

There are two great limiting factors.

The first theme is that of the fragmentation of medicine, with
which I deal in this chapter.

The second is that of the limits of clinical decision. A decision
to do what it is impossible for you to do is no decision. And many
cases now pose that paradox. 'What this patient needs is an
operation to restore the hip joint: but there is a two-year waiting
list.' 'What this patient needs is a kidney transplant: but the
availability of a compatible kidney depends on complex administrative arrangements outside my sphere.' And so on. Such cases
do not predominate; there are greater possibilities than ever
before of giving effective treatment, and I have often been a

beneficiary myself. But it is a by-product of technical advance that doctors work predominantly in large organizations and depend on organizational allocation of resources. And they are faced more and more with decisions about human and social priorities which are not in a technical sense medical. I attempt to deal with these organizational problems in Chapter 7.

Professional fragmentation

There is some consensus among organization theorists that technology moulds organization. There is for instance the Burns and Stalker (23) contrast between administrative styles, mechanistic and organic; a rigid style which is appropriate to straightforward repetitive machine processes, a flexible and spontaneous style which is appropriate to situations which require quick decisions in face of rapid changes of technology and situations. Likewise the late Joan Woodward (24) proposed a complex and subtle theory which she sums up very briefly (p. 50): 'firms with similar production systems appeared to have similar organizational structures'. But the technological imperative is not absolute; the manager operates within a social system which is given, and that system almost always includes what Pareto (25) calls 'residues', 'hang-overs' from previous states of organization. Some of these were once purposive and rational, but have been cast ashore and abandoned by tides of change. The origins of others are lost in mist—'old, unhappy, far-off things, And battles long ago' (26) which now have mythological force only, symbolic and yet powerful. To borrow a quotation from Rosemary Stevens,

> As the Pharisee thanked God he was not as other men, do not Physicians preen themselves ever so slightly on not being Paediatricians, Psychiatrists, or Pathologists? (27).

These 'residues' are present everywhere but are thought to be particularly characteristic of the English way of doing things. To explain the present English situation, one must go back at least to the reign of Henry VIII and to the foundation of the Royal College of Physicians, a self-appointed elite of London doctors practising largely for other elites in Court and City. There were two other ancestors; the surgeons—men of sharp instruments, razors, scalpels, lancets, and bone-saws—gradually detaching themselves from the old association with barbers; the apothecaries, and retail tradesmen in drugs, who acquired a working knowledge of the use of medicines. The distinctions once upon a time had a practical working basis, but by 1800 they were obsolete and there began to emerge the all-purpose doctor, the 'general practitioner' (28), who could do a bit of medicine, a bit of surgery, a bit of obstetrics, and knew enough about drugs to write simple prescriptions in gibberish Latin. It could be said that the GP was invented by the *Zeitgeist* to meet the needs of country people and of the new middle class; after perhaps half a century of unpleasant battles his position was sanctified by the Medical Act of 1858 and by the syllabuses of the new GMC. This was not as tidy a solution as those found by France or Prussia or even Scotland, but it served its time very well.

But it brought with it a new distinction which has perhaps not worked out so well. As early as 1797 Dr Percival, an inventive Scot who finally came to rest in Manchester, wrote a little book called *Medical Ethics,* prompted by quarrels between those members of the profession who served the Manchester Royal Infirmary. Its theme was that a doctor should behave like a gentleman (though I don't think he uses the word) towards his patients and towards his colleagues. Doctors owe to their patients (the emphasis is primarily on recipients of charity in Manchester Royal Infirmary) 'their skill, attention and fidelity. They should study, also, in their deportment, so to unite *tenderness* with *steadiness*, and *condescension* with *authority*, as to inspire the minds of their patients with gratitude, respect and confidence' (29) (his italics). But there is little more about patients, a great deal about doctors; and much of it arises out of the situation in which a GP calls another doctor 'into consultation'. The patient is still the patient of the first doctor, in the sense discussed in Chapter 4; but he may feel that some services (such as some forms of surgery) he cannot perform himself, or he may be young and faced with a new situation, or the patient and the family may be very anxious and also wealthy and are prepared to pay for a second opinion. The doctor called in would not be in any modern sense a 'specialist', and was properly called 'a consultant', who might well be himself also a GP. Very gradually there arose the career distinction between consultants and GPs, which survives to haunt us: the great majority were GPs, full-time consultants were very rare, except in London, where 'Harley Street' grew up to serve the wealthy throughout England, at any time of grave crisis.

Consultations could lead to situations of great 'delicacy' (one of Percival's favourite words) and he was mainly concerned to avert quarrels, in particular 'ungentlemanly' quarrels over fees.

'Residues' of this kind serve partly to explain the peculiar form which fragmentation has assumed in England. But there has also been a more recent invasion, that of true technological specialization; first a world-wide scientific revolution which has been on the move since the middle of the nineteenth century; then the establishment of a particular form of specialization by the National Health Service Act of 1947.

The scientific revolution of the last century is so familiar that it needs only a few sentences to describe it. One may envisage the structure of scientific knowledge as a vast loose-leaf book (I find this metaphor clearer than that of a computer information store) which is (in principle) unified in theory and comprehensively indexed. But it is continually growing and is continually being revised, and its neatness and order are subject to all manner of strains. New chapters are written which are found to disagree with chapters already there. There are awkward gaps between chapters which have to be plugged by new knowledge and new concepts; the new concepts may be hard to reconcile with old concepts, and every now and then there has to be a general 'spring-cleaning' of the book's conceptual order, a 'scientific revolution' in one of the senses implied by T. S. Kuhn's book (30).

One of the characteristics of 'the book of science' as it now exists is that low in its logical hierarchy come facts and procedures which have been tested to varying degrees of reliability. It is known that within these limits they are effective. That is to say the great structure is not only logical, awe-inspiring, and elegant, as was (say) the structure erected by Aristotle; it is also very useful.

Doctors, like the rest of us, have to come to terms with it; being above all practitioners, they have to be particularly sensitive to the fine print which tells you *exactly* what to do in *exactly* what circumstances. It is a bonus for the doctor if he can understand also the intellectual structure of the relevant section of the great book. But this has not the same priority for him or her as it has for the professional scientific worker. Of course, some doctors double the parts of healer and of scientist: but it is not necessary that lines of medical specialization should follow the same lines of cleavage as those of scientific knowledge (31).

Indeed, they do not. Here is a list derived from Rosemary Stevens's book (p. 111):

General surgery and related specialities
    Urology
    Neurosurgery
    Plastic surgery
    Thoracic surgery
    Hospital dentistry and orthodontics
Gynaecology and obstetrics
Ear—nose—throat
Ophthalmology
Anaesthetics
General medicine and related specialities
    Chest diseases
    Neurology
    Cardiology
    Pediatrics
    Geriatrics
    Physical medicine
    Infectious diseases
    Venereology
    Social medicine (or community medicine?)
Dermatology
Psychiatry (and its subdivisions)
Pathology (and its subdivisions)
Radiology and radiotherapy

It is at once painfully obvious that this is a form of organization based on no single principle; parts of the body, age cohorts of patients, types of disease, and types of technique (such as anaesthetics and radiology). It is in fact a historical rather than a logical structure, never wholly stable, affected both by the needs of patients and by the needs of other doctors: a structure concerned not only with skills but with ambition and prestige.

This type of structure is not necessarily ineffective, though it may be. Its advantage is that scientific categories cut across organizational forms. Geriatricians (for instance) have done a great deal to 'civilize' treatment of old people in a social sense: in a scientific sense, an energetic and able geriatrician is also concerned with the phenomenon of 'ageing', which is not necessarily correlated with chronological age. Indeed, it raises fundamental questions about the mechanisms of all life. Given able doctors, this pattern of 'cross-cutting cleavages' may stimulate work in both directions, social and scientific.

In one aspect, then, the structure of medical practice is political, and every doctor (like every man and woman) is in some sense a political animal. The NHS is structured in various ways, economic, social, and administrative as well as technical; like all complex organizations it has a political structure, in which a great part is played by the organizations of doctors. On the whole these operate in public, with a tremendous output of printed documentation. The researcher's problem is not so much to find information, as to organize it in a way which is clear, accurate, and realistic. One is bound to abbreviate the facts and impose a structure on them, and it is simplest to impose a simple structure—which is by definition inadequate. I have earlier rejected simple theories of professional organization for dominance or monopoly. Towards pressure-group theory (32) I feel more friendly, and also to the theory of elites. But on the whole, I think the most helpful concepts and images are those of interaction in a field or arena or on a stage (33).

My argument throughout is that in the show here staged the protagonists are doctors and patients but that neither group is homogeneous nor tightly organized. Furthermore, there are other important roles to be played, in particular those of nurses, of ancillary technicians and helpers, of accountants, and administrators. Occasionally, even elected party politicians come on stage and make as if to change the framework of the drama.

Their interventions are not trivial; the stage is set by great public statutes, such as Lloyd George's Act of 1911, Nye Bevan's Act of 1946. But the community of national health is something bigger than its legal framework.

Organizations of doctors

More than twenty years ago (34) I defined 'pressure groups' for the purposes of political analysis as 'the field of organized groups possessing both formal structure and real common interests, in so far as they influence the decisions of public bodies'. That formula contains a number of tricky words (in particular, 'real common interests', 'influence', 'decisions', 'public'); and it can fairly be argued that formal structure always lags behind social reality. I have already referred very briefly to the technological, social, and economic factors which underlie the historical development of medical politics; now I must try to explain the pattern of organization which emerged and which has done much to influence the present structure and present controversies. This structure is very complex, and I am unashamedly dependent on secondary sources, in particular on Rosemary Stevens and on A. J. Willcocks's book on *The Creation of the National Health Service* (35).

It is logical to begin with the British Medical Association (though it is by no means the oldest organization in the field) because it was founded specifically as a fighting organization with a claim to represent the profession as a whole. The second quarter of the nineteenth century was a time of active medical politics and journalism and in particular of the rise of general practice outside London (36). 'The Provincial Medical and Surgical Association' (1832) '. . . was largely set up to counteract, in the provinces, the power of the Colleges' (Stevens, 1966, p. 22). In that period (in so far as we can use modern categories at all) there were about 13,800 GPs, about 580 senior hospital doctors, about 600 junior hospital doctors. By 1853 London GPs were admitted to the Association, which became the 'BMA' in 1856 (the creation of the GMC followed in 1858). Most doctors joined, partly because the BMA became a provider of various necessary facilities (including its indispensable journal). But the working of the BMA depended on the

existence of a 'political class' of vocal and argumentative doctors, not yet much studied by academics. There is an excellent
example of such internal faction fighting to be found in Jean
Donnison's book (37), in the campaign led by Dr Robert
Rentoul of Liverpool 'who had set himself up as the champion
of the less affluent medical practitioner' (p. 120) and led a violent campaign against the training and registration of midwives,
which was not finally achieved until 1902 (seventeen years
before the registration of nurses). It is probably true that the
existence of midwives in private practice in working-class districts was a challenge to doctors attempting to earn a hard
living there. Certainly Dr Rentoul (he had his own journal)
provides plenty of evidence for the theory of doctors as organizers
of monopoly.

> The *Medical Times* warned that the 'fatal results' of allow-
> ing chemists to be registered outside the control of the
> medical profession would be repeated in the case of mid-
> wives. Moreover, the Bill would be a precedent for the
> registration of nurses, also independent of medical control
> (p. 155).

There was, however, another faction within the BMA, whose
journal, *The Practitioner*, denounced Dr Rentoul's party as
'scribblers and stump orators', 'with a shop-counter attitude',
'disgusting all reasonable men with their agitation for monopoly' (p. 155).

In the end, this case tells against the thesis of professional
monopoly. The BMA did not follow Dr Rentoul solidly and the
Royal Colleges kept out of the controversy. Reform in this case
came (as so often) through a small persistent group, including
some doctors with a social concern, some stern upper-class
ladies, and a few men or women who were prepared to speak
clearly for the under-privileged.

Since these days the BMA has built up a reputation for
political incompetence (38). Already at the end of the nineteenth century, some security was provided by the association
of local doctors with working-class provident societies; and this
was for the first time given statutory backing by Lloyd George's
Act of 1911. But the BMA's 'political class' led the BMA
into outright opposition, and then to a ludicrous collapse;

a story which repeated itself in the struggle over the Act of 1946.

The immediate result of that Act was to change the balance of numbers within the medical world. These figures (which relate to the UK) are not very precise, but there is no doubt about the situation and the resulting changes of perspective:

	*1860**	*1938/9†*	*1949‡*	*1959‡*	*1974‡*
GPs	13,800	18,000	18,000	25,012	25,844
Senior hospital doctors	580	2,800⎫			33,137
Junior hospital doctors	600	2,381⎭	15,950	20,950	
	14,980	23,181	33,950	45,962	58,981

* ABEL-SMITH, BRIAN (1964). *The Hospitals, 1800–1948* (London: Heinemann).
† STEVENS, ROSEMARY (1966). *Medical Practice in Modern England* (New Haven: Yale University Press).
‡ *Medical Manpower—The Next Twenty Years* (1978). (London: HMSO).

The leaders of the BMA had concentrated on what they were *against*, in particular against a salaried service and against any proposal to subordinate general practice to the elected local authority and its salaried MOH. In the end they were repudiated by their members; some of them secured promotion into the privileged ranks of the consultants (39), and the rest valued increased security even as 'independent contractors'. In general, personnel statistics were then very poor, and none of the parties seem to have foreseen the quite abrupt change from the predominance of GPs (mainly working from their own surgeries) to the predominance of hospital doctors, working from institutions owned and paid for by a public organization.

During the next twenty years statistics (which in this case deserved their old name, 'political arithmetic') swung from a predicted deficit of doctors (Goodenough) to a predicted surplus (Willink) and back again to a predicted deficit (Todd, 1965–8), and the university system responded (40).

This had relatively little effect on the political problems of the BMA. The NHS was constituted from the first on the theory that there would be a well-financed and coherently organized national system of hospitals and an equally well-equipped system of health centres staffed by teams of GPs. But very early in the life of the NHS (41) its costs escalated in a way which was alarming politically, and it was realized that the simple model of health care which was sufficient for Lord Beveridge had no relation to real life. There did not exist a back-log of ill health which could be cleared so as to produce a 'healthy' nation, with reduced medical needs. On the contrary, increasing medical possibilities produced new medical demands, escalation seemed infinite, and that during a period of economic gloom. In consequence, there was virtually no new health service building, and in particular no building of health centres, which no one demanded earnestly (except perhaps for the wives of single-handed GPs and for the Socialist Medical Association (42)). There was, however, a slow change of generations, and the perennial crisis over the pay of doctors escalated in 1965 when the BMA rejected the report of the Standing Review Body (Kindersley) on the remuneration of GPs and their relativities with hospital doctors. The situation was like that of 1911 and 1946, and yet subtly different. There was the old radicalism (in this case that of the Medical Practitioners Union (43) and the local medical committees in the 'provinces'), and the old threats of withdrawals. But by this time there existed a much more elaborate negotiating structure for all doctors in the NHS, an alternative to the Whitley Councils which covered between them all other NHS employees. There was a Joint Consultants Committee, representing the colleges and their affiliates; the General Medical Services Committee represented the GPs; and they had come together to present joint evidence to the Standing Review Body (Kindersley) constituted in 1962 on the recommendation of a previous enquiry (44) that there should be an arbitrating body to stand between the Ministry of Health and the doctors. Through this maze of institutions the BMA leaders managed to steer its Charter for the Family Doctor Service (March 1965, revised October 1965) to the point of approval in a ballot by a huge majority of the profession.

The resulting compromise was extremely complex, and it was followed by a period in which consultants complained that GPs (at least some of them) were now the financial elite of the profession. The principle of 'independent contract' and payment by capitation was sustained, but there entered also a diversity of new concepts: an increase in the (relatively small) salary element, a special element for elderly patients, a special element for work done 'out of hours'; special elements for seniority and for distinction; a special element for practice in an under-doctored area. Various 'fee for service' items have since been added.

The Labour government of 1964 came into office in a period of enthusiasm for coherent and vigorous government ('the planning mood' and 'the forward look'); the economic situation was not too bad, at least up to the devaluation crisis of 1967; and the settlement (though the principles were old) did indicate that the profession for the first time since 1946 was on the move. The GPs had awakened as if from long slumber and had begun to look for an ideology and for prestige. The ideology was that of the family doctor, specially concerned with social medicine and even with community medicine (the new title of their old enemies, the MOHs, who were also on the move). The land-mark was the foundation of the College of General Practitioners in November 1952, dignified by Royal patronage in April 1967. The College grew quite fast (6,200 members and associates by 1962), and its status was recognized in the merit awards and training payments of the 1966 settlement. This meant (perhaps) that there would at last be health centres, properly equipped at public expense, and that GPs would no longer be forced to pay for premises and equipment out of their own pockets. There would at last be a hope of predictable hours, adequate ancillary staff, and a set of records effectively tied in to a national system. There was even hope of reciprocal relations with the district general hospitals (still to be built) and even a prospect (perhaps illusory) that there would be some hospital work for GPs.

Progress towards these goals has been very slow in England and Wales (45), perhaps relatively a little faster in Scotland. But these negotiated objectives still stand.

And at this point the third factor in the structure, the Junior Hospital Doctors, first (in Mr Gladstone's words) 'come within the pale of the constitution'. Mr Gladstone's remark was made in 1864 (46), and referred to the general enfranchisement of working men. Its relevance is that there had been a very slow development in the status of junior doctors over 200 years from a position of servile apprenticeship, dependent on the personal patronage of the senior hospital doctors whom they served. They might in the end succeed to their master's prestige, status, and emoluments. Meantime, there were 'blood, sweat and tears' (47), and they were deemed by their superiors to enjoy it, on the good public school principle that fags like being beaten by prefects.

There was gradual improvement in the twentieth century, as higher qualifications began to presuppose a recognizable pattern of training, the centre of medical practice shifted from GP to hospital, and the old local authority hospitals began to give full-time salaried employment to competent doctors. The coming of the NHS enhanced and stabilized this trend, and by the 1950s there had emerged the concept that there should be a hierarchy of posts and an expectation of advancement through it, at least for doctors trained in Britain and in the 'Old Commonwealth'. The progression should be through grades of house officer, senior house officer, registrar, senior registrar to consultant, with planned progression through a variety of training posts at first, then a gradual narrowing to a particular field of specialization. The pattern was confused by the invention of Senior Hospital Medical Officers, Junior Hospital Medical Officers, and Medical Assistants, largely to increase numbers at the junior and middle levels without commitment to promotion—inevitably, after the rapid expansion in the early days of the NHS, there was now a promotion block for consultant posts and a silting up of good new people at the Senior Registrar level.

Silting up and frustration created solidarity and leadership; a junior hospital doctors' association was formed in 1966, and was given proportionate financial recognition in the financial settlement of that year. But while this was happening the nature of the problem changed. The provision for junior medical staff increased piecemeal, without any attempt at comprehensive planning, and quite suddenly (as it seemed) the NHS found that it was totally dependent on doctors qualified in universities outside the UK, predominantly in India and Pakistan. The UK medical profession, to its credit, had given help generously in building up medical schools in the old empire, where doctors were very badly needed. Now the graduates of these schools came to Britain in search of higher qualifications, were hired at decent enough wages to block gaps in the NHS establishment —and were desperately unsuccessful in the higher examinations.

A few qualified, and have given indispensable service as consultants in the scarcer specialities; a few have gone into general practice; there remains a stock of some 16,500 foreign-born doctors, product of continuing flows into the UK and out, still not adequately measured. An association of overseas doctors has existed since 1975; but its constituency is in its nature extremely difficult to organize, and it is certainly not yet 'within the pale of the constitution'. We talk *about* them (mainly with a view to getting rid of them, without damage to ourselves), we do not talk *to* them, either about their problems or about ours. They are essential to the working of the health service (25 per cent of the total active NHS medical staff); and yet they are in effect excluded from its political system (48).

Consultants

The argument so far has been that medical education did in the past, and still can, create very strong solidarity among medical graduates. The nineteenth century saw the rise of the 'general practitioner', and the British Medical Association was created largely to advance and consolidate his interests. For reasons not clear, it proved to be inept politically, and ridden by faction; a radically selfish faction, a radically public-spirited faction, and a soft centre. At times of crisis, the centre has generally moved, timidly and late, towards the radically selfish wing, and has been by-passed by the mainstream of events. Meantime the number of GPs has declined a little in absolute terms and has declined enormously in relative terms. Hospital medicine now dominates.

Yet, because of the nineteenth-century emergence of a special relationship between GP and consultant, we the patients deal with the system primarily through GPs. Perhaps the GP's surgery is no more than a sorting and despatching office, an issuing point for official 'chits' of many kinds. But we like it (I risk saying); indeed, we should endorse Rosemary Stevens' epigram (p. 359) that

> If the GP did not exist he (or someone like him) would have to be invented . . . The English referral system provides one very relevant answer for the provision of personal medical care in a specialized environment.

To paraphrase Dean Acheson, like Britain, the GPs have lost an empire and have not found a role. But there may have been a turn of the tide during the 1960s, towards a realistic doctrine and a long view.

The position of the Junior Hospital Doctors is rather different. In the nature of things, they are not motivated to seek power and dominate policy, as the GPs once were, and perhaps are still. Their problem is to keep in being the effective wage-bargaining organization that now exists.

In so doing they may sustain their coloured colleagues indirectly, but the latter surely are doomed to remain passive participants.

In the search for medical power, then, I must now tackle the difficult problem of consultants in general, Royal Colleges in particular.

First, some facts and distinctions. In 1976 there were 12,879 consultants in the NHS in England; a consultant is one who holds an established post as consultant; in the nature of things, there will always be vacancies, and therefore there are more posts than there are consultants.

A consultant is defined by his post as being a specialist. A specialist is defined by qualifications: training, experience, examinations, degrees, diplomas, and so on. He is not a consultant until his name is put forward by a selection committee for an established post: there may even survive a few elderly consultants qualified for specialism only by experience and not by examination.

Specialisms proliferate. The Americans (it is said) recognize eighteen, and have an appropriate process of accreditation for each. The English (49) position is quite similar in terms of scientific structure, but is greatly complicated by its history.

The oldest of the existing institutions is the Royal College of Physicians, approved by Henry VIII as a young man, and designed primarily as a gentlemanly monopoly for physicians to the wealthy, in court and city. It moved into the pre-modern world in the latter part of the eighteenth century, when the great London hospitals became centres for training and (to a limited extent) research; and Fellows of the College between them exercised virtually a monopoly of 'beds' (50). Surgery, still without antiseptics or anaesthesia, had nevertheless achieved similar social distinction, and claimed its own Royal College in 1800 (51).

The political character of the two Colleges differed somewhat from the outset. Rosemary Stevens (52) quotes a remark of Sir Robert Platt's (the late Lord Platt of Grindleford):

> Surgeons, I suspect, see themselves in a setting of glamour, conquering disease by bold strokes of sheer technical skill. Physicians quietly remember that they were educated gentlemen centuries ago, when surgeons and apothecaries were tradesmen. They see themselves as the traditional thinkers of the profession.

This is accurate enough, within the conventions of ceremonial persiflage, but it is much less than the whole truth. The tradition of the Physicians is one of leadership by a closed circle of Fellows, and of a 'holistic' conceptual scheme in medicine. Medicine is an art as well as a science; the patient must be perceived as a person, and must be treated as a unique single entity. The Surgeons were not managed in the same way by a tightly knit caucus; and they were, by the nature of their skill, concerned primarily with particular conditions which could be cured or at least ameliorated by dexterity and technical inventiveness. Their College was much more hospitable than was that of the Physicians to new developments in medicine, and to their practitioners.

The College of Obstetricians and Gynaecologists was set up independently of the Physicians in 1929, after a very interesting social and political battle, and gained the title Royal in 1938; it is of course the only Royal College in which women doctors have substantial (though by no means predominant) influence (53).

The College of General Practitioners (set up in 1952 and dubbed 'Royal' in 1967) has a different political and social origin; indeed it stands apart, as it seeks to give those who are not 'consultants' an equal but distinct standing within the profession.

There is also the special problem of the organization of psychiatry, 'the other half of medicine, and not just another specialty', as one of its leaders is reported to have said in 1946 (54).

The case is perhaps one of social change rather than of medical advance. Mental illness and mental deficiency are not new problems, and the NHS inherited a large number of 'beds', largely for long-stay 'patients' who had little hope of release. Social policy and social attitudes have changed and there are greater possibilities of 'care in the community'. But still half the NHS beds are in mental hospitals, and these still include a number of long-stay patients, even though the average length of stay has come down sharply since the 1950s. Hence psychiatry is one of the biggest 'specialisms' (55) and one of the most difficult to staff. Yet psychiatry for long remained within the structure of the Royal College of Physicians, represented by a rather unusual body, the Royal Medico-Psychological Association; a Royal College was not established until 1971.

Other new foundations reflect technical rather than social change. The College of Pathologists, founded in 1962, was chartered as 'Royal' in 1970; it is the only College which admits scientists who are not medically qualified. The radiologists (confined to doctors) secured their own Royal College in 1975, and complete the present list of seven. The next candidates in line were the anaesthetists and the community physicians, but they have decided that the wisest course in their own interests is to remain as Faculties within the Royal Colleges of Surgeons and of Physicians respectively.

The following other specialisms have consultant posts assigned to them and complex organizations of their own, mainly within the scope of the Royal Colleges: Paediatrics, Otolaryngology, Dermatology, Geriatrics, Orthopaedics, Urology.

The forms of organization vary; some act as 'qualifying associations' in terms of Geoffrey Millerson's book (56), some are primarily scientific, some combine various functions. But all are 'recognized' associations, 'within the pale of the constitution', which have in some informal sense the right to be consulted, though not the right to veto. It would serve no purpose to elucidate all these complexities here, provided that three points are understood.

Firstly, the familiar cry 'is there a doctor in the house?'; the scene of a motor smash, a nasty-looking accident on a playing-field or ski-slope. What will you get? You will probably be lucky if you get a GP; you risk getting a pathologist who has not laid hands on a patient for thirty years, or a specialist in mental deficiency, or a salesman for a great pharmaceutical company. In fact you may be better off with a State Enrolled Nurse than with any of these. But I have a feeling (which I cannot document except anecdotally—a gynaecologist saw me through very well after a nasty skiing accident) that each of these would in fact feel a professional obligation to serve, and would summon up from the recesses of memory knowledge and skill sufficient to control the situation temporarily. At least so far as the UK is concerned, the case for the effects of fragmentation and disintegration has been overstated. The status of doctor is still socially recognized and reacts upon the identity of its incumbent.

Secondly, there are important differences in pay and status, even among those who all rank equally as consultants. As George Orwell might have said, all consultants are equal, but some consultants are very much more equal than others.

The principle of equality means that the etiquette of relationships is at least as prickly as it was in the 1790s when Percival attempted to formulate a code of peace and dignity for medical gentlemen. Also (as will be explained more fully in the hospitals chapter) it weakens the authority of doctors in hospitals, in that the associated consultants attempt to formulate their priorities through a committee system, within organizations which are otherwise disciplined and hierarchical.

But in status and prestige consultants are unequal in subtle ways which are hard for the layman to perceive and to evaluate. There are problems of differentiation in relation to differences of region, class, and culture. Probably there still exists a stereotype of the successful Harley Street practitioner, drawn from the Victorian tradition of carriage and top hat, the Edwardian tradition of Rolls-Royce and chauffeur. Probably such characters are extinct: but probably there is still among the successful a predominance of public school, Oxbridge, London medical school, London experience. But there has been a big contribution by central Europeans, particularly in psychiatric medicine, and by Australians and New Zealanders, particularly in general medicine and surgery.

Scotland has its own distinct traditions and snobberies, less centralized than those of the London region; and progress has been made towards establishing parity of esteem between London and the English provinces, which now have almost an equal share of teaching hospitals and medical students. As I understand it, the Royal Colleges have all been wisely led towards an equal allocation of presidencies and other high offices between London and the provinces.

There is differentiation of prestige in terms of accomplishment in research. The *Annual Reports* of the Medical Research Council contain very full information about those who are members of the Council and its awarding committees, about the distribution of grants between specialties, about research units and individual grants, and about contract research sponsored by the DHSS, the Department of Employment, and the Health and Safety Executive. This is very difficult for the layman to 'read', and I risk no hypotheses—except that it can be read fluently by those in the inner circles of sponsorship.

Thirdly, there is the extremely complex process of negotiating remuneration. A settlement with the consultants was agreed with the DHSS in May 1978, after a great deal of bargaining, but final acceptance awaits the addition of actual cash figures to the framework of categories negotiated. One of the remarks often attributed to Nye Bevan is that 'I stopped their mouths with gold'; I cannot find it in his biography and perhaps he never said it—it is much too crude a summary. It is true that he won his battle in 1948 by dividing the embattled forces of the profession, but what emerged was a remarkably adaptable system which suited the needs both of consultants and of the NHS.

This is not the place for a detailed description of terms of service for consultants. The details are indeed important, but one can perhaps distinguish two main themes.

There is that of distinction awards, bonuses for status and prestige decided confidentially by a committee chaired by Sir Stanley Clayton, FRCP, FRCS, FRCOG.

There were four grades; the lowest awards are no more than a useful *pourboire*, the highest (only 113 for nearly 13,000 consultants) virtually double the basic salary (57). About one-third of all consultants receive some award, but among specialties there are very wide deviations from the average. At the top are cardiology, thoracic surgery, and neurosurgery, with over 60 per cent: in the lowest rank are community medicine,

geriatrics, rheumatology, and mental health—all of them under
25 per cent.

It is easy to guess at one dimension of this spread. The work of
community doctors has a large element of administration, and
relatively few (except perhaps the epidemiologists) can make
high professional reputations as practitioners or as research
workers. The other three bear much of the burden of work which
is still slow-moving and custodial, in areas of medicine which
are of vast social importance and yet depressingly static. There
is indeed some progress, but no present hope of any radical
innovation.

The new settlement retains the system, which gives a very
great salary spread between the highest and the lowest career
consultant. But it gives some assurances that the differentials
will be narrowed, between London and the provinces, between
brilliant innovation and steady meritorious service, between
fashionable and unfashionable specializations.

There is also the question of private practice, a theme which
appeals particularly to party politicians on both sides; it is seen
as a theme of equality versus elitism, as was the question of
comprehensive schools versus grammar schools. It is tempting
to extreme ideologists on both sides to say to doctors 'come in
or stay out'. But, in fact, at the working level, neither side can
afford a break. It is possible (much depends on the existence
of very rich patients, such as Arab princes and multinational
companies) that scope can be found for a few private hospitals
and a few consultants in fashionable specialties. But even the
high fliers need the national hospital service in the first years of
their careers; and those of lesser eminence are of necessity
committed totally to the service as it is to them. Hence, the
original formula for remuneration not by salary but by sessions,
eleven sessions in a notional week, the consultant committed
to a maximum of eleven sessions, a minimum of two.

This system also has been retained, except that sessions are
renamed 'notional half-days', NHDs, ten per week, but with an
option (by mutual agreement) of adding up to five more NHDs
a week for those who abjure private practice. This is a slight
concession to ideology: but, in fact, the vast majority of
consultants will be (as they always have been) virtually
whole-time servants of the state.

In parenthesis, it can be read between the lines that in 1978 the negotiators for the consultants know much more than in 1948 about the realities of pay in modern industrial societies. There are careful provisions for paid overtime; and they seem to have negotiated hard for untaxable benefits such as the cost of telephones and of travel.

This looks as if it may be the basis of a framework to last for a generation, as did that of 1948. But one more gap remains, that between university clinical professors and other consultants in the same specialties (58). One of the revolutionary changes introduced by the NHS was that it was made mandatory that professors teaching clinical subjects in the universities and their allied hospitals should accept full-time appointments involving care for patients, teaching, and research, as equal and necessary components of their university work. These became full-time salaried appointments, and for the first time the work of the medical school had priority over the private practice of consultants. But the best consultants could earn much more than a professor's salary, and from the outset the University Grants Committee and the universities accepted (to the prejudice of other professors) a provision that clinical professors should have a salary scale higher than that of preclinical professors in the Medical Faculty, and indeed above that of all their 'equal' colleagues in the University Senate. What is more, they were also in the field for NHS distinction awards, and with salaries thus reinforced their rewards might not be so much below those of fashionable consultants in private practice. I have seen somewhere a comment that, even so, the professors first appointed in London hospitals (or some of them) were by no means at the top of the prestige hierarchy in their specialty. But outside London, in the English 'provincial' universities the results were excellent, and medical faculties fully integrated into a regional university of many faculties had for the first time intellectual and social facilities better than those of London teaching hospitals, most of them very weakly integrated with the University of London (59).

It is possible that this special position may be endangered because consultants, like general practitioners, are beginning to see the advantages of a fee-for-service system (including fringe benefits and tax relief), as a supplement (not as an alternative) to present forms of remuneration, and as I write, there has appeared in *The Times* (5 April 1978) a long and carefully reasoned letter from almost 150 clinical professors in the university making the case for special recognition of their position.

Negotiations continue.

Retrospect

This chapter has been long enough, and yet scarcely does justice to the complexity of these interacting organizations. Traditionally, the BMA is politically inept, the Royal Colleges are slow to move, the average doctor, whether GP or specialist, is politically rather naive. But the system is held together by its peculiar relationship with the Ministry of Health (or DHSS), of which much more will be said in Chapter 9. In one sense, all doctors (and this effectively includes even the very small private sector) are its clients; it holds all the 'goodies', in terms of personal emoluments and of professional equipment; and its strength in bargaining is not weakened even though the Treasury lurks behind the arras, a formidable Polonius. In another sense, the DHSS is weak, it cannot move without the doctors. The doctors are weakly led, but they are indispensable. Rosemary Stevens writes somewhere of the stage army of sixty to eighty senior doctors, mainly Fellows of the Royal Colleges, who move through a network of Departmental Committees, headed by the Central Health Services Council and its subordinate bodies. Departmental officials, lay and medical, are always present, and so are some token lay-persons from outside. But the inner circle of doctors know one another by sight and by reputation pretty well; will influence the addition of new recruits to the circle; and will have a continuing influence on NHS policy and the allocation of resources. They are, by definition, middle-aged or even elderly; basically very able and tenacious; with high reputations as practitioners and research workers, but now past their prime in these respects; by no means representative of the profession as a whole, but nevertheless selected (and self-selected) as the 'political class', the unifying factor in a confused and changing situation.

Yes, the medical elite is powerful in the central management of the health service: but not all-powerful. Where medical power lies is at the level of clinical decisions, and it can be argued that for this reason local consultants are dominant at the level of local hospitals and in relation to the management of their specialty through local GPs.

Yet here too there are built-in limits, of which more is said in later chapters.

CHAPTER 6 WHAT IS A NURSE?

> What is it to feel a *calling* for anything? Is it not to do your
> work in it to satisfy your own high idea of what is the *right*,
> the *best*, and not because you will be 'found out' if you don't
> do it?
>
> FLORENCE NIGHTINGALE (1876), *Notes on Nursing*, ed. Drew, p. 99
> (London: Harrison)

The latest figures I have (those of the DHSS *Annual Report* for
1976) give a total of 338,997 staff in nursing and midwifery
(including part-time equivalents) in England alone; there are
separate statistics for Scotland, Wales, and Northern Ireland.

These figures are related to the work of 54,679 doctors (1), of
whom 22,015 are general practitioners; to a total NHS staff of
778,150; and to the experience of some 50 million patients. But
it is not easy to offer a total for patients, because an out-patient
is an elusive creature, who may appear once at an accident and
emergency clinic and never be seen again. On the other hand,
there are records of the number of patients on the lists of GPs;
records known to be inaccurate because of deaths and removals,
but good enough for practical purposes (not much worse than,
for instance, the electoral register). But it is not easy to get
comparable figures for the work of GPs at their surgeries and in
their home visits, except by an organized sample survey and
some arbitrary definitions. For instance, I usually get a monthly
prescription by post; last month I forgot and went along to
surgery for a signature—but I did not in fact see the doctor who
signed it. Similarly, it is not easy, it may even be meaningless,
to give figures for patients attended by domiciliary nurses and
midwives, health visitors, industrial nurses, school nurses, and
so on. But the official figures give the following for the year
1976:

Hospital in-patients	5,254,000
Out-patient attendances: clinics	32,396,000
Out-patient attendances: accident and emergency	13,077,000
(NB. These are *attendances*, not cases.)	

Notes and references for this chapter begin on page 198.

The population of England in 1976 was estimated to be about 46 million.

NHS statistics are notoriously difficult to handle, but nothing can modify the first impression that a very high proportion of the population is directly affected by the NHS at some time; and that a very large proportion of the work of the NHS is done by nurses and midwives. They (like doctors) are at the centre of the system.

But their distribution within the system is quite different. Roughly two doctors out of five work in the community as GPs; for nurses the proportion is more like one in eleven (2). To put it in another way, for every hospital doctor about ten nurses, for every GP perhaps one nurse. Hospitals are very largely nursing institutions. Indeed hospitals as we know them have been shaped largely by nurses (3). The legend is that of Florence Nightingale; not that of 'The lady with the lamp', but that of the ferocious invalid who bullied the male establishment and who constructed a women's profession from her couch. It is not true that she invented modern nursing; there were Catholic nursing orders and (writes Abel-Smith) (4) 'The reform of nursing in Britain owes something to the example of the Protestant Institute of Deaconesses at Kaiserswerth' in Germany. But the centre of construction was the Nightingale School of Nursing at St Thomas's Hospital, opened in 1860 with funds collected to commemorate Miss Nightingale's work in the Crimean War.

> Between 1860 and 1903 the Nightingale School certified 1,907 nurses as having had one year's training . . . the new order spread by geometric progression as each trained nurse trained others. Miss Nightingale herself . . . acted as a clearing house for nursing appointments throughout the country and steered candidates of whom she approved into the key positions of the nursing world (5).

These key positions were as matrons of the great voluntary hospitals, which were also teaching hospitals for the medical profession. It is not true that Miss Nightingale set out to provide scope for the thwarted energies of upper-class ladies like herself. Indeed Abel-Smith (6) quotes a report of 1862 which she doubtless drafted:

> Persons of superior manners and education, ladies in fact, are not as a rule the best qualified, but rather women of somewhat more than ordinary intelligence emanating from those classes in which women are habitually employed in earning their own livelihood.

So far as I know, no one has attempted (it would be a very hard task) to 'sociologize' the early graduates of the Nightingale School; certainly 'upper-class ladies' were among them, but probably there was a higher proportion of daughters of the successful middle class, able people who sent their able daughters to the girls' grammar schools and boarding schools which came into being at this period (7).

The new matrons were able, they were well trained, they were afraid of no man. And

> they possessed one weapon which could be kept in reserve; in the event of serious trouble they could appeal above the heads of the doctors or lay administrators to Miss Nightingale herself. . . . In nearly all cases the new matrons triumphed. And in the voluntary hospitals they carved out for themselves positions of undisputed authority between the medical staff and the lay administrator (8).

This was 'main-stream'. Much came from other sources, as will be explained later. But hence came much of the image and the ideology. The image is conveyed to all by a uniform which (as Abel-Smith says somewhere) seems to combine the style of religious orders with that of Victorian domestic servants— 'a pride that apes humility'. The ideology is in part that of hierarchy, of discipline, and of precise distinction of roles and ranks. But there is also an ideology of 'tender loving care'.

'Care' not 'cure'; care is for the nurse, cure is for the doctor. The distinction cannot logically be sustained. Everyone knows that the best medical treatment is sometimes to leave the patient alone to recover, cared for 'in good hands': everyone knows that in some emergencies a well-trained self-reliant nurse can be of more help than an inexperienced doctor; and the protective relationship of the ward sister to the young 'house-man' in training is one of the many themes available to those who write hospital 'soap operas'. One definitional refuge is in

terms of specified nursing 'procedures'; there are drills to follow, observations to be made. These can be and must be defined
precisely; and they are in principle 'ancillary' to the medical
work of diagnosis and treatment.

But in practice the distinction is maintained by a delicate
set of understandings learned by long experience of work together on the wards and in the operating theatres, and guarded
by seniors in the two professions. This etiquette of subordination
is perhaps endangered by rising standards of academic training
for nurses, at least for the select few who enter degree courses;
perhaps it is also endangered by the rise of the professions which
claim to be 'supplementary' or 'complementary' to medicine,
rather than 'ancillary', as will be described in Chapter 7. A
staff nurse or theatre sister is not likely to accept lower status
than a physiotherapist, an occupational therapist, or a speech
therapist, all of them professions which claim the privilege of
'therapy'. And in hospital life status is perhaps more valued
than is salary, though the two are very closely linked.

There is also the organizational argument, that doctors are
expensively trained, are in short supply, require equipment too
sophisticated for most cases in most of the developing world.
Hence arguments in favour of the pre-1914 Russian *feldscher* (9),
the 'bare-foot doctor' in China, the medical assistant in charge
of a simple dispensary in the African bush (10). This pattern
will certainly not be adopted here: but it is first cousin to our
current proposals for care in the community. These are still
rudimentary, perhaps even unreal: but domiciliary nursing in
all its forms enforces self-reliance, and to some nurses this is in
itself attractive.

Midwives

Doctors need nurses, are dependent on nurses, but are not
jealous of nurses; and so it is likely to continue. But I have been
writing hitherto of nurses, not taking into account that the
proper phrase is 'nurses and midwives' and that there are two
bodies of equal dignity, the Royal College of Midwives and the
Royal College of Nursing; State Certified Midwife (SCM),
State Registered Nurse (SRN).

We forget the old distinction because practically all qualified
midwives are now also qualified as nurses; but Jean Donnison's

recent book for the first time made clear the radical distinction between the two traditions.

Childbirth is not an illness, but it spells crisis, a climacteric, a time of decision and danger. From the moment of conception the mother passes through a time of complex physiological changes which continue for some time after the birth. Knowledge of this has been a mark of the solidarity of women since time immemorial; in a good community, however primitive, the stages of pregnancy would be observed and encouraged by older women, and a few of these would be 'wise women', *sages-femmes*, midwives who were experienced and trusted. Probably they helped most by physical skill and contact in handling mother and baby; but they also had a heritage of herbs and charms and protective spirits (11).

The Hippocratic doctors were well-informed about childbirth and its dangers, but a 'man midwife' was scarcely heard of in Europe till the latter part of the seventeenth century. In France, in *Le Grand Siècle,* some midwives became fashionable and sophisticated; some even wrote textbooks. England lagged somewhat; nevertheless this was a respectable women's profession centuries before women aspired to be doctors. But this stronghold was attacked by men at the beginning of the nineteenth century, and by the middle of the century 'obstetrics and gynaecology' became part of the medical curriculum and every medical student was given some sketchy practical training in delivery wards (it was part of the changing pattern that hospital 'lying-in' began slowly to displace childbirth at home).

As Jean Donnison describes it, there then began a period of direct competition between doctors and midwives. It is true that incompetent and dirty midwifery was one contributing factor in the high infant mortality of the period, and that this was itself part of the 'cycle of deprivation' among the poor of the urban slums (12). Doctors could point this out truly: but they were also driven into financial competition with midwives, in that if a young doctor 'put up his plate' in an industrial area he might well find it easiest to build up a practice first in midwifery. The ironic consequence was that one faction among doctors was trying to drive the domiciliary midwife out of business, while another faction was trying to achieve what France and Germany had achieved many years before, a state service of trained and registered midwives. For nurses, Florence Nightingale preferred voluntary association to regulation by law, but she distinguished the case of midwives as independent practitioners and supported their case, though she did not take the lead.

Agitation for improved training and status began about 1870; a bill for registration reached the floor of the House of Commons in 1890, and the Midwives Act was eventually passed in 1902, after able and persistent lobbying in face of political and public indifference. This was seventeen years before the Nurses Registration Act of 1919, and it was only possible because the midwives in effect struck a solemn compact with the doctors; a midwife might attend a normal birth single-handed, but she must not use an instrument to aid delivery and she must call for medical help at once if there was any indication of abnormality.

But since that settlement was reached the scene has changed. Domiciliary deliveries went out of fashion, slowly but steadily. They survived into my day (1909). But when my own family were born (in the 1940s and 1950s) the children of the middle-class were born largely in small 'nursing-homes' run as private enterprise by qualified 'nurse-midwives' to serve local GPs. But at the same period, that of the adolescence of the NHS, hospital deliveries were steadily increasing, and now (in my daughters' time) they are virtually obligatory.

That is to say, the midwife, the *sage-femme*, the priestess of childbirth, is now 'a member of a team': a very important member, but one among others who work on a production line. Production is not quite as perfect as in some other European countries, but the gains of fifty years in reducing maternal mortality and infant mortality are quite startling (13); there were many factors, but it is unlikely that these gains could have been made without this centralizing discipline. Mothers oriented to psychology and sociology dislike it very much (14), and there is statistical evidence that in the Netherlands (which has 'one of the lowest perinatal mortality rates in the world') only 29 per cent of births take place in hospital as against 90–95 per cent in the UK (15). It may be that routinization has now achieved all that it can, and that the time has come for a swing back to the single-handed domiciliary midwife and to childbirth within the family. It could be more satisfactory for the midwife; but birth pains obey no clock, and it would be a complex business to organize a humane and reliable stand-by system for midwives. It could be cheaper than hospitalization; but production line costs are already cut to the bone—mothers are brought in promptly, may be 'induced' if they occupy a bed too long, and are pushed out into the world after very little bed-rest in hospital.

There are many forces at work on the present trends, and I dare not prophesy. But I hope enough has been said to explain that a midwife is not a nurse, or at least not *simply* a nurse.

Mental nurses

Professor Kathleen Jones (16) has described very perceptively the process of social change which led from a custodial view of madmen and mental defectives to a therapeutic one. The process involved a growth in scientific knowledge; a shift of influence from lawyers concerned with *habeas corpus* and individual rights, to doctors who saw the need for early medical intervention; a movement of public opinion and the use of language from 'madhouse' and 'idiocy' to 'mental health'; from the Lunatics Act of 1845 to the Mental Health Act of 1959 and the White Paper of 1978 (17). Scientific enquiry into abnormal mental states had begun before 1800, and it led quite early to the concept that a therapeutic environment for those mentally disturbed should be quiet, friendly, and orderly (as in The Retreat at York, founded in 1792), the antithesis of the old madhouses or the private custody of lunatics of good family (18). This concept was never lost, but unluckily its path was crossed by a different stream of reforming activity, that of the break-up of the Poor Law. All England revolted against the confinement of 'paupers' in huge undifferentiated 'Bastilles', in which were housed together young and old, physically and mentally sick. But the first efforts at reform, public and voluntary, were of necessity pretty rough: orphanages, Poor Law Hospitals, and Poor Law Asylums. In some respects, these efforts were mean and poverty-stricken; in some respects they were an attempt to segregate from the public things that it did not like to see; but they also founded new traditions of reform which have not yet fulfilled themselves. Legislation and official action change slowly; but not so slowly as places and people. The great asylums of the Victorian age, housing up to 2,000 patients, still stand, though vigorous attempts are made to humanize them; so do the special conditions which discourage recruitment to mental nursing and tend to segregate mental nurses from the rest of the profession (19).

The Victorian institutions were primarily custodial; lunatics and idiots were to be kept from harming themselves and others. Given the existing conditions of public opinion and scientific knowledge, no other line of action was possible (except to a very limited extent for wealthy sufferers). A lunatic asylum had to be built like a gaol and managed like a gaol. Men and women were strictly segregated; it was expected that physical strength would be needed to handle madmen, and the staff might be thought of as 'warders' or 'keepers' or at best 'attendants'. The conscience of the outside world was perhaps mainly concerned that no one should be locked up improperly and that there should be careful legal machinery to protect sane people against incarceration.

The theme is set by the evidence which Shaftesbury gave to a House of Commons Committee in 1859 (20). 'Wages were low—in many hospitals no more than twelve guineas a year— "the wages of a housemaid".' The hours were extremely long, and the work exacting. There was no great shortage of female nurses. Good male attendants were far more difficult to recruit. Commissioner W. G. Campbell, another witness, said of male asylum attendants: 'They are all of too low a class. They are an uneducated class.' He considered there was truth in the assertion that they frequently used force against their patients when they could do so undetected by authority. The development of professional standards could, he thought, best be assured by the institution of formal qualifications and a higher wage-scale.

To quote again (21)

> I have been cut down with a hatchet once; and shut up for three hours in the strong room of a private asylum with a patient suffering from *delirium tremens*, who stood 6 ft. 2 ins., hanging at my throat . . . and all for £25 a year.

That was in 1877.

> Already in 1930 we were learning that it is almost impossible to staff mental hospitals in times of national prosperity; and only too easy in times of depression. And there was, during these years of financial crisis, a considerable influx of new recruits, particularly men, into mental nursing. Many of them came from depressed areas—among them small tradesmen, miners, and craftsmen. The hospitals usually required that they should be physically fit, and able either to take part in organized games or to play a musical instrument. On these slender qualifications, they started training; and . . . a surprising number remained to make excellent trained mental nurses (22).

This was the main source of recruitment of male nurses into the NHS (23), and the best of these brought not only a keen desire for advancement but some experience of industrial organization. They were responsible for the creation in 1910 of the National Asylum Workers' Union, the first health service trade union, and from this descended the Confederation of Health Service Employees, one of the essential constituents of the Whitley Council system when the NHS was created in 1947.

Examinations had been started on a national scale by the Royal Medico-Psychological Association in 1891 (p. 102). When the General Nursing Council was set up in 1919, it instituted a special Mental Nursing Certificate at a rather higher standard, and there are now separate certificates in Mental Nursing and Mental Deficiency Nursing. The RMPA exam ended in 1951; but the system now provides intermediate qualifications for those able to attain them.

Nursing and midwifery staff at 30 September 1971

	Total	(Whole time equivalents) Male	Female
Acute	142,420·8	6,977·0	135,443·8
Long Stay	15,578·8	1,600·8	13,977·8
Mental Illness	36,340·3	13,883·5	22,456·8
Mental Handicap	17,624·8	6,375·2	11,249·6
Maternity	8,941·9	—	8,941·9
Geriatric, etc.	42,545·3	2,508·7	40,036·6

This interesting little table has been put together from Appendix IV to the Briggs Report (24).

That is to say, the old situation continues; male nurses are mainly concentrated in institutions for mental illness and mental handicap. In other hospitals, they are a tiny minority.

No word of sex war or sex competition has reached me; a contrast with the situation in the medical profession. But there clearly exists a third tradition with the nursing profession, with traditional weaknesses and also great strengths.

Nursing students and nursing auxiliaries

This may be a convenient place at which to give a glossary of nursing qualifications as they stood in 1975.

The basic general qualification is that of SRN (State Registered Nurse); the Scottish equivalent (which I do not attempt to treat separately) is RGN (Registered General Nurse). RMN (Registered Mental Nurse) and RNMD (Registered Nurse for Mentally Sub-normal) have already been discussed, as has SCM (State Certified Midwife).

Registered Fever Nurse (RFN) and Registered Sick Children's Nurse (RSCN) raise no special problems in the present context; nor does that of Registered Nursing Tutor. That leaves two broad categories; on the one hand, State Enrolled Nurse (SEN), on the other hand the additional qualifications for nursing in the community, that of the Queen's Institute of District Nursing (QIDN) and that of Health Visitor (HV).

The latter used to be essentially the field force of the MOH, along with his sanitary inspectors and the school nurses who served him in his capacity as school medical officer. Each of these has a distinct and distinguished history and tradition, and there must be an important future for them, because of the fundamental policy division in 'philosophies' of health service organization, as between hospital care and care 'in the community'. In the latter, leadership has passed from the old MOH to the new 'consultant in community medicine', referred to in Chapter 5 above, but the community nurses are now directly responsible to a Nursing Officer at the level of the Area Health Authority who delegates authority to a Nursing Officer at the level of the District. To that extent, they are brought closer to the main body of nurses, but in the process of negotiating on the recommendations of Briggs, district nurses and health visitors fought hard to maintain their separate identities and have largely succeeded in this.

The position of the State Enrolled Nurse involves a different perspective.

Returning to the convenient tables in Appendix IV to the Briggs Report, one finds the following figures for nurses in Great Britain, whole-time and part-time (to simplify I disregard the figures for midwives).

SRN and RGN (i.e. fully qualified)		
Senior Nursing Grades		13,504
Ward sister/charge nurse		39,623
Staff nurse		36,858
		89,985
Enrolled Nurses (SEN)		43,687
In training		
Students for SRN & RGN (and for special courses)	55,801	
Pupils for SEN	24,834	80,635
Other nursing staff		71,089
		285,396

In fact, the number of individuals employed is substantially higher because of the number of part-time workers employed; and this differs radically between the sexes. The figures given above were for 'whole-time equivalent', disregarding sex; if one takes actual 'bodies', by sex, the figures are:

	Whole-time	*Part-time*
Male	34,275	2,703
Female	190,327	123,783

Indeed, part-timers predominate among female staff except at the level of ward sister and above, and except for student and pupil nurses. One could almost say that the place is run by the ward sisters and by the students, backed by a shifting body of part-timers, SRN, SEN, and unqualified.

One has to be a clever and observant patient to make out what is going on. The language of dress, badges, belts, and gradings is hard enough in itself; and it is made harder because faces change from day to day. The situation of course reflects society; women's path through life is still dominated by marriage, children, and domestic management, a continuous career is still exceptional. A woman's life may be a series of expedients; so is the management of any industry staffed mainly by women. (The closest analogy is that of teachers in primary schools, which are also haunted by the problem of 'married women returners' and 'part-time teachers'. But teaching organizations dislike part-timers and to some extent can get by without them, perhaps because school hours and school holidays are easier for the married woman with children than are conditions in hospital.)

Traditionally, the life of a student nurse is very hard; so is the life of a newly qualified houseman or a junior registrar. In both cases, the experience, once safely passed, has very strong binding force and gives a strong and characteristic social identity to a nurse, as to a doctor. But student nurses work in worse conditions and the wastage rate is higher. They come to it younger, and with less preparation (an important recommendation of Briggs is for the extension of 'preparation for nursing' courses in local technical colleges). Their work is essential to keep the wards going; work comes before study. Because of the necessity to recruit students every hospital that could possibly do it has in the past sought to establish its own nurse-training-school. This has pushed down the academic standard of admission to training and this in turn has produced a teaching atmosphere of rote learning and of weary cramming for dull examinations. The teaching by the Sister Tutors (RNT—Registered Nursing Tutors) is not necessarily very inspiring, nor very closely related to what is being learnt practically from different Sisters on different wards.

It is not surprising that there is a high wastage of nurses in training; a 30 per cent wastage rate is not regarded as abnormal, with special emphasis on the shock and stress of experience in the first year. But where selection for entry has been lax (and this may have arisen from the necessities of the service) repeated examination failure is common, and kind and careful girls may be lost to the profession. Traditionally, the Royal Colleges, having fought for recognition, have become in their turn exclusive, and it was not till the Second World War that they recognized a two-year training and a lower examination standard, for the grade of State Enrolled Nurse, SEN. As can be seen from the figures given by Briggs, the SEN is now a central pillar of the service; yet still marked by inferiority in symbolic status (for instance, their trainees are 'pupils' not 'students').

Probably there are also a fair number of student 'drop-outs' among the category of 'other nursing staff'; a few thousand men, but about 90,000 women (26), an army without which the hospitals would collapse. These are emphatically nursing staff; not ward clerks, ward orderlies, or cleaners. They are allowed to touch the sacred 'bed' and even the patient in it, and I can testify that they are pleasant people to have around, largely because they are less pressed for time than are the qualified nurses, less tense than the students. But they are recruited separately at local levels, and I have never come upon any thorough statistical or sociological study; nor any study of the variety of different local situations. Nor has there been any effective induction or progressive training; not worth it if the turnover is high? But it will continue to be high if no effort is made to involve them emotionally and intellectually with the service.

On the face of it, pupils, students, and 'other nursing staff' are among the weakest of all creatures (except patients?) in the political world of health care. Yet there has been quiet steady pressure to raise their status, and there has been some progress. Many of the old puritanical restrictions on students have gone, and there is better understanding of what education and social experience these girls have had before entering hospital. Wastage rates have dropped, and there is no reason to believe that standards have dropped. There is a long way to go before the standards of the weakest training schools reach the levels of the best: as always the best schools get the best, and the weak scramble for what is left.

Organization

It is not easy to assess the organizational strength of the nursing profession. Certainly, it enjoys high public confidence, and even a sort of affection which is not given to doctors. Certainly, 'the leaders' in the Royal Colleges are conscious of a great tradition and have ready access to top management in the NHS. Certainly, a responsible place for nurse administrators has been built in at every level of the reformed health service. Yet it will be clear from earlier sections of this chapter that a profession largely of women, largely of part-timers, is extremely difficult to convert into an instrument of policy. More will be said in Chapter 10 about the impact of trade unionism on the health service. But certainly there was a breakthrough in the 1960s; inter-union competition for members weakened the old domination by the Royal Colleges, but it also weakened the old inhibitions about stating wage claims forcibly and acting to support them. Nurses will not endanger the lives or even the comfort of patients; but they can be very effective demonstrators in their own interests. Their interest on the whole is favourable to wage restraint, in that their paymaster is the Treasury and they cannot expect to lead in a round of pay increases. But they have established parities with comparable grades, such as those of teachers, who are well organized; there does exist a private sector, in which the market price of trained nurses is high; and the profession does seem to hold its own pretty well.

These improvements, due quite largely to trade union organization, have been bought at the cost of bad relations between unions. It is by no means easy to get reliable figures for TU membership, partly because the figures are themselves weapons in competition, partly because there is some duplication of membership, partly because the office organization of the unions is much weaker than that of the Royal Colleges, which are under a statutory obligation to keep a register. It is perhaps fair to say that the source of strife is that there are two old-established negotiating bodies, the Royal College (limited to qualified nurses and to student and pupil nurses) and the Confederation of Health Service Employees, referred to on page 90 above. The invaders are NALGO, primarily an office workers' union, and NUPE, primarily a manual workers' union, which offers a militant image and appeals in the first instance to unqualified auxiliary nurses.

The battle continues, and perhaps weakens the influence of the profession as a whole. The image certainly is not as 'lady-like' as it once was; but these are fighting organizations, and Nightingale herself was always a fighter, as were her contemporaries and immediate successors. Nursing politics continues, though by other means.

Policies for the profession

I hope that I have contrived to make two points clear so far. First, the image of the profession is very strong, in its own eyes and in those of the public. The latter is not simply a blurred expression of sentiment. 'You can always tell a nurse', says my wife; and she means that irrespective of colour, accent, and dress. There are ways of doing things and ways of speaking which are common to all nurses, even when far away from their professional duties. Of course she exaggerates, but the remark makes a good talking point, because we all (regardless of class) have some personal experience of nurses to chat about. A trained nurse is careful, disciplined, and exact, also somewhat authoritarian, and curiously detached, as if armoured against painful personal involvement. One gets, I feel, 'tender loving care' more readily from junior nurses than from those with more experience, because juniors have not learnt how to make themselves professionally invulnerable. This is not a criticism; the trained nurse is the dependable backbone of a great variety of different human situations, and I think she sees herself in that role. The Briggs Report has an interesting chapter (Chapter II) on 'Nurses, Midwives, and the Public: Images and Realities', in which it quotes a nurse responding to a questionnaire: 'I've never met a nurse who can't find something to moan about. Yet, whenever I am asked if I enjoy nursing . . . I say, yes, it's a wonderful life.'

That is what makes it so difficult to talk in general terms about the 'morale' of the profession.

My second general point is that though the image is pretty solid the reality is diverse. Briggs was not particularly interested in the social background of nurses, but I believe it to be very diverse, much more diverse than that of doctors. Clearly, there is likely to be a concentration of girls from 'privileged' families in the 'best' teaching hospitals. But girls from poor families are acceptable, provided (a large proviso) that they have the ability and persistence to stick to the job; and this includes of course Irish nurses and many from the Third World.

There is also great diversity of status and of skill within the profession; there is great diversity in practical conditions of service; and the NHS inherited much diversity of ranks, grades, and titles.

There have in recent years been two attempts to establish an orthodoxy for this apparent chaos: Salmon and Briggs. The Salmon Committee was appointed in July 1963, when Enoch Powell was Minister of Health, in the last days of Harold Macmillan's tenure of office. Its chairman was Brian Salmon, one of the younger generation of the family which founded 'Joe Lyons' and still manages it; apparently not a graduate, but a thoughtful and experienced 'businessman' with a strong commitment to doctrines of scientific management. With him were four nurses of varied experience, all of them qualified Nurse Tutors, one physician, one administrative doctor, one lay hospital administrator, and a social scientist.

The terms of reference were:

> To advise on the senior nursing staff structure in the hospital service (ward sister and above), the administrative functions of the various grades and the methods of preparing staff to occupy them.

The Briggs Committee, appointed by the late Richard Crossman in March 1970, in the last days of a Labour Government, was charged:

> To review the role of the nurse and the midwife in the hospital and the community and the education and training required for that role, so that the best use is made of available manpower to meet present needs and the needs of an integrated health service.

The chairman, Professor Asa Briggs (now Lord Briggs of Lewes) is an economic and social historian, very perceptive and industrious, and also an experienced university administrator. His team included eleven nurses (one of them Professor of Nursing in Edinburgh University, and two of them men), a hospital administrator, a psychiatrist, a surgeon, an administrative doctor (a lady), a teacher, and an economist and the able wife of a Tory Front-Bench politician.

Salmon reported in December 1965, to a Labour government in which Kenneth Robinson was Minister of Health; action followed almost at once. Briggs reported in October 1972, to a Conservative government in which Sir Keith Joseph was Secretary of State for Social Services. Nothing happened— except more committees (27). I quote from the *Nursing Times*, 24 November 1977 (28):

> If those of us whose job it is to follow the twists and turns of the Briggs Bill are now totally confused, heaven help *Nursing Times* readers who must fit the profession's politics twixt bedside and kitchen sink.
>
> All we are trying to do—remember?—is to create the statutory framework around which the reform of nurse education can be introduced. This part at least of the Committee on Nursing's proposals should have been simple and uncontroversial, but already we are reliving past antagonisms—and discovering a few new ones—with the Bill not even drafted . . .
>
> As a profession we are politically gauche. We never bothered to find out how a standing committee differed from a statutory one and how both might fit into the statutory framework, until now, the eleventh hour, when we suddenly notice that it matters. So we are confused because we do not even know the language in which we are negotiating.

A piece of political analysis which is not gauche at all. If we could understand why Salmon went through and Briggs stuck we should begin to grasp the political working of the NHS.

On the face of it, Briggs is a calm and virtuous document, well researched and well written, indicating a wide consensus about the next steps; in Kenneth Wheare's terminology (29), it was a committee to negotiate rather than to advise or to enquire. There was perhaps not much in it (apart from good research) that was not in the *Lancet* Commission Report of 1932, the Horder Report of 1940, and Sir Robert Wood's Report of 1947 (30), but it led logically to organizational conclusions which seemed to provide scope for all. Perhaps that was its weakness, that it offered scope, but it did not offer gains to particular interests or solutions to continuing practical problems. It could cost not much, but something, in public money, and in the short run it would subtract from the daily nursing force, by giving better facilities for training. It could not expect much help from the Treasury, the DHSS, the other Departments, the working hospital administrators—nor even politicians. The nurses were on their own, and still are. But they do not possess sufficient unity to feel warmly about a scheme which would increase unity.

Salmon, on the other hand, is written in a way that shocks the careful academic. It is not researched but is deduced from supposed principles of management; the principles are those of the first generation of scientific management, perhaps never better formulated than by the founding father, F. W. Taylor himself, whose long paper on 'The Art of Cutting Metals' (31) had an enormous symbolic influence on the development of the ethos and techniques of production management.

The principles were very simple: that management is an exercise of authority, workers are tools in the hands of authority; that there are two sorts of authority, structural (position in a hierarchy or on an organization chart), sapiential (possession of relevant knowledge or skill); that each job should be exactly defined, and that the working of an organization should be set out on a comprehensive organization chart. Unfortunately, Salmon goes no further, and in that way he omits the guts of the theory; the definition of an output, and the measurement of the relation between inputs and outputs which we call 'costs.'

One hardly knows how to cope with this stuff intellectually. The report neglects the whole course of organization theory since 'the Hawthorne experiment', influential in the 1930s (32). The experiment began the long process of demonstrating by observation that 'classical' management theory was not 'true'; that, on the whole, organizations did not work like that. Was it then valid practical advice that they should attempt to work like that? There was a period in which the Salmon theory of management was an object simply of derision; from that it was rescued by the growth of serious attempts to measure costs, both in ergonomic terms and in terms of input/output analysis. But Salmon is written as if the last phase, essential to rescue its logic, had never been.

Add to this that the writer of the Report seems wholly un-
aware of certain linguistic traps. The work of the professional
nurse can be described accurately and unambiguously (as
might the work of the surgeon, or the garage mechanic) in
terms of certain procedures. There may indeed be argument as
to which of two procedures is 'better', and this may in practice
be resolved in terms of established habit, or that 'this suits me'.
Nevertheless, at this stage of the argument one is still in the
realm of mechanical and instrumental action.

But, as the Report so rightly says, 'management' begins at
the level of the Ward Sister. She does procedures and she demon-
strates procedures; but also she 'leads a team'—and even these
commonplace words bring in an element of personality, idio-
syncrasy, and imagination (33). As one goes higher up the
management hierarchy, the vague words proliferate: top
managers are apt to find themselves defined as 'co-ordinating',
'informing', 'liaising', 'communicating', 'studying', 'advising',
'publicizing', and even 'policymaking'. All these are words
from Salmon; they defy operational definition; and indeed
(ever since the days of Sune Carlson's pioneer study (34)) it
has baffled empirical researchers to define what top managers
'really' do, and how one distinguishes (except by triumph or
disaster) between a good leader and a bad one. It is not part
of the Salmon perspective to think of 'observing' matrons and
finding out what they 'really' do. It would in fact be sickeningly
hard to do it; but failure to make the attempt defines the
character of the report.

What it does is to produce a grading structure for the whole
great army of nursing staff. The pivot is Ward Sister, Grade 6;
below her come Grade 5 Staff Nurse (SRN), Grade 4 Qualified
Nurse (SEN), and three years of student nurses, 3, 2, and 1.
Above Grade 6 comes Nursing Officer, Grade 7, head of some
sort of nursing unit with a technical task to perform (for instance
a maternity unit, or a suite of operating theatres, or a team of
community nurses), and we can still envisage this in practical
terms. But above Grade 7, Grades 8, 9, and 10 ascend into the
empyrean (like figures in a Tiepolo picture of the Ascension)
and one is left hoping that they know what they are doing,
because we do not.

It is easy to make fun of Salmon, and after the event there was great hostility to it, particularly from consultants. But its frame-work was clamped upon the system almost instantly (35). Why?

One would like to find some relationship between the system of management and the ideology of political parties. We have heard a great deal at various points since 1945 about the Tory Party's view that the nationalized industries (including the NHS) could be much more efficient if they used the experience of private industry, to which this particular management theory belongs. But I can find no confirmation; a project begun by Tories was executed by Labour.

It is much more plausible to see this as a scheme attractive to lay administrators at each level, from the Treasury, through the Ministries, down through the hierarchy of lay administrators and finance officers. It purported to clarify a very confused situation; the clarification might be more apparent than real, because the real situation was indeed intricate and confusing. But the experienced administrator knows that even the attempt to simplify may help clarification and agreement. It brings to the surface the deep-lying concerns of the participants.

Perhaps one should add that there was a certain vested interest among the technicians of work study and of organiza-tion and methods, who had done a great deal of hard work for Salmon, and would find much more work to do in the process of sorting out old jobs into new grades. There is a good deal of established conventional gamesmanship in the process of negotiating for grades as between the personnel officers and the spokesmen of trade unions; there is a common language which the negotiators understand. I doubt if their influence was decisive; but it was certainly not in opposition.

The nurses had nothing to lose except an old and confusing language. But no one could stop them using it, provided the grade was also specified; and the new system seemed to offer financial advantages in terms of improved career structure. I doubt if it did. The chief obstacles to the promotion of sufficient really able nurses beyond Ward Sister, or perhaps beyond Nursing Officer (Grade 7) is that they prefer the work they are doing and that further promotion would damage their domestic situation, their self-image, and their easy relations with col-leagues (36). In the old phrase, *nolo episcopari*—I am a parish priest and I do not want to be made into a bishop (37).

One may suspect also that by definition of this kind the status of a Matron has been diminished rather than enhanced. A Matron of the Nightingale School had full power, by divine right, to poke her nose into every aspect of *her* hospital and to insist on action. Not so a Grade 8, in charge of nursing and of nursing only.

There are more queries; but every consultant one meets is ready to say that Salmon was a disaster. This seems to mean that it interfered between him and *his* nurses. He could no longer see *his* Ward Sister and *his* Theatre Sister as acolytes in *his* empire. The mannerisms of consultants often invite this sort of irony: but nevertheless they could be right. 'Team' is one of these embarrassingly ambiguous words, but there could be substance in their unreasonable feeling. It is a pity to do anything to dislocate an established personal relationship that works smoothly; real costs are involved in the process of re-learning.

There seems to be no record of what has actually happened. Has there in fact been dislocation because Ward Sisters aspire to higher things and (once they have reached the top of the Grade 6 scale) begin to look elsewhere for promotion? I doubt it; but if it is true then there is a negotiating base already available in the Scientific Civil Service. A limited proportion of working scientists who loathe the idea of becoming administrators may be given a step up without change of job; a rather invidious expedient, as consultants themselves find in relation to their own merit awards.

This surely is negotiable, if the situation demands it. But I suspect that consultants have been taught by experience to keep out of business that lies between Matron and her nurses, and that they simply do not notice the politics of nursing until their own work is directly affected (38).

CHAPTER 7 WHAT IS A HOSPITAL?

This time the chapter heading is paradoxical. Would it not be common sense to say that the interactions of patients, doctors, and nurses should constitute—not a hospital, but a health service? Yet surely the unreflecting Freudian response to the words 'patient', 'doctor', and 'nurse' would be 'hospital'? And this is also the impression given by NHS accounts; about 80 per cent of current NHS money and manpower is spent on hospitals, an even higher proportion of NHS capital expenditure. We had *Doctor Finlay's Casebook*; A. J. Cronin's *The Citadel* gives the author's more direct and radical image of the profession; both of these reflect a bygone age, that of the 1930s. During the whole life of the NHS, the share of the hospitals in total resources has increased—and total resources have increased to meet that demand, without an absolute decrease in the resources allocated to the other partners. Crude percentages are perhaps slightly unfair to the hospitals, in that there must surely be gains from hospital services to offset against costs; on the one hand, by cutting the costs of ill-health and of premature death; on the other hand, by reducing the burden of work carried by the rest of the NHS system? Such a global calculation would be impossible. Yet it is of crucial importance to any attempt to assess policy rationally rather than politically, and I know of no economist, statistician, or accountant who has tried to face it.

One aspect of the difficulty was explained in Chapter 4. Health care is in principle distinguishable from the NHS, not simply because of 'private medicine' but because the patient's concern for his/her own health and that of his/her closely connected 'folk' leads to self-care (1) (2); the patient need not

Notes and references for this chapter begin on page 200.

(and does not) trouble the NHS unless he/she fails in self-care, and is aware of failure—or unless he/she needs a certificate to show to some 'authority'.

To parody an eighteenth-century attack on the growth of central power; the power of the hospitals has increased, is increasing—and ought to be diminished (3). This is one of the platitudes of policy. GPs should come together voluntarily into health centres, which can be equipped to do immediately some of the tests which can now be done only by sending a patient to a hospital clinic, with costly and dangerous delay, and with greater expenditure over all. Health education, from the schools onwards should be done much better than it is, so that the quality of self-care can be improved. The epidemiologist should be better equipped to forecast critical situations and to alert community physicians and GPs in good time. Above all, something should be done about 'care in the community', and that involves social services which are not part of the NHS. The NHS reaches out into the community through district nurses, health visitors, and domiciliary midwives; but community care involves also local authority services of many different kinds (housing, education, and social work), and also cash benefit services such as those of the Supplementary Benefits Commission.

All these things are aspects of approved policy; it is unfair to say that nothing happens at all. But more happens in the hospital sector. Why?

There is one over-riding reason: that hospitals cure people. Not every time; I know of no record of the trend of deaths in hospital in relation to all deaths, but I suspect that death in hospital rather than at home is now normally expected. One of the dilemmas is that hospitals need vacant beds, and yet are reluctant to send patients out to die in homes which cannot provide decent care, even though supported by domiciliary nurses.

But in person, and within the family, I have been the beneficiary of bits of orthopaedic carpentry which could not have been done at all before 1939; hospitals grow because they succeed. In spite of the declared policy of diverting resources to geriatric care and to the care of the mentally ill and mentally handicapped, and the care of acute cases, surgical and medical, is bound to have the upper hand, in public opinion and medical opinion, by an accumulation of specific cases in which there is absolute consensus that a valuable life must be saved, at all costs.

It is true that Struldbrugs (4) have votes, and that their number is increasing fast. Certainly, they will vote for higher pensions in cash; but I doubt if even they would vote unanimously for prolonged geriatric care, the fate of those whom Swift condemned to never-ending old age.

The second reason for the predominance of hospitals is that both doctors and nurses are trained there. Even those who prefer to practise in the community (and there are many), take with them the knowledge that hospital procedures set the highest standards of health care, and that it is dangerous to fall short of them. The WHO have published a most valuable *Working Guide for the Primary Health Worker* (5), in effect, 'be your own bare-foot doctor'. But each 'Decision Tree' of observations and procedures ends with the option in case of failure; 'send the patient to the hospital or the health centre'.

This chapter is concerned largely with the trend to hospitalization: there is also a trend towards shorter stay in hospital. The latter may be in part a reaction to financial constraints. The figures are not easy to make precise, but clearly it is an axiom of cost-accounting that speed of turn-over reduces unit cost; the quicker the flow of patients the lower the cost per patient. The effect may in part be the transfer of costs from the hospital to the patient and his/her family. But it is also an incentive to ingenuity and activity in treatment. Not all patients like this; there is a record of protests about brutality from patients in a new-style geriatric ward. But (as an enquiry reported in that case) activity at all costs is now an orthodoxy; 'bed rest' is quite out of fashion as a panacea.

At present, 'implementation' is a good word in administrative theory, as a result of an amazingly effective short book by Jeffrey Pressman and Aaron Wildavsky: *Implementation; How Great Expectations in Washington are Dashed in Oakland* (6). A policy is no better than its implementation, and in a complex organization action (the promotion of real change) follows the lines of least resistance. At present action flows most easily on these two lines; more people hospitalized, for shorter stays. Whereas it flows sluggishly or not at all towards care in the community and towards the use of relatively advanced techniques by GPs and nurses in health centres. This may be due in part to compartmentalization of finance as between different authorities, and to flows of money which take no regard to incentives for implementation. In the end, every trend hits a limit; a platitude which is useless unless one can read the first 'true' indicators of a bend in the trend. At the moment, I can see no such signs. Therefore, I feel it right to place the hospital still in the centre of the picture.

The hospital as history (7)

A hospital at first was no more than a resting-place, or even a doss-house; a place where passing strangers in wild country could find a relatively safe night's rest. The map of Scotland is full of them: Spittal Berwick, Spittal on Rule, the Spittal of Glenshee, Dalnaspidal. It was an act of public service to provide these; particularly suitable for the medieval religious orders whose members were often on the move themselves. So, for instance, the Hospice on the Great St Bernard Pass.

The religious orders were also involved in a rather different institution, the infirmary; at first, a dormitory for sick monks, with crude facilities for care, then a resting-place for the sick poor in which they might recover or might die. In many places the tradition of the religious orders is unbroken; in England the oldest of London hospitals—St Thomas's, St Bartholomew's—bear religious names, but they bear also the marks of successful businessmen seeking to earn merit; direct ancestors of Lord Nuffield. And in the period of enlightenment there grew out of these second foundations the beginnings of scientific observation, scientific practice, and practical schools of medicine. London led, but the rest of the country moved on the same lines, which were in fact rather idiosyncratic, in that the hospitals gained the lead (except in Scotland) over the University Faculties of Medicine, and the old divisions are not healed even yet. The Todd Report (1968) devoted a chapter to the relation between the London Medical Schools and the University of London; once again the crux lies in implementation, which has run into very great difficulties (8).

Probably the lead in this respect, as in others, was taken by

Scotland in the latter part of the eighteenth century, and Scotland has ever since been a net exporter of doctors (9), trained in a sparse but intellectual environment.

The central tradition therefore is that of the teaching hospital, supported primarily by charitable funds and staffed largely by unpaid doctors, men ambitious for success in private practice and interdependent with the voluntary hospitals because these alone could offer 'beds', as laboratory, and as testing-ground of skill.

One can risk the equations, Beds=Status: Status=Power, power being understood in various senses; as disposable income, as decision-making in respect of patients, as scope for intellectual enterprise, and as scope for moulding successors in the profession.

These are the 'great' hospitals, and they hold the eye. Their tradition is that of healing, and in particular of innovation in healing. The reverse or underside of that tradition is that they do not want to block beds with patients whom they cannot cure. Do not allow 'silting up' in the wards; exclude 'uninteresting' cases; and do not become 'custodial'.

There is therefore also a complex and depressing story of the hospital as custodial institution.

A tribal or medieval society had little choice but to contain its own 'incurables' within society; the main categories being cripples, blind, deaf-mute, those with chronic diseases such as leprosy, bedridden old people, madmen, and idiots. From this list one can extemporize recollections of marvellous social adaptations within the community; from blind Milton, for instance:

> Blind Thamyris and blind Maeonides,
> And Tiresias and Phineus, prophets old; (10)

The Hunchback of Notre Dame; the madmen, fools, and jesters of Shakespeare and Walter Scott; the leper with his warning bell. All very romantic: but for the vast majority sparse charity and early death.

The Age of Reform shuddered at the medieval relics of public concern, embalmed in the old parochial poor law; and one aspect of the New Poor Law (it had many others) was that it attempted to sweep together into centralized residential

'Institutions' all who were not capable of living on the wages of their labour. True, there was a provision for 'outdoor relief' for those not able-bodied, but that category was to be restricted so far as possible, and the consequence was to sweep together into 'the Bastilles' a miscellaneous and anomic mass of all categories of the 'impotent poor'.

The Victorian age was not at heart cruel (though it had a great capacity for ignoring cruelty), and it was prepared to give at least limited support to reformers who could gain access to the channels of effective influence. In consequence, while the New Poor Law was still being integrated, it began to disintegrate; a beginning was made to provide separate Poor Law accommodation for different categories of disabled paupers. Hence the poor law infirmaries, started by the more active Boards of Guardians; and the very serious efforts made by good medical superintendents and by matrons of the Nightingale school (11).

To some extent, this movement was seconded by separate movements intended to remove from the public gaze those who might be dangerous or polluting; hence the growth of huge asylums for those mentally ill or mentally deficient (set up by energetic county administrators under the supervision of the Board of Control) and of fever hospitals, and tuberculosis hospitals, under the public health authorities.

Medical change has virtually wiped out the special hospitals for infectious diseases, but the other custodial institutions still stand, a monument to Victorian certainties, a disgrace to our lack of certainty.

The existence of this historical gap between the different categories of institutions called 'hospitals' was one of the forces which generated the NHS. On the one hand, a Domesday Book of England's hospitals, compiled in the late 1930s and during the Second World War, revealed a situation both ridiculous and tragic; on the other hand, the 'custodial' hospitals, backed by public conscience and public funds, were making real progress against enormous odds, whereas the voluntary or charitable hospitals (still the leaders) were finding it increasingly hard to meet the increasing costs of technical leadership. It was extremely fortunate that a unique political situation made it possible to legislate this extraordinary union before the parties to it lost the euphoria of national unity and began to look at the actualities of the new law. There evolved rather slowly an ideology of the new situation, and there are still ambiguities (not to say 'hypocrisies') lurking in the question, 'What is a hospital?'

The new ideology was complete in the Hospitals Plan of 1962; was given a legal basis in the Act of 1973; and is enshrined financially in the plan for the eventual equalization of financial resources in the Resource Allocation Report of 1976 (12).

In principle, there shall be a District General Hospital, with about 800 beds, serving a population of about 125,000; about 90 new hospitals for England and Wales (13). Each such hospital will have a full range of specialties and will include wards (and consultants with their 'firms') for geriatric cases and for mental illness. Both will be committed to the same doctrine as the acute wards; 'get on with it'—'do not let beds silt up'— 'get them back into the community'. But on the one hand there are patients (especially in geriatrics and mental deficiency) for whom no treatment is possible; on the other hand, there are patients with whom the community cannot cope—neither the private network of family and kin nor the publicly organized social work services. Hence custodial institutions survive (often with better paint and a generous supply of TV sets); hence a tendency (which is by no means new) to shuffle marginal patients around between different public authorities, each anxious to evade responsibility. And there also survives a status hierarchy, so that low status doctors, low status patients, and low status nurses, interlock to perpetuate the low status of certain hospitals.

Some very bad things have happened in some of these, and an inspectorate (tactfully called an Advisory Service) was created in 1969 to reduce the chances of recurrence. The Advisory Service has some resources of power in that it has political influence with Ministers who hate scandals, bureaucratic influence with low status institutions, and who see in it one of their few chances of enhancing their low priority. But the last published report (14) is really not encouraging; there is still an implied advice to 'Struldbrugs', which Keith Joseph is reported to have made explicit. 'Take my advice and do not be old or frail or mentally ill here—at least not for a few years' (15).

The hospital as complex organization

So much for the gloomy backstage world of memories embalmed in hospital structure. One can also answer the question in quite a different way.

For those who look at humanity from the point of view of management and technology, the modern world is one of complex organizations (16). The first steps of the chain of argument are easy. The power of man over environment depends partly on technology, as textbook knowledge plus the skills of craftsmen, partly on organization for combined action.

The simplest case is that of straight-line hierarchy. Pharaoh tells A to tell B to tell C to tell the overseers each to tell his slave gang to carry earth on their backs to block a breach in the flood works of the Nile. But even the simplest case is not simple. Pharaoh himself has no idea where and how to block that leak and to anticipate further leaks. All he can say, effectively, is 'I want that leak blocked'. That model is extended in even the simplest account of military organization. Victory over all-purpose tribal levies goes to those who can organize a coherent army out of distinct 'arms'; the legionary foot soldier, the cavalry, those who attack with missiles such as bowmen, slingers, and crossbowmen. And by Roman times, the supply services, in particular the military engineers, had also become special parts of the organization. A general might still be able to make his own plans in his own head, but to do so he had to know extremely well the capability of each of his 'arms', and the complexity of weapon technology has now made this virtually impossible.

Hence the invention of the General Staff, a process completed by the emergence of the Prussian General Staff in the 1860s, and the Prussian victory over France in the war of 1870–1. The principle is simple enough. The general remains supreme commander, and passes his orders down the chain of command to his forces on the battlefield. But at each level there are 'advisers'; the general is 'advised' (and his orders are put into written form) by his Chief-of-Staff, who is in his turn 'advised' by a team of officers, each of whom contributes knowledge of the capability of one specialist corps. And so on down the line to the ultimate unit of action, platoon or battery or engineering unit.

This model has earned an immense reputation, is still deemed essential to all military organization, and is taught in academic courses on management as relevant to complex organizations of civilians. One of its weaknesses is that in a highly technical organization of specialists it blurs the location of power, decision, and responsibility. The German 'team' in the First World War was led by the combination of Hindenburg, supreme commander, and Ludendorff, his Chief-of-Staff; the responsibility was that of Hindenburg—but where did power lie? All one can say with certainty is that Hindenburg was a man who could project the image of command, as could (for instance) MacArthur and Montgomery in the Second World War. 'The image' is not to be dismissed as trivial, even though it can be manipulated by good PR men; the image is itself a tool of organization. But there may be a dangerous gap between image and reality. Hitler (aided by the skills of Goebbels) was a gifted image-builder; but he acted (for a long time successfully) as 'front' for a political organization and a military organization, at odds with one another and each deeply, even murderously, divided.

The more complex the organization, the more difficult it is to locate the point of decision for the organization as a whole. A military organization attempts to combine unity with initiative by two methods, discipline and doctrine. By discipline men are standardized and made interchangeable; by doctrine they are taught how to think independently, and yet on parallel lines. There is for instance the old military maxim, 'march to the sound of the cannon'. This reflected the experience of a time when an army advanced across country in parallel columns at walking pace and with no intercommunication except by dispatch rider. The point of the maxim is to secure local superiority in numbers at the first point of contact with the enemy, even though the supreme commander and his staff are themselves in the dark. If columns converge instantly towards the point where advance is checked by a defensive line they stand to increase their chance of achieving local superiority and a breakthrough. Modern communications (as for instance at a fighter control war room in the days of the Battle of Britain) may make it possible for the commander to see the whole pattern at a glance and to issue relevant commands in time to be effective;

nevertheless, the concepts of discipline and doctrine are still essential and they can be applied to many civilian organizations.

But they encounter various difficulties. One of them lies in the increasing complexity of specializations, each teaching its own discipline and doctrine, and reluctant to accept those of other groupings. A second lies in the impact of technology upon organization. An advanced machine—such as a supersonic aircraft or an intensive care unit—requires certain humans to be placed in certain positions to watch certain indicators and to react to them—an even more advanced machine might dispense with all or some of these human controllers. Nevertheless, it is unwise to talk of technological determinism because technology has flaws, it 'makes mistakes', and it is continuously in process of change. Finally there is the character of the end product; there is for instance the assembly line, there is batch production, there is the management of huge continuous flow complexes such as oil refineries, there is the one-off job—which may itself be a unique piece of construction; for instance, the building of a medieval cathedral, or of the new art gallery now being built to house the Burrell Collection in Glasgow, or the creation and performance of an opera, or the work of one man's hands and mind (like this book, in which many borrowings are brought together, in an attempt to unify them).

The hospital organization is subject to all these influences. It is complex in the diversity of its staff; it includes many different technologies and working processes; the daily and hourly patterns of activity vary greatly. Chapters 5 and 6 have shown the extreme, perhaps growing, diversity that exists within the professions of doctor and of nurse, although each of them is unified by a relatively strong tradition and discipline; 'relatively', that is to the other three components of a complete hospital.

These might be labelled supplementary, ancillary, and logistic; but the words themselves are badges of status, and are quite sharply contested. The figures given for England in the DHSS *Annual Report* for 1976 (para. 243) are not easy to interpret but as far as I can judge rather less than half the staff of hospitals in England are doctors and nurses.

One of the other classes is that of professions supplementary to medicine (17); and the word 'supplementary' is carefully chosen. On the one hand, it admits that medicine holds the centre of the stage; without the hero there would be no play. But it implies also that all actors who play speaking parts are (as it were) equal members of Equity, the actors' union. There are two kinds of people in the supporting cast; those who have (as it were) the right to treat by laying on of hands, which they share with doctors and nurses and with no one else (dentists being outside the scope of this study); and those who may never see patients, who certainly never touch them, and very rarely are at the bedside or even in the ward.

The former comprise the therapeutic professions, at present seven: in no particular order, physiotherapists, radiographers, remedial gymnasts, occupational therapists, speech therapists, orthoptists, dieticians. To these are added, rather irrelevantly, medical laboratory technicians, who have a different role (18).

On the whole, these supplementaries do not seek to establish themselves on the same plane as doctors, though they grumble a good deal about the ignorance of some doctors. (There is always a shortage of supplementaries to fill established posts, but the real value of their work may vary according to the experience and temperament of individual consultants.) But there is possible status conflict with the profession of nurses, which now covers so wide an educational span. Very roughly (and at the risk of contradiction) supplementaries are at the same sort of educational level as the SRN; but on the one hand they claim cure not care, on the other hand they are for the patient (perhaps) a side-show, whereas the nurse is the patient's whole life (19).

The other category is that of 'back-room boys', on whom doctors are increasingly dependent. The most general case is that of pathologists, who now have a Royal College in their own right. But the range of skills required is immense, covering almost all branches of science and technology; and these special skills are required not only for diagnosis but also for treatment, and for the maintenance and development of advanced machines required for diagnosis and treatment. A single example, chosen simply because of the publicity given to it—lives can be saved by the provision of more kidney dialysis

machines. The government (which recently provided £4m
extra for the NHS), generous private donors, and the Association of Kidney Patients, all write and speak as if the crux of the
matter is to provide machines; but it is pointless to provide
machines without staff (20). In a hospital unit the crux is how
to find nursing staff except at the expense of other nursing
services; for home dialysis the problem is how to find and train
skilled men for routine maintenance and to provide a technical
service on call for emergency repairs. The cost of staff is likely
to exceed many times over the cost of depreciation on the
capital sum spent; and in some fields staff do not exist unless
diverted from some other field and re-trained extensively.

At present publicity is at last being given to the problem of
commissioning the new hospitals which are now coming into
service under the programme of the 1960s. Of course the
accountants must have known, but the innocent public (and
perhaps also the administrators?) thought that it would be
cheaper to run a single purpose-built modern hospital than to
provide services dispersed among decrepit Victorian buildings,
scattered in built-up areas and in the countryside, patched
with clumsy adaptations and supplemented by old army huts.
Not so; disregarding depreciation and inflation, the increase
in annual cost per patient treated is usually of the order of
20 per cent, and the main reason is that good new facilities
require the recruitment of special people.

I have distinguished the categories of ancillary and logistic
in the hope of distinguishing between 'patient care' and 'hotel
services', a distinction made by Beveridge which now has some
political importance, in that one Conservative proposal for
shifting the burden of costs from taxpayer to patient is to
distinguish between free treatment and the sort of costs in-
curred by a patient living at home or in a modest boarding
house. The difficulties are most easily seen by giving examples.

By ancillary staff I mean those who would be rated as semi-
skilled or unskilled workers, but are indispensable to the work
of health care staff. Perhaps one would put the ambulance men
at the top of this category, in that fairly often they find themselves to be first at the point of crisis and must act to get the
patient into skilled hands as fast as possible and with the least
damage possible. Hospital porters often have to act in close

contact with patients and with their families, and their help is appreciated. But of course there is also a legion of less conspicuous jobs; cleaners, kitchen workers, laundry workers, the staff of central sterilized stores departments, gardeners, hairdressers (to shave before an operation), and so on.

Total numbers are hard to state precisely because many of these workers are part-time and temporary. Some of them become familiar and essential figures in the social character of the hospital, but on the whole labour turnover is fairly high, at least in areas where there are other jobs. As a round figure 200,000 is a good approximation, perhaps two-fifths of the total staff of hospitals (they are quite rare elsewhere in the NHS).

Traditionally, this has been low-paid labour, and even now the hourly rates are such that living standards depend greatly on overtime. But in recent years their trade unions have added one more theme to the complexities of the health service, largely because their rivalry has led them to join in a political campaign for the abolition of 'private beds'.

1974 was the year of two elections; in 1973 the issue of private beds had been raised in the House of Commons, and it became 'an election issue' between the two parties, which had almost reached a consensus on other aspects of the NHS. Between two elections three competing unions, COHSE, NALGO, and NUPE, all became embroiled in the issue, to the point of threatening to blockade private beds in London hospitals; the Charing Cross hospital yielded to the threat, but apparently there never was a strike—to the death.

The incident has attracted myth, and should be analysed carefully (21). It may be that it made it impossible for Mrs Castle as Secretary of State not to engage in the confrontation with London consultants which led to the Health Services Act of 1976. But to the rest of the country (Scotland in particular, with 184 private beds (22) for private patients, and these not fully utilized, in relation to a population of 5½ million) the issue was ideologically interesting, in practice insignificant. The question now open is whether the socialist decision will or will not improve the prospects for investment in private medicine; there is as yet no consensus among entrepreneurs (a private hospital is a big risk even for big gamblers).

Perhaps the most important effect has been to enhance the status of the unionized workers. This has been at the cost of some ridiculous stories. For instance, the theatre porter who insisted on stabling his bicycle in the doctors' changing room and chaining it up, and thereby provoked a quarrel with the theatre sister, and a bitter little strike which had to be settled with the full tool-kit of industrial conciliation. Or the dear, good ward cleaner who could not resist chatting with the patients and fussing around with their beds. Sister warned her many times; in the end she was sacked, and the sacking was upheld on appeal.

Other factors helped to change the climate; junior doctors and junior nurses would doubtless have become militant even if NUPE had never existed. But certainly the hospital (if one dare postulate such an identity) has begun to see itself collectively as an industrial organization, and not simply as a humanitarian one.

Finally, logistics: I choose the word partly to avoid saying 'administration' or 'management', confusing words which I shall try to face in a later chapter. In one sense, these are the men who sit in offices, who do nothing and whom nobody loves, the descendants of local authority clerks, the NALGO members. In another sense they are indeed (as they see themselves) those who sustain the fabric of the hospital. It is generally supposed that their numbers have increased greatly since the 1974 Act, but I have seen no reliable figures, and this may be no more than a piece of 'political mythology'.

Essentially, there are two characters, under various titles: the Hospital (or District) Secretary, and the Hospital (or District) Finance Officer. The former is served by those who literally keep the fabric in being—architects, surveyors, electrical engineers, heating engineers, and boilermen. The latter is custodian of regularity in terms of cash; and also he has the difficult and invidious task of cost accounting, of measuring resources supplied and in relating them to output. In a sense, they have much power and carry much responsibility; but one must also see them as 'men in the middle', squeezed between the distant outside authorities who supply funds, and the immediate demands of the diverse groups who constitute the hospital. It is generally supposed that the consultants are the most demanding and the most disorderly; the over-mighty subjects, the reckless consumers of resources; a dynamic element in the system, powerful because they mobilize patients' concern for cure and convert it into a demand for staff, resources, and money. But a sequence of strikes in 1978 (particularly that by supervisors and engineers in October) has illustrated the blocking power of other groups.

The hospital as community

What follows may be construed as critical of hospitals in particular, of complex organizations in general, and therefore of the condition of post-industrial man, who is thus enmeshed. That is a possible argument, but a different one. I am not concerned to criticize but to unravel; the mere existence of the acute hospital, greatest of all complex organizations, is a challenge to the imagination.

First, the dimension of command and discipline.

If one can slip unnoticed into the corridor of a general hospital (which is easy) one's impression as one strolls around (a white coat will make you invulnerable and invisible) is one of vagueness, planlessness, and irresponsibility. This is not an irrelevant impression; a hospital is in some sense a loosely constructed self-motivating institution. But discipline is there.

In the first place, it is there in the doctrine of command at the point of impact between doctor and patient. The 'ideal type' of consultant (by no means all actual consultants) leads a 'firm' through a rather complex set of human relations; he is not necessarily the same man to specialists in training with him, to housemen and clinical students, to his theatre sister and ward sisters, to junior nurses, and to ancillary staff. But it is essential that at the point of impact there be exact discipline, exact understanding, and exact timing. The television image of the operating theatre stamps this on the public mind; procedures exist to eliminate error (the swab left in the wound), but the procedures themselves depend on discipline within a group. After an operation, or in non-surgical cases, the centre of discipline passes to the ward and to the ward sister, also supervising disciplined procedures. In my experience, sister is less alarming to patients than she used to be: but it is remarkable how well her training serves her in sustaining regular behaviour with a mixed crew of junior helpers, and a very mixed ward of patients.

Once upon a time this capacity for doing things exactly and to a time-table dominated geriatric and psychiatric practice as well as that of acute wards. Doctrine has now turned against this, because geriatric patients and some psychiatric patients may accept discipline too gladly, and may sink into lethargy and 'institutionalization'. This doctrine asks for a new and even more difficult pattern; orderly but relaxed, a discipline in which some responsibility passes from doctor to nurse, and the nurse as agent of cure attempts to sustain responsibility in the patient. This is so difficult that no one need be horrified if there is sometimes a slide from therapeutic to custodial care.

Without this kind of discipline, with all its complexity, the community (whatever it may be called) is not a hospital. But it is sustained largely because each consultant's firm, each 'division' of specialism, exists like the primeval giants in Homer, the Cyclopes:

> they have neither assemblies for consultation nor rules of procedure, but every one exercises jurisdiction over his wives and his children, and they pay no regard to one another (23).

The other kind of discipline is deduced, just as rigorously, from another aspect of the situation, that a consultant's firm has no cash income. A wise consultant, or a division of consultants, can establish a complex set of exchange relationships which do not depend on cash; the exchange of symbolic satisfaction with matron, with the pathologists, with the works staff, and so on. But in the last resort, extra staff, extra equipment, extra accommodation cost money, and money is controlled elsewhere. The NHS was of course put together thirty years ago out of a great variety of organizations, each with its own financial procedure. The evidence is not easily available, but one may judge that, after thirty years, accounting procedure has been pretty well standardized, and that the service has advanced some way beyond regularity in accounting to the more difficult phase, that of cost accounting; and even a step further to the study of cost/benefit and cost/effectiveness.

And that means that a rival order, that of financial control, is intruding upon the discipline that links doctors, nurses, and patients. This is a source of stress and conflict built into the character of the institution.

Another source of stress lies in the character of the hospital as status hierarchy. It is difficult to define status except in terms equally vague, such as deference and condescension: and to define these, in turn, one takes refuge in symbolic verbiage about 'down' and 'up' (24); or in examples—'who (of the same sex) goes through the door first?' I do not think hospitals (like old colonial societies, or the world of diplomacy) are troubled by the formal hierarchy of precedence at table. But the patient can from his bed fruitfully observe status in action, himself for the moment *déclassé*.

I puzzle myself as to whether this status hierarchy among people who are virtually all state employees is at all susceptible to Marxist analysis; does the hospital polarize into classes? The question is hard to put fairly, in that the hospital is only one aspect of a wider society. There has been a vague NUPE ideology, which sees private patients as finance capital and consultants as their lackeys. But this is grossly unfair to the main body of consultants who never see a private patient from one year's end to the next, and who are servants of the public at large just as the nurses are. Certainly there are divisions between weekly paid and monthly paid staff, between unqualified and qualified, according to length of training. And certainly any NHS hospital, including its patients, is a very mixed community of all professions, trades, colours, and forms of speech.

But to me solidarity (however weak and variable) seems stronger than polarization.

There is one final question raised by social theorists, in particular organization theorists; the scope for adaptability, innovation, and social learning. The hospital (with few exceptions) is an organization without a head. Medical superintendents filled that role in local authority hospitals, and in mental institutions; in some voluntary hospitals, the Secretary or Steward held a position of influence, especially if he were the effective manager of fund-raising campaigns. But the NHS has settled (there are some exceptions) for an odd sort of consensual government, in which Administrator, Finance Officer,

Nursing Officer, and Community Physician work together in consultation with a District Medical Committee, which 'brings together GPs and hospital doctors in a formal body' (25) (the District may include several hospitals, but they are, at least in principle, run as a single institution to serve one local community).

'Headless' societies and 'segmentary' societies are well known in the anthropological literature about pre-literate cultures. It is not true that every tribe, every institution, must have a 'chief', a spectacular figure who embodies metaphorically the identity of the community. Often headless societies (for instance, the Kikuyu in Kenya) prove more adaptable than those (like the Zulus, the Matabele, the Baganda) who look for leadership to a chief or king. And some management theorists recommend an argumentative association of equals as the most flexible organization in conditions where rapid change requires very quick reactions (26); as for instance an advertising agency or an innovative group of physicists and engineers, such as TRE, the Telecommunications Research Establishment, was forced to be by the pace of radar development on both sides in the Second World War (27).

To be 'headless' does not of itself entail adaptability and readiness to innovate. Indeed such organizations may prove extremely resistant to change and to new ideas, in so far as they contain many separate centres of resistance, each with power to fight a delaying action, as has happened for centuries in such conservative organizations as the Universities of Oxford, Cambridge, and London. But such organizations may prove hospitable to small nuclei of gifted people, who can find space for manoeuvre in a loosely organized community and can give practical shape to new and effective ideas. It has been said that the most original work in the hospital is done in the oddest old hutments and attics, because the innovators had no power to encroach on the existing allocation of beds and of laboratory space, but had sufficient drive to do what could be done by extemporization and peaceful penetration.

These paragraphs reflect the administrative theory of incrementalism or piecemeal social engineering (28). In its extreme form it would maintain that 'small is beautiful', that big enterprises are so 'lumpy' that they are obsolete before they are operational, that mobility of organization is essential in a period of rapid technological change. A Victorian hospital enclave, in which innovators have been at work, will look shabby and confused, and it may indeed disgust many of those who have to work in it (unless they are so excited about the job in hand that they scarcely notice their surroundings). But we are now in 1978 reaping the fruits of magnificent new hospital plans, rationally worked out ten years ago: and it is clear that the debate continues behind the scenes. Hence the concept of the nucleus hospital, of perhaps 300 beds in the first instance, to which 'modules' of further beds can be added quickly as social and technical patterns change (29).

On this third point, that of adaptability and the capacity to learn, the verdict is therefore mixed. The historical development of hospitals within the NHS has produced a form of organization which is in its nature leaderless and confused. It does not look good, but it has advantages. In particular, it may offer scope to leadership from below; not from the lowest level, but from that of teams or firms of enthusiasts who know one another face to face and who have the patience and ingenuity to drive their way through the loose fabric of the organization (30).

There can in fact, within this system, be very good hospitals; or hospitals with some very good departments; or very bad hospitals; or hospitals which keep ticking over in a sustained and reliable routine. There is no league table of hospitals, based on a scale of measurement, nor could there be. But there is certainly a hierarchy of prestige with measurable effects on attractiveness to different groups of staff; and certainly the system as a whole depends for innovation in therapy upon the work done in the 'best' hospitals. But probably, taking the health care system as a whole, the character and power of hospitals makes for conservatism rather than for adaptability. That monster of complexity and power, the hospital, might yet go the same way as the great battleships and aircraft carriers of the Second World War.

CHAPTER 8 COMMUNICATION AND INFORMATION

This book started with the concept of political system; a pattern of human interaction distinguishable from other patterns of relationship but not isolated from them.

The words 'power' and 'responsibility' are (at least in my language) words that spell out the concept of 'political'. The concept of 'system' has often been stated in terms of energy and information; words which acquired their present meanings largely in the context of electronics and the biological sciences, and in the interplay between these. This is not simply a matter of an analogy between *The Computer and the Brain* (1); the overarching concept of systems theory is that of survival in an environment. A 'thing' seen as a distinguishable part of the environment (a cloud, for instance) sustains its 'thingness' so long as it does not fail to sustain its boundaries and its 'shape'. Partly this depends on its having a favourable balance of energy: to be pedantic, of mass/energy, as these are in the last resort physically interchangeable. But the balance must be precise; not too little, not too much, a balance between over-feeding and starvation. How is this balance to be maintained? By the proprocess of negative feed-back, now familiar in so many sciences; every 'engine' developed as a source of power has at least one 'governor', a device which levels out every deviation from the norm, and thus in a sense sustains the entity and continuity of the machine. An engine, if it is to be an engine, needs not only fuel but controls. These a cloud lacks.

Perhaps the earliest application of control theory to human physiology was in the book by the Harvard physiologist, W. B. Cannon, *The Wisdom of the Body* (2) in which he sought to generalize about the many regulators which maintain within

Notes and references for this chapter begin on page 202.

limits of tolerance the levels of each of the chemical components invoked in the living process. Each substance has some device for regulation; 'information' of the flow of each component is monitored and fed back, so as to increase or decrease the supply appropriately. The concept is suggestive, but without precision it is not very powerful; you cannot do much with it until it is made measurable. And here digital computers enter the argument; given their fantastic speed, 'information' can be spelled out by an immense succession of what might be called 'dot-dash' signals, or 'on-off' switches. The 'information' is carried by 'energy', but it needs only a tiny amount of mass/energy to support an immense amount of 'information'. Much larger amounts of energy, steered by that information, can then build a machine capable of surviving by adjustment to a fluctuating environment.

These concepts, mathematically stated, have proved to be powerful in many branches of science, both physical and biological: for instance, the rather later work on the chemical basis of heredity (usually dated from the publication of Watson and Crick in 1953 (3)) has adopted the same language in its explanation of the genetic code and of the transmission of information by the replication of the giant molecules of the gene.

Why not pursue the analogy further, and try out this conceptual tool in the analysis of social and political structures? The way was shown by the mathematician, Norbert Wiener, in a book called, *The Human Use of Human Beings; Cybernetics and Society* (1950) (4); it was not taken up by Talcott Parsons in his work on the social system, nor in David Easton's book, *The Political System* (1953) (5). But its use was foreshadowed in that year by Karl Deutsch's study of *Nationalism and Social Communication* (6) and it was elaborated by him in 1963 in *The Nerves of Government: Models of Political Communication and Control* (7). The problem, of course, is whether these concepts, so fruitful empirically in many quantitative sciences, can be quantified in the study of politics in such a way as to yield usable empirical conclusions. Experience so far indicates that quantification is difficult to operate effectively in a field in which controlled experiment is impossible. The enterprise yields the useful negative maxim (almost a tautology) that without communication no political system is possible; it yields positive results sometimes in some micro-studies of human co-operation; and it yields insights and conjectures on a larger scale. Perhaps these are not very different from those arising out of the very ancient metaphor, that a political system is like a living body. But we know more than the ancients did about the living body, and to that extent the metaphor is sharpened.

In particular, it forces us to distinguish between 'information' and 'communication' in a way which goes beyond the ordinary usage of these words. One wants if possible to fix the use of the word 'information' in the context of mechanical, or electronic, or biological, 'information stores'. For these there are adequate mathematical expressions, and there are empirical techniques for measuring 'bits' of information stored or transmitted. There is a moving research frontier about the storage of biological information in the gene: John Young's work (and that of many others) has pushed forward the frontier opened by the late C. Ross Ashby, to the point that it is legitimate and illuminating to write of *The Memory System of the Brain* (8).

One would like to fix the use of the word 'communication' in the context of social interaction between human beings. The difference is easy to illustrate. To 'command' a cybernetic device is to set in motion a set of impulses which must follow, logically and mechanically, upon the command given. One 'commands' an electronically programmed lift by pressing a button; one commands a space-craft or an advanced computer in more complex but analogous ways. The response must follow precisely upon the command; if it does not, then one must set to work to trace a fault. Faults are of course common; they can never be completely eradicated, but one can reduce the risks by duplicating the system and by including various back-up and fail-safe services.

By contrast, one 'commands' people by talking to them or even shouting at them, or by writing them letters. Unless you know another extremely well you can reckon that before the command is translated into action various questions spin around in the respondent's head—Who's he?—What exactly does he want?—Is it urgent?, and so on. Human communication is loaded with ambiguities, to an extent that it is a miracle it should work at all.

In this field also there has been great activity in recent years.

It has been usual to associate human communication primarily with human speech and language, and much has been written both about clarity in the use of language, and about the complexity and richness of natural language, which generally communicates much more than is said explicitly. In addition, it has been realized, partly from the study of communication between animals, that though words are special they are only part of human communication. The written word is (as it were) sterilized; the spoken word is reinforced, or weakened, or subtly modified, by facial expression, gesture, movement, accent, and intonation. Indeed, we identify ourselves socially by the sounds that come out of our mouths, and by the way we conduct conversation.

I hope this distinction between information and communication will help to structure this chapter, and also to clarify the view that all political systems are systems of information and communication as thus defined. But the distinction cannot be made absolute. It is true that the attempt to programme computers to talk natural language has produced jokes rather than discoveries; but the research has given important negative results in illuminating the character of living human language, by contrast with the limits set by the capacity and rigidity of even the greatest computers. On the other hand, much of the power of science depends on the possibility of reducing natural language to symbolic language, as in mathematics and logic. One can give 'algorithms' to human beings as to computers, by defining symbols exactly in an interpersonal way; hence the immense scientific power of modern mathematics and symbolic logic. Highly skilled co-operative action also depends on absolutely unambiguous communication between persons, and the possibility of programming people for exact co-operation is essential in surgery and in other aspects of medical care. But it is equally important that discipline in science and in action does not reduce men and women to programmed behaviour, except for short periods, and even in these short bursts the person as a whole will remain vigilant and reflective outside the constraints of the artificial situation.

This introduction might give scope to another and different book; I hope to use it here to justify the briefest possible summary of a field necessary to the understanding of the health service.

Information (9)

The NHS began blindly, in the dark, because its information was so poorly organized. One can perhaps risk a division into three: scientific data, data about patients, and operational statistics.

DATA ABOUT THE SCIENCE OF MEDICINE

The organization of modern science (and this includes medical science) is a peculiar affair, in that it depends very largely on interaction among groups of people. 'A knows all about that—ask him.' A, if you consult him, may say three things: (a) 'Look it up in the following references.' (b) 'B is better on this than I am—talk to him.' (c) 'Indeed, there are other knowledgeable people scattered round the world; the ultimate authority might be to hold a small symposium or seminar.'

The character of scientific 'frontiers' is in this sense highly personal, but it is backed by a world-wide system of scientific reporting. Articles in the scientific journals are not always what they seem; human motives, ambitions, and competitiveness lie behind very formal presentation, and you will need a man or woman who 'knows the field' to tell you whose articles are genuinely important. Nevertheless, the system of research is based on the principle of cumulative enquiry; a research report ought to record a search for relevant published work and should note its own 'take-off point' in relation to what is already known, and its implications for further work.

There the problem begins to come within the scope of 'information science'. Any growing branch of science has hundreds of journals, thousands of research reports, and an enormous stock of abstracts. The culmination of the process of indexing and cross-referencing is to put the whole index of abstracts into a computer; this can be done and is being done, with great labour and at considerable expense, yet evaluation of the enterprise is still rather ambiguous. A wide sweep of computer memory may produce too much that is irrelevant; a narrower sweep may miss something that a knowledgeable person would consider specially important just because it is slightly off main stream, is not yet conveniently labelled, but opens up new lines of thought.

This probably concerns only research scientists, thesis writers, and industrial technologists who must make haste to learn a new field thoroughly and quickly. The average NHS consultant will look regularly at a few specialist journals, and especially at 'review articles'; the average GP will do well if he keeps abreast with the general journals of the profession, such as the *British Medical Journal* and the *Lancet*, which exist partly to serve him. Such journals (virtually all professions have them) exist also to carry advertisements aimed at their readers; and floods of advertising material, particularly from the pharmaceutical companies, pour through the GP's letter-box. In addition, he will have a few essential reference books of which one (*MIMS, The Monthly Index of Medical Specialties*) is in fact produced by the pharmaceutical industry as a service to doctors and to its own scientific workers (10).

These stocks and flows of technical information are an important aspect (not the only aspect) of the structure of the medical world, and they are a very odd lot, ranging from high science and strict computer indexing to commercial advertising and personal chat. To practise actively as a doctor (or as any other sort of professional) one has to have a feeling for the character of this continually changing network; and some efforts have been made to estimate the effects on medical decisions of different sources of information. This is a particularly difficult kind of research; worth doing, as a reminder that this is a topic of extreme importance, but not likely to produce conclusions precise enough to justify action—for instance, for the control of advertising by the suppliers of 'ethical' drugs.

DATA ABOUT PATIENTS

Any observer of a GP's surgery will have a simple introduction to the problems of record-keeping, especially if he can sneak a glance at his own envelope.

One aspect of this problem of records is that there now exist projects for computer diagnosis. Stock a computer's memory with the equivalent of a medical dictionary, add the records of the social, occupational, and medical history of a particular patient, then feed in the symptoms now presented, and the computer can be programmed to spell out the diagnosis or various possible diagnoses. This can be done, and may be one more valuable cross-check on the fallibility of doctors. But is it much more than an expensive toy?

That remains an open question; whereas the maintenance and preservation of patients' records, individually and collectively, is one of the central problems of the health service. The technological problems of a collective memory are immense, but they are now soluble, at least conceptually. Every patient can be given a reference number and some identification in the great computer's memory. At each 'medical encounter' the relevant data can be typed in, in standardized computer language, by the GP's secretary, the consultant's secretary, the ward secretary, and the record can be produced instantly at any output point in the system. This is certainly not merely a clever toy; within the last week the Glasgow daily paper has printed two reports of deaths shown by formal enquiry to have been due to lack of relevant records at the point of medical decision.

The records are as important to epidemiology as they are to decisions about the treatment of individual patients. The computer can readily be programmed to print out tables of numbers of cases, cross-referenced and correlated by type of patient, of area, of job, and so on. By analogy, the adaptive capacity of a health service, as of any other organism, depends on speed and accuracy of feed-back. Hints, at least, could be gathered of correlations, such as that between smoking and lung cancer, far more swiftly than at present; and these could be followed quickly by field studies and by detailed research.

Thus in the interests of community medicine each of us would become a number in an electronic data store. There are only two discernible difficulties.

One of them is embodied in the old adage 'garbage in, garbage out'. Records at present are physically a mess; scraps of paper stuffed into tattered envelopes. Under a computerized system tidiness would be perfect, a neat computer console in a corner, the print-outs thrown away soon as used because they could always be instantly reproduced. But would the doctors brief the secretaries promptly, completely, and accurately? Would the secretaries translate the data accurately into formal computer language and type them in accurately? There is no answer, I think, except that even at the worst the percentage of error would be immensely less than it is at present.

The other objection is that 'Big Brother is Watching Us'. It is at least ten years now since public anxiety was first aroused by the existence of data banks for many spheres other than that of health; the story is extremely well summarized by Paul Sieghart's book, *Privacy and Computers* (11) and a White Paper (12), with proposals for action, was issued in 1975. Nothing has been done, and it is not surprising that there is now a deadlock between the BMA and the DHSS over the question of computerizing medical records (13). The Secretary of State has now written soothingly to all MPs (14) and he has good technical advice at his disposal. But no safeguards can be absolute and impenetrable especially if public security is involved.

The doctors are certainly right to stand their ground until the whole question of comprehensive data banks has been handled thoroughly. Paul Sieghart's view is that safeguards can be contrived, and indeed that other countries have already done so. But this is a highly technical subject and one which does not have much attraction for politicians. I do not think that the question of medical records can be handled on its own; but it will be a public service if the doctors and the DHSS can see that the fullest possible publicity is given to both sides of the case, both to the bonds of professional confidence, and to the necessity of good records to protect the health of individuals and of the community.

DATA ABOUT THE SERVICE

The Service started blind in 1947—not that there were no administrative and financial statistics, but that they were scattered among literally hundreds of separate agencies— hospitals, local authorities, insurance committees—and could not be cumulated to give any general guidance about administrative policy. They varied in definitions; in coverage; in period; and also in skill and accuracy. In consequence there were no common measures of effectiveness and efficiency in such vital matters as bed occupancy, staff turnover, stocks and flows of essential stores, building maintenance costs, and so on through an endless list of matters which looked as if they might be relevant to cost, but not directly relevant to standards of care. Questions continually arose which seemed simple but which could not be answered except by mounting a slow and costly special enquiry in each case.

It would be misleading to say that these problems have now been solved; one still finds that common sense questions are asked and that the answer comes back 'it would be nice to know about that, but we have no usable figures and we can't get them without a special enquiry, and the staff will hate us even more if we send them more forms to complete'. A store of administrative data is always vulnerable in various ways, as I learnt through handling aircraft production, maintenance, and availability data in the Second World War, and the relevant manpower statistics (15). The initial collection of data and preparation of data was generally left to the lowest dog's-body on the Station; returns came in late or not at all; technology was changing continually so that definitions could never be held stable—hence endless battles between the Air Ministry and the Ministry of Aircraft Production about the silly question 'What is a complete aircraft, ready for operations?' Indeed, the interpretation of data was an important weapon in inter-departmental warfare; one of the real services to Churchill of F. A. Lindemann, Lord Cherwell, 'the Prof.', was to set up a small statistical unit to see that in case of dispute the basic figures were agreed (right or wrong) before they went to the Prime Minister, so that a dispute about policy (in our case generally one about aircraft allocation) was not transformed into a wrangle over figures (16).

I met the same problem in another form as a co-opted member of the Manchester City Education Committee in the 1950s. Inevitably there was controversy—was Manchester Education extravagant or was it niggardly?—and inevitably there was recourse to the comparative financial statistics produced for all LEAs by the Institute of Municipal Treasurers and Accountants—and inevitably our officials had to explain to us patiently that all cases were special cases, and that the figures would not really bear the conclusions we wanted to place on them.

It is not unfair to take Karl Deutsch's analogy, of 'the nerves of government'—a complex organization cannot react either speedily or rationally except on the basis of adequate data. By virtue of size and complexity and speed of change the data system of the NHS can never be wholly adequate. What has been accomplished in thirty years, however inadequate, is nevertheless miraculous. In the old Highland jingle:

If you'd seen these roads before they were made,
You'd lift up your hands and bless General Wade.

Communication

'The essential unit of medical practice', wrote the late Sir James Spence, 'is the occasion when in the intimacy of the consulting room or the sick room a person who is ill, or believes himself to be ill, seeks the advice of a doctor whom he trusts. This is a consultation and all else in the practice of medicine derives from it.' It is with communication between the ill person and his doctor in a consultation that I shall first be concerned and shall then go on to look at communication about 'all that derives from it'. This is usually just a matter of reassurance and explanation or advice about a simple course of treatment, but it may be necessary to tell a patient he will need an operation, which is always a disturbing prospect, and there may be complex investigations to be done in hospital. Not only doctors and nurses but also technicians and receptionists can play their part in explaining what is being done and why.

In a consultation, a doctor has first to acquire and then to impart information. The skills needed for these exchanges are rather different but both need privacy and time which, all too often, especially in hospital, are inadequately provided. In their absence full communication between doctor and patient is not impossible but is much more difficult to achieve. The processes of acquiring and imparting information do not end with the consultation; they must continue throughout the patient's illness.

CHARLES FLETCHER (1973), *Communication in Medicine,* p. 7
(London: Nuffield Provincial Hospitals Trust).

The processing of information is a dull subject to laymen, however important the content may be; it entails a combination of exact drudgery with great mathematical skill, and its history cannot be 'glamourized'.

By contrast, anyone with any spark of imagination takes fire at once at speculation about the nature of human communication, its marvels, its flaws, and its silly jokes. One of the funniest books about the health service is an official publication called *Doctors Talking to Patients* (17) which reports a really brave piece of research by a group of GPs who were prepared to have their surgery conversations tape-recorded over a period. Anyone who has tried similar experiments knows how humiliating they can be to the participants, and in a sense they prove nothing that we don't know already. But they remind us and make us more sensitive, and they make fascinating material for teaching. The same has been accomplished visually or in various TV simulations of doctors and patients in conversation; and on a larger scale in the series of camera reports on the District General Hospital at Bolton, screened by BBC Television in 1977 and 1978.

All this is 'anecdotal', it may be said, and unsystematic. But social science has in fact done a good deal of basic work on human communication in the last thirty years; there is theory which can be taught—yet practice remains very difficult. Some are born with the gift, it seems; others never acquire it, even though they recognize their own repeated failures.

Much of this literature has been surveyed and summarized by Charles Fletcher in his Rock Carling Lecture for 1972, on *Communication in Medicine* (18), and I cannot improve on his statement of topics.

Part One: Communication between individuals in the National Health Service

1. Communication with patients.

2. Communication in hospitals.

3. Communication between the three divisions of the National Health Service.

Part Two: Communication with the public about medicine

4. Introduction

5. Communication with the public about preventive medicine: 'Health Education'.

6. Communication with the public about treatment of illness.

7. Communication between consumers and providers of health services.

8. The mass media and the medical profession.

Each of the topics is inexhaustible, and I choose only three for discussion here.

'They never tell us anything.' Virtually every opinion poll brings a response from the public which indicates a mood of thankfulness for the existence of the NHS and for the work of its staff. But along with this there goes the almost universal complaint that the patients and their close kin find it hard to understand what is going on.

There are various built-in reasons for this. One is that there is a division of opinion among consultants as to whether it is even possible to explain things to patients; and if it were possible would it be good for them? A large part of the population is quite spectacularly ignorant about the internal arrangements of their bodies; they are better (but not good) in understanding the injuries which they can see and localize—cuts, breaks, sprains, and skin troubles in general. Basic health education (with diagrams) really is not a thing that can be done in hard-pressed hospital wards and out-patient departments. A good GP can do more, if there is indeed continuity of care in his practice (not easy to ensure in metropolitan conditions); in particular, he can (but it needs sensitivity and experience) make realistic individual decisions about the psychological effects of full explanation.

Another inescapable difficulty is that hospital medicine is of necessity organized hierarchically, and that the dosage of information to patients is regarded by some consultants as being part of the treatment and therefore a prerogative of their own. Of course this attitude is not universal, but its effect is that junior staff find that it is a good rule to say nothing without guidance from higher authority. Ingenious patients (if they are feeling reasonably well) are always striving to break this censorship by putting two and two together from scraps of talk and from unspoken indicators—and they may get it wrong.

But there are also difficulties arising out of the character of our society. Our dependence on foreign doctors raises this communication question in an extreme form; it is no use pretending that we are not uneasy when we find that a coloured doctor is the man directly in charge of our case. We do not know how to convey information to him in a way which leaves no room for misunderstanding; he on his side does not find it easy to talk to us. But this is a familiar enough problem of language teaching, which ought to have been recognized long ago; not that it is easy to work in a language of which one is not a native speaker, but such talk is almost as essential to the practice of medicine as is technical knowledge (19).

What is not so easy to grasp and assess is the extent of 'social bilingualism' within our own society. Doctors share a common medical language and are to that extent a special 'caste'. In addition, they are inescapably 'middle class' in status; a tiny proportion have grown up in 'rough' families, and have learnt the 'rough' language of a poor home, a poor school, and a poor neighbourhood, but even these must necessarily learn to talk and write like professional people. The bulk of the profession have grown up as middle-class people, and many are in fact sons and daughters of professionals. Teenagers now are far better than they were in my time in seeking a social mix, and parents tolerate their rough ways more patiently than they once did. But it is not easy to sustain bilingualism of the kind described in Basil Bernstein's research reports (20), and to be able to switch from what he calls an 'elaborated' code to a 'restricted' one, from professional speech to the vernacular. Some doctors handle this problem marvellously well; nevertheless the opposition of 'we' and 'they' is built into our society and into our system of professionalized technologies, and it cannot be abolished by any political programme. Even if all doctors in future began as pupils in comprehensive schools (and that will not happen) the problems of social language would nevertheless remain.

Health education. The terms of reference are simple. Within limits, the body is a machine with a built-in repair service. Some models are issued with defects in manufacture which require constant skilled maintenance. But for most people most of the time there are only two sorts of trouble; short-range troubles which are largely self-curing; and long-range troubles which are largely due to long continued abuse of the machine. Preventive medicine is steadily getting a grip on infectious conditions, plagues, epidemics, and pandemics, for which there is no natural protection; it has no remedy for the bodily catastrophes which are endemic in a technological civilization, but a little forethought does reduce the risks. Various Victorian proverbs preached that a sensible man is his own physician (21), and modern preventive medicine preaches that if we were all sensible the role of the NHS would be quite small. Why do we not do better?

The official view is pessimistic. Here are two quotations.

The boundaries of health education are broad and imprecise. In general the field is more characterized by its good intentions and energy than by its scientific and intellectual rigour and objectivity. Uncritical and unsupported presumptions abound, principles often prove to be prejudices, and there is little factual evidence to support activities and claims. Among contributory factors to the under-development of health education are: the failure of epidemiologists to define the behavioural causes of the major diseases of unhealthy behaviour; doubts about the contribution of the behavioural sciences; the imprecisions of communication processes; and the essentially empirical and pragmatic bases of education. Until health education is based on more unassailable information, fewer unsupported deductions and a more sceptical assessment of objectives, its methods and achievements are unlikely to attract the interest of scientific workers (22).

The greatest difficulty with which health education has to contend is that the lower social classes have the highest morbidity and mortality but are the most difficult section of the population to reach. They have, on average, lower intelligence, a much readier acceptance of the inevitability of illness, and less acceptance of the view that man is master of his fate which characterizes the more successful sections of our society, and they make much less use of preventive services such as dentistry, cervical cytology, and family planning. When faced with appeals to better their health, designed by doctors with a quite different social background, their reaction may be hopeless apathy, anger, or simple resistance (23).

The institutions exist. A Central Council for Health Education was set up in 1927; in 1948 health education was made a statutory duty of local health authorities and local education authorities; a new Health Education Council was created in 1967 (24). In addition, the Health and Safety Executive was constituted in 1974 (25) to amalgamate the old Factory Inspectorate with other cognate inspectorates, and its authority carries great weight on all matters of industrial safety. The budget of the Health Education Council was £1·5m in 1976–7; that of the HSE in the same financial year was about £36m (26) which includes a substantial allocation for health education; there were also substantial sums buried in the education budget—how much, it is hard to say. These sums are trivial in relation to NHS expenditure, but the spending authorities do not seem to think that they can usefully spend more. Schoolteachers do not much like to be landed with this extra responsibility, and the latest DES handbook on *Health Education in Schools* (27) is a rather bleak and unimaginative document. And to judge from Dr Jones's article, quoted above, the medical educators are reluctant to fire larger sums of money into the haze until they have some means of getting reliable feed-back. They can justly claim that if they hit the public with a very large and expensive campaign with a distinct focus (as for instance over cigarette smoking or polio immunization) they will get results. But even in these cases they cannot measure cost-effectiveness in terms of lives saved and bodies repaired; and for the most part the public absorbs health propaganda, and gives no measurable response.

And yet 'the public', or some undefined sectors of the public, are intensely interested in news about their own and other people's bodies. While this work has been in progress I have diligently kept clippings on matters of health from the *Guardian* and the *Glasgow Herald*, and there is rarely a day which does not produce three or four items from each paper. It is hard to find a simple classification for these cuttings, still harder to put forward safe propositions about what they mean. Occasionally there are headlined items, emphasized by a write-up in the editorial columns. And occasionally there are contributed articles on topics of current controversy, such as fluoride and whooping-cough vaccine. But primarily there is a flow of small news items, doubly pre-selected first by the agencies and news sources and then by sub-editors.

Perhaps there is a certain bias towards sex (I did not really need to be told that a former Army Pipe-Major—named and photographed—has had a sex change operation and is to become a grandmother); still better, if the story includes babies as well as sex. But in general, what these two sober papers are

presenting is relevant news and discussion, a useful contribution to the day's casual conversation—the present status of
the Pill; why do wheels fall off ambulances in the West of
Scotland and nowhere else; trouble about the closing of small
hospitals; occasionally a delinquent doctor, occasionally something that has gone badly wrong with an operation; occasionally
the finding of an old person or an invalid who has lain dead for
weeks or months in a lonely place.

In other words, the public as seen through the eyes of news
editors is quite level-headed, not 'sex mad', ready to read and
talk about small gossipy items of local health news; in fact,
much like the people one meets in the GP's waiting room or in
the beds and day-room of a hospital ward. Certainly there is a
market for other styles in fact and fiction about health; TV
generally has some hospital soap opera in progress (more often
American than British); black farce about doctors (*Carry on
Doctor* and *M.A.S.H.*) holds its own; women's magazines (but
not men only magazines) carry a fair amount of good advice
about health (28) and also a fair amount of 'nurse/doctor'
romance. On the larger railway bookstalls one can see little
magazines dedicated to nature, health, and beauty in various
styles, and one can observe the steady growth of health food
shops in a particular sort of urban milieu. But the BMA failed to
find a market for its popular journal, *The Family Doctor* (29), and
one would judge from their rarity and from their odd time-
tabling that programmes of good medical advice do not get very
favourable audience ratings on TV. So far as I can judge, mail
order advertising for contraceptives has virtually died out, but
there are still many sad little advertisements reflecting the needs
of sad people—trusses for hernia, anti-incontinence pants, a
commode chair for granny, special beds for backache, and
so on.

In general, the public seems less stupid about health and
readier to engage in dialogue than one would judge from the
worst moans of health educators. But the old rule holds: those
who need help most ask for it least and get it least (30).

Communication with politicians and civil servants. This
is the chapter which is missing from Dr Fletcher's book. It is
clearly difficult to write, and yet it ought to be there, because

the ministers and back-benchers and their Whitehall civil servants are placed at a key point in the decision-making process. Even if one plays down the extent of their 'real' power and responsibility, one must nevertheless see them as 'cybernetically' important; the 'feed-back' process works through them, or rather (to put it negatively) if the ministers, the senior lay civil servants, and their professional advisors are out of touch with reality the existing difficulties will grow worse. To take one familiar example, each arm of the service seeks to extract better terms for itself by complaining of bad morale and imminent breakdown. Much of this, as we all know, is bluff; in a crisis these professional people will rally round and (cursing vigorously) they will adjust to levels of performance slacker than they were taught to respect. Does the Minister know when and how to call their bluff? Remember that he needs that bluff in his own negotiations with the Treasury, and dare not rashly deflate it.

One can count on it that the statisticans and the cost accountants know the figures better than anyone else in the world, including their outside critics in the universities and the independent research institutes. But they know no more than the rest of us about what is going on 'at the coalface'.

The public health doctors (now called 'community physicians') earn regard in the profession not as intellectuals and innovators, but as sound people who know what they are doing and who cherish the right contacts. A Chief Medical Officer and his deputies live and work some distance away from the direct experience of their early formative years, but part of their job is to seek contacts vigorously, and to introduce them to the Minister. They and their contacts are by no means a perfectly transparent medium, and the Minister must make his own judgements about the prejudices of which they are themselves ignorant. But they are his environment, just as admirals, generals, and air marshals constitute the environment of a civilian minister of defence.

As in that situation, the general civil servants (in Health as distinct from Social Security) have very little power over policy, and they are licensed idiots so far as technical knowledge is concerned. But they are the masters of what they themselves call 'presentation', experts in bureaucratic drafting and debate. More important, they are the channels of all financial business. There is (so far as I know) no close connection between the 'mandarins' of the Elephant and Castle and the financial hierarchy of the Regions, Areas, and Districts; indeed they are socially very different animals. But information coming through these financial channels and linked to the perspective of their masters in the Treasury, is essential to the continuing life of the whole system from year to year. There is no doubt that through thirty years of experience the NHS has gradually become closer knit financially. I avoid the word 'centralization', which can be misleading if applied to a system which is in its nature diffuse. But it is enough to say that if the Treasury mandarins sneeze, the hospitals in (say) Bootle catch a cold; and vice versa —if Bootle finds a new trick for exceeding its cash limits, the infection will spread through the system, and the Treasury will be forced to seek a remedy.

The Minister himself? We have no extensive first-hand printed source except for the *Diaries* (31) of the late Dick Crossman and one must remember that though Dick did not lie to his Diary he was a man who fantasized about himself a good deal. From his record, three things stand out.

First he was above all anxious to make an impact and to be seen to make an impact. At the Ministry of Housing and Local Government his desire to make an impact destroyed a long trend towards compromise, which might have corrected the anomalies of the English local government system with some measure of consensus. In his anxiety to avoid the embrace of Dame Evelyn Sharp, the Permanent Secretary, he involved the Department in a Royal Commission which re-opened all the old sores, and left the verdict to be given by a scramble between the local henchmen of the two political parties. In relation to reform of the House of Commons and the House of Lords he was similarly open to winds of opinion from all quarters, and his efforts (intellectually praiseworthy) led to nothing; the problems of a weak House of Commons, an even weaker House of Lords remain on the books, to which he contributed no more than an interesting chapter.

In his *Diaries* he writes rather contemptuously of his immediate predecessor, Kenneth Robinson, as a minister who was in the pocket of his officials, and was effective only as their spokesman.

And yet he was a well-liked and respected minister; he belonged to the NHS and spoke for it. Was that such a bad thing?

Secondly, there was Dick's effort to go out and see for himself. In London he was always ready to talk to serious academic observers. Clearly, Brian Abel-Smith was important, but he had no monopoly. Outside the Department, Dick did all that a man could do to visit places and to talk to unofficial people; and he had on his hands not only the empire of health but that of social security as well. Dick talked so much that one could never be sure that he was listening at all. The record of the *Diaries* shows that he listened more than one ever imagined, and that he learnt sympathetically.

But he was a man in his early sixties, a very strong man, but during his two years at the Department he began for the first time to feel a strain on his health and to grumble about feeling old. One feels that his style could not be sustained physically, and that he had no notion of how to change it.

Finally, it is clear that he felt keenly the distinction between a senior minister who was at the centre of political business and one who was merely master of a great department. In this period of transition from being Lord President of the Council and Leader of the House of Commons to being Secretary of State for the Social Services as a whole, with direct responsibility for a giant ministry, it is clear that Harold Wilson was gradually and tactfully edging his old patron and ally off the centre of the stage. And Dick did not like it. Hence his desire to cling to the title (which still survives) of 'S of S for S S' and his struggle to have it both ways; both to be one of an inner group with ultimate power over priorities, and to be master of a 'feudality' or fief which would give him a great independent sphere of activity. The dilemma was faced in January 1969, in his early days at the DHSS, when he had to expend much time and influence in fighting through Cabinet a pay recommendation for doctors which the Prices and Incomes Board thought to be inequitable and inflationary. He won; but so did Ted Short, the Minister for Education, fighting on behalf of the teachers. A Departmental Minister is inescapably bound to his clientele: 'I pointed out that to reject the recommendation would quite clearly be considered a breach of faith and that it would make my relations with the doctors impossible' (32).

Crossman in fact was fully conscious of his responsibility as communicator; his duty to pick up messages from the constituents of the service, to encourage the transmission of idea within it (he was particularly proud of the part he played in initiating the Hospital Advisory Service (33)), and to stand for NHS interests at the centre of government. It is often said that swift and easy communication is the pre-condition for effective 'team-work', and the team metaphor is widely used from the level of the health centre to the level of the Department and indeed to the level of the Cabinet. Crossman himself varies in his interpretation. In his Godkin lectures at Harvard (34) he had a good deal to say about the power and authority of the Prime Minister, and he certainly wished to exercise authority himself. But the *Diaries* tell a story not of authority nor of 'team-work' but of what Anselm Strauss calls 'negotiated order' (35). The phrase was first applied to the character of co-operation within a hospital.

> The area of action covered directly by clearly enunciated rules is really very small. . . . These house rules are much less like commands, and much more like general understandings . . . mostly they can be stretched, negotiated, argued, as well as ignored or applied at convenient moments. In addition, rules here as elsewhere fail to be universal prescriptions; they always require judgement concerning their applicability to the specific case (36).

> No one knows what the hospital 'is' on any given day unless he has a comprehensive grasp of what combination of rules and policies, along with agreements, understandings, facts, contracts, and other working arrangements, currently obtains (37).

These phrases apply equally well to the constitutional context within which a Cabinet Minister must work and I recur to them in the next chapter.

CHAPTER 9 WHAT IS THE GOVERNMENT?

OWEN GLENDOWER: I can call spirits from the vasty deep
HOTSPUR: Why, so can I, or so can any man.
But will they come when you do call for them?
SHAKESPEARE: *Henry IV, Part One*, III.1

Concepts of management

Management theory offers alternative models of the operation of large complex organizations, linking each with the conditions set by the technological situation.

One model is that of spontaneous co-ordination between those with special skills who must combine swiftly in face of rapidly changing situations. The favourite word is 'team' and the visual image is that of the ceaselessly changing pattern of a football game in which 'running off the ball' is no less important than running with it. Off the field, the players are under strong discipline. They have been taught skills and must continually refresh them; and they must keep themselves fit for the conditions of play. All this is supervised by 'the manager' but once play has begun the manager has very little to add to the performance.

The word 'team' has certainly been used *ad nauseam* in making recommendations about the health service—the surgical team, the ward team, the health team in the community, and the district management team. The metaphor has been worked too hard, so that we feel it merely as one more piece of bureaucratic jargon. But if it can be kept fresh it is still relevant. A health service must in some sense be run from below, because its technologies depend very greatly on individual contacts at the point of action.

I have argued throughout that the doctor is at the focus of this action; not that he or she is the sole agent or even the dominant agent. Doctor interacts with patient, with other doctors, with nurse, with social worker, with various hospital technologists, and with the innovators in scientific medicine

Notes and references for this chapter begin on page 204.

who are continually modifying the character of relevant skill and knowledge. None of these relationships is merely a command relationship. Each doctor has his own style, and some may sound more authoritarian than others. But even what seem to be direct commands, for instance to nurse or pharmacist, depend on the slowly acquired skills of these participants, and they always imply a question—'tell me at once if your knowledge and observation suggest that I may be wrong'. The system is one of communication rather than of command; of course there is hierarchy and subordination, but there is also egalitarianism in shared responsibility and shared language.

The contrasted model is military, or bureaucratic, or managerial. There is a boss who tells you what to do. If he is a wise boss, he treads warily, consults, draws in information, never bullies: but his commands carry authority and are in the last resort final and beyond appeal. They are to be obeyed, subject to the penalty of ejection from the system.

Of course this too is a communication model; much passes within the system which is not command. But command dominates the situation. Other kinds of communication are also used, but simply because they are necessary to the effectiveness of command. There comes to one's mind the old definition of sovereignty coined by John Austin in the 1840s:

> If a *determinate* human superior, *not* in the habit of obedience to a like superior, receive *habitual* obedience from the *bulk* of a given society, that determinate superior is Sovereign in the society, and the society (including the superior) is a society political and independent (1).

Students of law and politics have for generations sharpened their wits on that quotation, and the prevailing view is that it is not sound analytically in that it confuses two senses of the word 'sovereignty'; sovereignty as formal source of law, sovereignty as a factual description of the distribution of political power in the community (2). This is quite true, and yet Austin's phraseology is helpful partly because of that confusion.

In the community, society, or polity of the NHS the Minister is sovereign, but in two senses. Within the relevant Acts his word is law; but the Minister is hemmed in politically and is limited by the realities of the situation; this is how 'a determinate human superior' must live 'in the real world of democracy' (3).

Demands in the health service arise (very largely) from the concern of citizens for their own health and that of others, and in that sense there is consumer sovereignty. But resources are available (very largely) 'free at the point of service' and are financed from general taxation. This arises out of moral scruples about the allocation of life-giving and life-enhancing services by a market process, with its known bias in favour of the rich and greedy: 'unto every one that hath shall be given, and he shall have abundance; but from him that hath not shall be taken away even that which he hath' (4). But if there is not to be allocation by a market, then there must be allocations by 'a determinate human superior'. This principle may in part be qualified or pushed out of sight because allocation follows a customary or traditional plan: 'do the same as you did last year'. But this comfortable maxim cannot be sustained in a period of rapid change; population structure, technology, and human feelings are all changing very fast, and it is often impossible to do the same as last year because we can see clearly that we are not living in last year's world and that the precept cannot be obeyed. Decisions cannot for ever be blurred and evaded; allocation must depend on human choice, however we may seek to conceal it.

'Government' is the place where the burden of decision comes to rest; as things now stand it rests upon the office of Secretary of State for Social Services. The office (I use the word in a legal sense, as an abstract bundle of powers and responsibilities) stands at the crossroads of decision; it looks up towards the process of allocation of national resources to the health service and the other social services; down to the allocation of resources within all these services.

I shall go on to qualify all these abstract statements by empirical description; but the principle stands. In President Harry Truman's favourite phrase, 'the buck stops here'. Given the ethical and institutional principles of the health service, there is built into it an antinomy between the power and responsibility of medical care in action at the periphery, the power and responsibility for resource allocation at the centre.

The Minister in the political environment

It would be inappropriate in this context to spend much time
on the place of the Minister within the whole structure of
British government. Much remains a mystery until the files are
opened after thirty years; much remains a mystery even then,
because so much of the process of interaction goes unrevealed.
But we all have some idea of the interacting forces. The office
of minister depends (almost entirely) on statute law, which can
be changed by those who hold power in Parliament, but not
quickly except in an acknowledged emergency. The character
and role of the changing incumbents of that office depend largely
on the interplay of electorate, parties, and House of Commons,
and it is not easy to generalize about this. Choice rests with the
Prime Minister; but he has to find Ministers who will fit into
his own view of his own role and of the balance he wishes to
sustain in his Cabinet, who can play their part well in electoral
campaigns, who will not look foolish in the House of Commons,
who have sufficient good sense (however selfishly astute they
may be) to avoid rancour in Cabinet negotiations. In general,
these characteristics depend on mutual recognition among the
inner circle of party politicians, which takes time to develop;
it is only in exceptional circumstances that one finds rapid promotion—Sir Harold Wilson, a Cabinet Minister at 31, Dr David
Owen at 39, and Mr John Davis coming into a Conservative
cabinet straight from the offices of the CBI. Generally, the
Minister is one of a group of men whom he has known well for
years, and whose idiosyncrasies he must tolerate because their
fate is bound up with his own. Generally, he is not tied too
closely to the Ministry which he heads; there are exceptions, those of men and women whose reputations have been
built on the development of some single aspect of government,
but for most politicians the over-riding objective is to gain
status and advancement within the inner group of leading
politicians.

There is much academic debate about 'the power of the
Prime Minister', 'the collective responsibility of the Cabinet',
'the individual responsibility of each Minister', but there is no
consensus about the definition of these terms, and their practical effect varies according to the conjuncture of events. They

belong to the mythology and rhetoric of the constitution, and furnish a rich store of arguments on each side of every political question. One can say with confidence only that the Minister is one of a group of quite senior politicians, interacting with one another, with the House of Commons, with their respective parties, and with the public, in so far as the public frame any image of them through the media (5).

They also interact with the Higher Civil Service, in all its aspects, including the heads of professional services and of the armed forces. One key to this situation lies in the fact that here too there is a relatively small group of men who have been interacting (and observing one another) for years. Another is that the Treasury, in association with the Prime Minister and the Chancellor of the Exchequer, constitute a group within a group, and their interaction is crucial in the allocation of national resources between different sectors. Their power is great but subject to two well-known restrictions, which operate also within the health service: first, that changes in allocation are generally no more than marginal; secondly, that overall growth, especially if accompanied by inflation, eases the process of reallocation. Radical change is very difficult, because so many interests are involved in the *status quo*; nevertheless, slow modification adds up as if by compound interest, provided that there is continuity of direction.

But continuity is at the mercy of other elements in the situation; the parties and the electorate. Traditional theory requires that there should be two great parties based on distinct principles, offering to the electorate a choice between alternative packages of leaders, principles, and proposals for immediate action. In this way (says theory) the huge electorate is offered a real choice which combines elements of national feeling, sectional interest, gut reaction, and rational analysis. Political sociologists have so far failed to sort out the parts played by these elements in electoral choice (whether mass choice or individual choice), but there is at least 'anecdotal' evidence that the electorate would like to reject the dilemma, to mitigate party antitheses, to sustain continuity. There were stable Labour majorities in 1945 and 1966; a strong Tory majority in 1957, dwindling election by election till the defeat of 1964. At the same time the electorate has persistently cast a solid percentage of votes for parties which were neither government nor opposition; one could adjust the figures in various ways to accommodate complexities, but a figure of 20 per cent of those actually voting will serve as illustration, and the proportion of these voting for the Labour/Tory 'establishment' has gradually declined.

The drift of this tenuous argument is that the electorate has 'power' that it exercises it 'responsibly', and that it prefers continuity to polarization (6). Whereas each of the great parties is itself divided, one wing in each of them favouring polarization, the other urging the electoral and administrative advantages of continuity and adjustment.

The balance has worked out differently in different spheres of action. The greatest confusion has arisen over nationalization and de-nationalization and over the attempts (on both sides) to find ingenious devices for bridging the gap; with the result that there is an interpenetration of public and private institutions, and no one can give a simple statement in plain words about what sort of industrial society this is (7). In education, the situation is a little less complex; undoubtedly the public sector is predominant in scope and finance, but there is pretty general recognition that the private sector cannot be suppressed. It will break out even in a strict Socialist state in the form of payment (or other consideration) for private tuition for a son or daughter threatened by examinations; and it has often been said that there would be no point in closing Eton College, Windsor, as it would merely raise funds and reopen outside the jurisdiction, in the Republic of Ireland or elsewhere. Indeed, that confused English institution, the direct grant grammar school, has been forced to clarify its position, to be either private or public, and it is rather difficult to see clearly what the consequences will be; perhaps to strengthen the private sector and increase the power of money in education. The so-called Left of the Labour Party, in search of polarization, favoured a similar policy for the NHS; hence the Health Service Act of 1976, a compromise plan for phasing out 'private' beds in public hospitals, which may serve to strengthen the private sector in medicine (8). But the NHS is not greatly troubled at present by problems of polarization between public and private sectors. Its main problems lie elsewhere.

Perhaps no more need be said here about this complex environment in which the Minister has to play the hand, for his own advancement, for that of his Department, for all those (including patients) whose interests are bound up with the development of the NHS.

He operates largely on the 'inner circle' (9) of men of power, who are all alike prisoners of circumstances and of continuity, yet have 'real' power in that they can inject an element of policy into the unending flow of administrative decisions. But he is certainly also 'responsible' in the sense that he is 'answerable' in various 'forums' for a sphere of action constitutionally defined. He is answerable to his colleagues in the Cabinet, to the House of Commons, to the leaders of his party, to individual complaints, enquiries, and petitions, to the general public through the media; and particularly perhaps to the various organizations of patients and professionals which have been described in previous chapters.

Can he be 'punished' if his answers displease? Only in the sense that his career may be blighted by a sense of failure. The job is distressingly difficult, yet Ministers have on the whole enjoyed warm public support in standing up to sectional pressures. The mantle of Saint Nye Bevan is a strong shield, whichever party is in power.

The Minister and the Department

So much for the Minister, as seen by his equals and by those to whom he is in some sense responsible. The next step is to see the Minister in relation to his responsibilities.

As sovereign the Minister is in a legal sense a 'determinate human superior', his word, his signature is a legitimate authority upon which action can and must proceed. In that sense, he is as lonely as the commanding general on an old-fashioned field of battle. But his power to act includes power to delegate; even if he does not delegate formally nevertheless he must act collectively, as part of the system of which he is the head. The acts of the Minister cannot be separated in practice from the acts of the Department, the collectivity which supports him and brings his immense task within the bounds of practicability. This section is concerned with the scope of the Department, its internal structure, its attempts to allocate and to manage; the next section deals with the hierarchy of management; and finally, I try to deal with the problem of managing the unmanageable, the work of caring for and curing people in face of diffuse and deep personal concern.

All the departments of state are entangled and trammelled by their own history, partly because of continuity in the problems they face, partly because total administrative revolution is virtually impossible. Top people and their principles may be swept away, but their humble servants are irreplaceable; a few may be shot or shifted, *pour encourager les autres*, but on the whole the same little men (in complex organizations we are all 'little men') will come daily to the same desks and to the same heap of files in the same in-tray.

Sir George Newman (10) takes history back to medieval magistrates and to Bentham's inclusion of a Ministry of Health in his Constitutional Code, which belongs mainly to the 1820s. But he rightly gives a central position to the Royal Sanitary Commission (Norton) of 1868–71 which was followed by Liberal legislation in 1871 and 1872, and by the Conservative consolidating act of 1875. Disraeli was then Prime Minister; hence his parody of the preacher's message about 'vanity of vanities'; *sanitas sanitatum, omnia sanitas*. Hence also the claim of Disraelian Tories, that the Tories as 'national' party have a continuing tradition of concern for the people's health.

The Report and the Act attempted to embody the lessons of history. The 'germ theory of disease' was still to come, and the disasters of plague and of lesser epidemics were ascribed in the first instance to 'bad air' (a favourite foe of Florence Nightingale) and then (more accurately) to 'bad water'. The fear of death by infection was strong enough in the 1830s to launch the first sanitary movement, there was a first period of heroic figures; Dr Southwood Smith at the centre, other reforming doctors in London and in some at least of the great industrial towns. They made great advances in medical administration, but the institutional structure went badly wrong, and the first General Board of Health, created in 1848, was harried to death by vested interests in 1858 (11).

The accepted diagnosis laid the blame on the pattern of administration adopted by the reformers in the 1830s; the association of an appointed central body not formally 'responsible' to a minister or the Parliament, with elected local bodies charged with one function only. With many variations, this pattern was used for poor law, education, and roads as well as for health; it was by no means dead by the 1870s but educated opinion was turning against it, and was moving towards the contrasted formula, that of ministerial responsibility, the supremacy of the Commons, the creation of all-purpose local authorities. And so the Act of 1875 for the first time gave responsibility for public health to a responsible Minister and his department.

But here the modern world begins; for good administrative reasons health was yoked with Poor Law, and the Department (created by the Act of 1871) was entitled 'The Local Government Board'—a fictitious board like the Board of Trade, with a President who was an independent minister, a rather humble one but occasionally admitted as a member of the Cabinet. The new department inherited two distinct administrative traditions, both worthy but certain to conflict because they were harnessed together in closely related fields. On the one hand, there was public health in the person of Sir John Simon, one of the greatest of community physicians, and to him and his colleagues money was a secondary consideration in the battle for the effective and humane control of disease. On the other side were the administrators of the Poor Law of 1834, guardians of the public purse and of the principle of 'lesser eligibility'—a pauper should never be made better off than a self-supporting citizen. There were not on that side any great administrative names, but the principles and procedures involved were close to the hearts of the strong personalities who constituted the Victorian Treasury and generally persuaded Victorian Chancellors of the Exchequer.

Sir George Newman blames James Stansfeld, the first minister, for using his influence on the poor law side against Sir John Simon, who resigned in 1876. This is perhaps unfair to Stansfeld, a minor politician, but a man of strong humanitarian and feminist convictions, who withdrew from politics himself in 1874 to join in the fight against the Contagious Diseases Act, which in effect created licensed and inspected prostitutes for the use of the army and navy (12). But much of the underlying structure of public health as it existed before the NHS was created by Sir John Simon's successors, and of course there are some who argue (for instance, Professor Thomas McKeown (13)) that this phase of medicine did far more than the NHS has done to transform the mortality statistics of industrial Britain. Furthermore, the unenterprising policy of the local government side of the Department left scope for the growth of self-government in the great cities, symbolized by the great Victorian Town Halls of Manchester, Leeds, Birmingham, Bradford, and many others—quasi-cathedrals, erected competitively by the city fathers in their own honour. But they built sewers and waterworks with the same ostentatious grandeur, and on the whole they were responsive to instruction by their Medical Officers of Health, so that one can perhaps speak of this as the period of the second Sanitary Movement, which has handed on to the present Ministry many of its functions.

The third period is one of almost continuous movement leading to the National Health Service Act of 1946. In its prehistory, two events were decisive. One of them was the passing of Lloyd George's National Insurance Act of 1912 (14). Lloyd George as Chancellor ventured into a complex technical field, with no majority in the House of Commons, under pressure from many conflicting interests, and with little public support except such as arose from an English sense of inferiority in relation to the achievement of European and other systems of social security (the experience of Australia and New Zealand was relevant, and a New Zealander, W. Pember Reeves (15), was then Director of the London School of Economics). His Bill was not a response to pressure from the 'health professions'; indeed the BMA was in opposition. But when it came to the test, the majority of doctors saw the opportunity and took it; for the first time the practice of medicine (as distinct from sanitary administration) came within 'the pale of the constitution' (above Chapter 5, p. 70). General practice was given financial stability and ceded very little in exchange. Certainly it did not accept the 'sovereignty' of the Minister—though it took his money.

The second decisive event (if one can call it an 'event') was the ideological debate about administrative structure which followed the Majority and Minority Reports of the Royal Commission on the Poor Law (Lord George Hamilton), 1905 to 1909. The appointment of the Commission was itself due to a long course of lobbying orchestrated by the Webbs, and Beatrice was a member of the Commission and the leader of its Minority. The Commission was not in fact so bitterly divided in terms of personal relations and practical recommendations as might be imagined from the public agitation that followed. The important thing was that the Minority stood for a principle, that of the 'break up of the Poor Law'; that it managed to commit to this principle the trade unions and the emergent Labour Party; and that a very vigorous generation of young civil servants went along with them. The Poor Law of 1834 was a political target, a symbol of the degradation of workers not needed by the economic system; the Webbs tied this to a maxim of administrative science. Services (they said) may be organized either by category of clients (e.g. the poor, legally defined as paupers) or by function (e.g. defence, education, and health). In the modern world, the decisive factor in terms of effective service is that of function, because the modern world is organized functionally, in terms of relevant professions, such as teaching and medicine. For competent and humane service the category of the poor, 'paupers', must be split by the functions of health, education, housing, and so on, in each of which they should be grouped with other citizens; there would be left a residual category of 'income maintenance' for those who were much like other people except for one essential factor, that they had not money enough to pay for a minimum of food, shelter, warmth, and clothing.

The principle has been punched full of holes conceptually by administrative theorists from the time of Chester Barnard (16) and H. A. Simon (17); and it was in substance political rather than scientific (18). But it was above all powerful, in the scientific sense that it unified and 'explained' a wide range of phenomenon; and it remains powerful to this day.

The sequence of events, so far as relevant here, is that in the crisis of the First World War, Lloyd George, who had seized power in 1916, made it his programme to wage war and prepare for peace, both with equal energy. As Minister of Reconstruction, he appointed Dr Christopher Addison, Professor

of Anatomy at University College, Sheffield, then MP for
Hoxton from 1910; a man much under-rated by conventional
history (19)—to all intents and purposes, the only doctor ever
to be Minister of Health (20). Addison's Ministry sired a great
range of committees, including one on health (21), and (above
all) a committee on the Machinery of Government, chaired by
Lord Haldane, lawyer, Hegelian, restless reformer, and including
among its numbers Beatrice Webb and Sir Robert Morant, the
most alarming civil servant of his generation, then Chairman of
the Commission appointed to administer Lloyd George's Act
of 1912.

From that point matters proceeded according to plan. The
Ministry of Health was created in 1919, under an Act passed in
the first flush of victory, with Addison as Minister, Morant as
Permanent Secretary, Sir George Newman (then chief medical
officer at the Board of Education) as Chief Medical Officer;
an extremely far-sighted and resolute group, seeking long-term
objectives.

But Morant died suddenly in 1920; Addison became famous
for the Addison Housing Act, another forward-looking measure,
superseded by the post-war slump and the consequent attempt
to cut spending and stabilize the pound. None of Addison's
successors (except perhaps Neville Chamberlain, who was an
excellent minister in his own sphere) was of equal calibre, nor
were the successors to Morant. But Newman remained, and
by his own account (22) he established a number of principles
which are still valid and which define the rights and duties of
doctors working as civil servants.

> In August 1919 an official minute was issued by Sir John
> Anderson, approved by the Secretary and the Minister,
> which found a satisfactory solution. The Chief Medical
> Officer was granted the pay and status of the Permanent
> Secretary of the Ministry, without the duty of exercising
> any of the administrative functions of the Secretary. This
> was the first occasion when a medical officer received that
> status, which gave him direct access to the Minister for
> submission of proposals and discussion of any matters
> within his responsibility; and it raised the status and pay
> of all his medical colleagues to an equality with that of their

respective administrative colleagues. This was an end of all talk or assumption that either the administrative or the professional Civil Servants were in a position of subordination or of superiority to the other section, and it bears witness to the foresight and wisdom of Mr MacKenna in 1907 and Dr Addison in 1919, both having been thus advised by Sir Robert Morant. Consider what this arrangement meant. It meant that the status of the whole of the medical staff was safeguarded in two respects. They were never to be placed in the false position of carrying out a policy with which they did not concur from the professional standpoint, without having had full opportunity of urging their views upon their administrative colleagues and upon the Minister himself; and they were ensured that any proposals initiated by the medical Civil Servants were considered by their colleagues on their merits. No expert could fairly ask for fuller assurances. It is not for him to determine political issues, it is for him to place his considered and skilled advice effectively before a Minister.

Two pages later Newman refers to an Establishment Minute of August, 1920, issued by Sir Arthur Robinson after Morant's death; and he continues:

A medical man in the Civil Service has a duty to his profession as well as to the Service, and he should not enter it unless he is prepared to obey orders, and work co-operatively and harmoniously in a great organization.

These principles (like most great administrative principles) are extremely flexible and allow great scope for personal interpretation. Much history remains to be written; but a working hypothesis is that on questions of health policy the initiative lies with the medical side, on matters of resource allocation and administrative structure it lies with the generalist class of the Civil Service. Chief Medical Officers hold office for quite long periods, are well-known to the medical public, and speak quite freely about policy, so that it is relatively easy to know their personalities and their views, even though internal dealings in the Ministry are confidential. The lay civil servants, on the other hand, pass fairly quickly through the top posts, are not

well-known to the public, and leave little on the record. At
most one can say that the balance shifts according to the period;
and that we are now in a period of consensus over medical
policy, of crisis over resource allocation. The balance may shift
again.

In the period of Sir George Newman (1919 to 1937) the
Ministry was dominated politically by problems of housing and
by problems of local government structure and finance; Neville
Chamberlain's grasp of these two fields established him un-
expectedly as No. 2 in the Tory Party, Chancellor of the Exchequer from 1931 till he became Prime Minister in 1937. But
Sir George Newman's *Annual Reports* on the Public Health were
respected and influential; and by the 1930s the crisis of hospital
medicine was clearly foreseen and publicly debated. In the
war-time coalition a series of rather second-rate Ministers and
civil servants mulled over a sequence of plans for a 'true'
National Health Service; nothing was settled before the election
of 1945, but Nye Bevan then had before him ample material with
which to work. With a sweep of national opinion behind him,
and a powerful majority, he was able to negotiate a new system
with remarkable speed, and his system still stands virtually
unchanged at the centre.

The one great change is that the Ministry of Health became
in 1968 the Department of Health and Social Security, headed
by a Secretary of State. This had political and personal advantages, in that it provided an honourable move sideways for a
restless politician, Dick Crossman, who had created a good deal
of confusion during his time as Minister of Housing and Local
Government and as Leader of the House of Commons. It also
had what the Civil Service call 'presentational advantages', in
that it could be said to be in line with Labour principles and
also with modern theories of social medicine, that questions of
health and of poverty were not separable.

On the other hand, the expert Whitehall-watchers were
sceptical. Crossman records a discussion with Titmuss and
Abel-Smith in 1968 (23), in which he sensed their reluctance to
see their 'splendid Ministry of Health', yoked to the 'vulgar'
Ministry of Social Security. They have indeed been yoked together, but it is not certain that there has been inter-penetra-
tion. Indeed, it could be argued that the Department has been

weakest precisely at the centre point of current policy, which emphasizes the continuity of medical care and community care. The latter is almost entirely a matter for the elected local authorities, and it has not been easy to cajole and bully them into close collaboration with local health authorities. But this is the outcome of a deep underlying fissure in English institutions, and the gap cannot be closed simply by doodling with administrative structures.

It is worth quoting the carefully drafted statement of the Department's scope which is included in the *Civil Service Year Book* (24).

> The Department of Health and Social Security is responsible (in England) for the administration of the National Health Service; the social services provided by the local authorities for the elderly and handicapped, socially deprived families and children in care; and for certain aspects of public health.
>
> Throughout Great Britain it is responsible for the payment of benefit and the collection of contributions under the National Insurance and Industrial Injury Schemes; for the payment of Family Allowances; and through its Supplementary Benefits Commission for determining awards of non-contributory benefits and Family Income Supplements, for reception centres and for assessing the means of people applying for legal aid.
>
> It also makes reciprocal social security arrangements with other countries; represents the United Kingdom in the World Health Organization; and is responsible for pensions and welfare services for United Kingdom war pensioners throughout the world.

What this means is that (on the one hand) this is not the only Department concerned with health even in England; it is responsible only 'for certain aspects of public health': other aspects are scattered between various Ministries and semi-independent bodies—Education, Home Office, Industry, Agriculture, Environment, and the Health and Safety at Work Commission. The DHSS has some responsibility for taking the initiative if it sees dangers that require co-ordination; but this involves its officials (medical and lay) in a maze of committees and committee work. Whitehall administration is remarkably good at extemporizing action in face of 'clear and present danger' (25); but it moves very slowly towards long-term objectives.

There is no cure for this, since questions of health are built into every kind of human activity.

On the other hand, the DHSS has to take responsibility for various activities which seem remote from the NHS and from social security. There is a whole list of formal and inspectorial functions derived from the public health movements of the nineteenth century, things older than the NHS and not in total unimportant. More striking is the recognition that the management of disease is international; the DHSS is a 'Foreign Office' in relation to the World Health Organization and its various agencies. This is not a starry-eyed commitment nor yet a purely formal one; every baby born in the UK is involved in the question 'is smallpox extinct throughout the world? Is vaccination obsolete?' And we all watch news about the advance of rabies across northern Europe and the coming siege of the Channel Ports.

Two final comments. The essence of the Department still lies in the balanced relationship between administrators and doctors within it. But (firstly) this is not the whole Ministry even on the side of health; it is hung about with implements like Lewis Carroll's White Knight. Here is a succinct list from the *Civil Service Year Book*: operational research service, computers and research division, information division, statistics and research division, industries and exports division, supply division, office of the chief scientist, social work services, pharmaceutical division, catering and dietetic branch, domestic services management branch, architect's division, and divisions for engineering and for surveying. Clearly all these are relevant; precisely for that reason, anyone who knows how files move within a department will blench to think of the paper circulated (quite properly) to every one of those who may possibly be concerned.

Secondly, great pains have been taken to ensure that the Department is not professionally isolated and closed in on itself. Sir George Newman reports (26) the small beginnings of the present extraordinary system of consultation.

At the Board of Education, soon after the Medical Department was established in 1908, the Chief Medical Officer was permitted to have an informal committee of outside medical experts and subsequently at the Ministry of Health the Minister himself, at the request of the Chief Medical Officer, appointed such a standing medical Advisory Committee consisting of the Presidents of the two Royal Colleges (Sir John Bradford and Lord Moynihan), the President of the Royal Society of Medicine (then Lord Dawson of Penn) and Sir Henry Brackenbury of the British Medical Association. This body proved invaluable in presenting medical issues to the Minister.

This was a very small and very formidable group; thus armed, the CMO might dominate the Minister in relation to matters clearly medical. But this very important political concept has perhaps now got out of hand.

The Act of 1946 places squarely on the Minister of Health 'the duty . . . to promote the establishment in England and Wales of a comprehensive health service . . . and for that purpose to provide or secure the effective provision of services . . .'. The Minister is without limit or qualification sovereign of the service. But Section 2 adds unto him the Central Health Services Council, which looks as if it might be intended as a rival; the focus of the NHS as a self-governing institution, the governing body of an autonomous polity within the state. There are to be 41 members (27) headed by the Presidents of the Royal Colleges (by this time including the RCOG), the Presidents of the BMA and of the GMC and the Chairman of the Council of the Medical Officers of Health. To these are added 35 others (I abbreviate drastically, as there has been much amendment in detail, though the principle of the main Act stands unchallenged):

15 doctors (two of them with interests in 'mental health')
5 laymen concerned with hospital management
5 laymen from local government
3 dentists
2 experienced in mental health services
2 nurses

1 midwife
2 pharmacists

all to be selected after consultation with 'representative organizations'.

This is an immense organization with no power except to tender advice solicited or unsolicited; the Minister pays, the Minister appoints, the Minister can sack, and the Minister can refuse to publish. But the Council is explicitly encouraged to appoint standing advisory committees, which it does lavishly. The latest *Hospital and Health Services Yearbook* (28) lists 6 of these and it is perhaps worthwhile to call the roll: Medical, Nursing and Midwifery, Dental, Pharmaceutical, Ophthalmic and the Joint Committee on Vaccination and Immunization. The Council's Annual Reports list many more.

To this list of advisers one must add the list of those committees, rather different in character, which serve the Medical Research Council. Sir George Newman writes of Robert Morant that

> Another of his peculiarities, or rather principles, was to get much out of little, which led to one of his nicknames, 'the magician'. He made the fabric of the school medical service out of half a dozen lines in a second-class measure, which passed Parliament in the late summer of 1907; and out of an obscure clause in the National Insurance Bill he drew forth the fertile institution of the Medical Research Council (29).

In its first year as Medical Research Council (1913–14) its revenue was about £53,000; in the last year (1976–7) for which I have a full report it was over £52m. And it was fertile not only in research but in committee structure. That report lists 13 main committees: Finance and General Purposes, Training and Manpower, Neurobiology and Mental Health, Cell Biology and Disorders, Physiological Systems and Disorders, Tropical Medicine, Environmental Medicine, MRC/Cancer Research Campaign and five research grant committees; one can count on it that each main committee has spawned sub-committees, and Appendix I to the *Report* gives the basic details of 70 MRC 'establishments'.

It is easy to be ironical about the paperwork involved; about the labours of those who take minutes and pay attendance expenses; about the 'seventy or eighty' people who constitute the circulating elite of pluralist committee-sitters. I suppose I used to qualify as a member of it, though not in the health service sphere; and often one does not know whether to laugh or to cry about the process of 'government by committee' (30). But underlying the process are serious questions which are extremely hard to answer.

The Department, complex enough in itself, is enveloped in a network of 'advisory' bodies, of which the Central Health Services Council and the Medical Research Council are examples rather different in character (these two types are by no means the only ones). One can build from their reports long lists of Who is Who in the health service, and one can make guesses about power and influence. But no one knows how to confirm or refute such guesses; or even whether to 'model' the Department as spider with finger on the threads, or as merely one ganglion among many in a complex cybernetic nervous system.

One can say with confidence that access to the Department is easy, once you are admitted to this Inner Circle (31). But the complexities of this departmental world are beyond the scope of any single enquirer.

The subordinate levels

So far I have considered the 'government' of health as extended only in administrative and intellectual space. But the service is also extended in geographical space, over the whole surface and population of England; space which is also communication space in many different media. These last were discussed briefly in the previous chapter and in some respects they condition the whole operation. But enough trouble for the present chapter arises out of the fact that the service is by its nature localized into every part of a country which is complex in its social and geographical structure.

It would be fair to say that no one was ever very happy with the tripartite structure of the service as it was created in 1946. Three geographically distinct organizations were superimposed on the same map; the areas of hospitals, the areas of local health authorities, the areas of general practice Executive Councils. This was the result of historic compromise, it was difficult to defend except by historical arguments, and it took the blame for many of the gaps in NHS provision. Opinion hardened against it in the 1960s, at the same time as medical and sociological opinion turned towards the analysis of medicine in its social setting. The arguments for unity grew stronger as analysis showed the predominance of categories (above all, old age, mental health, mental deficiency, and severe disablement) which placed great burdens on the NHS, and yet had relatively little hope of medical remedy. It seemed increasingly clear that what was needed was a continuum of care—which would be very hard to secure whatever the organization, and was certainly not helped by the existing division of responsibility.

A plan for unification was built up tentatively by a series of Conservative and Labour ministers, and provoked no storm of opposition at any time before the NHS Reorganization Act of 1973, which passed virtually on the basis of inter-party agreement on principles, though not necessarily on detail. The essence of the matter was that (with all its weaknesses) there existed a centralized and managed organization of hospital services; there was no such organization for general practice nor for local authority health services. In consequence, the only feasible solution administratively was to hang the other two services on the existing framework, and to modify that framework so as to accommodate objections and foreseeable difficulties. Given the rather cantankerous character of organized GPs and organized local authorities, it is surprising that things went so quietly. Perhaps to some extent the Ministers 'stopped their mouths with gold', as Nye Bevan may or may not have said about his relationship with the consultants in 1947 (32). Certainly, the GPs (though stoutly maintaining their status as 'independent contractors') had gradually become convinced by the attraction of better organized and financed practice. Certainly, the MOHs saw attractions in the status and career of 'community physician' and may have under-rated what they would lose in losing the 'power base' of an elected local council. Perhaps local government was exhausted by 25 years of wrangling over its own structure, and was preoccupied with very difficult problems of reorganization arising from the English Local Government Act of 1972.

There might also have been opposition from the point of view of the separate organization for teaching hospitals, embodied in the 1946 Act mainly for the benefit of London hospitals and London consultants. But Scottish experience of an integrated organization had been favourable; the English provincial medical schools had grown greatly in stature over these 25 years, and were closer to Scotland than to London in their problems of medical organization and practice; and perhaps also the balance of power, which generally tips towards London, had in this case tipped a little against it and toward the other English regions.

The upshot of these slow manoeuvres was to create a structure strictly hierarchical in form, but hung about with concessions to special interests and to the principles of 'participation' and 'democracy'.

There were to be in England three tiers of hierarchy under the Department; 14 Regions, each with a medical school, 90 Areas, and 171 Districts (33). A District held in its hand responsibility for several hospitals, for GP services, for the old local authority services, and it would inherit staff from each of these services. No lay persons would be included in its management, which would consist of four full-time professionals—community physician, chief nursing officer, administrative officer, and finance officer—with two part-timers, one representing consultants, the other representing GPs. They are enjoined by the Grey Book (34) to act on principles of corporate management and team responsibility, ideas then in vogue in the management of large business organizations, which had been preached also to local authorities after their reorganization. They are obviously in conflict with another set of principles, those of individual responsibility and 'negotiated order'. A Scottish Committee which reported in 1966 made a strong plea for the former, basing itself on the strong Scottish tradition of the Medical Superintendent. Indeed it went further and introduced the concept of a combined administrative service, which would give equal opportunities to lay administrators to reach the level of Superintendent. Such a scheme would clarify responsibility and make clear the chain of command; looking at the service from outside, I like this scheme—but I fear that it is Utopian even for Scotland, out of the question in England. Too many prejudices are allied against it.

The lack of provision for administrative leadership adds emphasis to the concept of teamwork, which remains appal-- lingly vague. It implies perhaps that each member of the team has a concept of the interests of the firm (perhaps reinforced by some profit-sharing device?), and that where there is conflict the firm's interests take priority over those of individuals and departments. The result should be 'management by consensus'. They tell us that in business (particularly in American business) this does happen. I remain a little sceptical about the facts: but would in any case maintain that the concept does not fit public service organizations either descriptively or normatively.

Hence my adoption of the phrase 'negotiated order' (35). The public service, and in particular the health service, brings together persons of many professions and skills. Each partici- pant stands personally by the dignity of his own (or her own) profession and its contribution, and in any co-operative situa- tion he or she acts also in a representative capacity as spokesman for the group to which he or she belongs. This is not a game, as the reference to 'team spirit' might suggest; it is a continuing and most serious way of life, which demands mutual respect and an understanding not of the skills of others in any detail but of their 'self-image' as necessary parts of a great service. A group of such professionals newly assembled will be somewhat wary, even prickly, about one another and about their claims on each other. But if all goes well, there supervenes rather slowly a set of understandings about who does what and who claims what; mutual respect can be combined with mutual deference, and these constitute an 'order' in that mutual expectations become almost second nature, a confident basis for action and co-operation.

This is a difficult form of management, harder than the form which requires subordination to an imposed but respected leader, and the 'District Team' faces other difficulties also in that it is at the 'cutting edge' of the service. The principle of management by professionals has been accepted at this de- cisively important level. But it must (given the character of our society, as it sees itself in this day and age) be hedged about by provisions for democracy and participation. Much has already been said about these in the chapter about patients; complaints procedure, the possibility of legal action, the Health Service 'Ombudsman', and the Community Health Councils. To this one must add that at one higher level, that of Area Health Authority, one meets the principle of lay representation on the governing body. At this level also there is a 'team' of officers, but they are responsible in the first instance to the board of their Area Authority, and 'one-third of its membership should be drawn from the local authorities' (36).

It remains to be seen whether these provisions, taken together, will make the work of the District Management Team not only difficult but impossible. There are not only the built-in problems of consensus management in a complex technical setting, fraught with intense human emotion. There are also the problems of responsibility laterally to the various organs of 'patient power': and of responsibility upwards through two separate lines of command—through a hierarchy of professional superiors in each profession, through a hierarchy of mixed public bodies to the Secretary of State himself or herself.

Criticism has so far been concentrated on two matters which are clearly of importance; the unreality in conditions of great financial stringency of 'the complementary concepts of "maximum responsibility delegated downwards" matched by clear lines of accountability upwards' (37); the delays consequent on a structure of four general administrative tiers (including the Ministry) and of a proliferation of professional hierarchies in parallel with them. A third problem of which much less has been said is that of the quality of the hospital administrative service (secretaries, treasurers, supplies officers, and so on) at District level. The Lycett Green Committee (38), reporting in 1963, experienced very serious doubts about the age structure and about the intellectual quality of the service as it then was. It can hardly have been improved by the transfer to it after 1973 of blocks of lay staff from the Executive Councils and from the local authority health departments. It is very difficult to attract much public interest to the apparently humdrum problems of the great middle class of British public servants; the executive officers and higher clerical officers who run many Departments of the Civil Service; the tax men; the Customs and Excise; the officials of local authorites below the top levels; and many others. We take their negative virtues for granted. They are not corrupt; they are not arbitrary nor dictatorial (except perhaps sometimes to those whom they think socially inferior?); they are not (on the whole) careless nor incompetent. They are not perhaps on the whole very imaginative; but then they are not hired to be imaginative, and indeed gifts of imagination might increase their liability to the stress of boredom. The fabric of our welfare state has depended very much on these people and they have on the whole taken the strain well. Perhaps they do so in the health service also, but the human problems of their work deserve more attention than has been given to them (39).

On the other hand, almost too much has been heard (in particular, the sound of Sir Keith Joseph beating his breast in public, and confessing his guilt) about the problems of a superfluous tier. As explained above, the English pyramid is one of 14 Regions, 90 Areas, and 171 Districts. In terms of classical management theory, this shape is relatively narrow, relatively deep. It keeps the span of control at higher levels rather narrow; in so doing it makes possible, at each level except that of the Department, rather close control of subordinates, and indeed intermediate officials may find themselves short of work if they do not keep themselves busy with such control. If we grant that such control is now too strict and too repetitive, there is no doubt that in principle one of the answers (perhaps the only answer of a general kind) is to change the shape of the pyramid. If one abolishes the Areas (at present the favourite solution) then each Region would be responsible for about twelve Districts. If this is judged to be too many, then add new Regions and amalgamate some Districts. So far the argument is easy; as soon as one contemplates action it becomes much harder. The present boundaries are not fortuitous; they represent traditions and compromises which it would be painful to renegotiate. What is more, they have been re-staffed recently by the filling of many new appointments; an expensive business, as compensation must be paid to those who cannot be re-employed at their old levels or who choose to retire prematurely. Are we to go through this again?—so soon? It is at least possible that politicians will draw back when their officials explain the difficulties, and that there will be no new Act, as yet. Perhaps these difficulties would fade away if there were more money available? But if there is no more money, will not even wise circulars be resented? (40).

What does the Department do? This train of thought leads directly to the central question of the health service polity—who runs it? (41). And one must recognize that it would be a valid answer to reply 'no one runs it'; that is to say that the appearance of command is deceptive, that the great Department and its political head are the captives of the service, not its masters, in that they are dominated by the historical complexities of the situation, and can make choices only within very narrow limits, if at all.

It is worth keeping that picture in mind, as a limiting case, even though it cannot be wholly true. But meantime let us proceed on the basis of a more orthodox analysis. The Department exists to govern a sphere of operations defined functionally in the quotation given earlier in this chapter (p. 156). That sphere is coterminous with a polity or commonwealth of human beings. Taken at its widest, the polity of concern for health includes every person within the territorial boundaries of England: but that concern is organized, within the larger polity, by those who earn their living in and by the NHS. This includes contractors as well as employees; not only the GPs working on contracts of a rather artificial kind, but also suppliers of goods to the NHS who are in some instances monopoly suppliers to a monopoly purchaser. The service, including GPs, employs directly, in England alone, about 800,000 people; one cannot tell from the available figures how many more jobs are supported by over £850 million (42) which the service spends on purchases in the market, nor where these jobs are located.

One part at least of the Department's work is that it secures resources, which it then allocates. This can be illustrated most simply by quoting a table and a paragraph from a paper which deals with the Government Expenditure Plans, 1978/9 to 1981/2 (43).

> 24. About 40 per cent of public expenditure by the central government, excluding debt interest, is on goods and services, the largest elements being defence and the national

health service. The remainder consists of transfer payments—including social security benefits, housing sub-
sidies and industrial support—and net lending, which
includes loans to nationalized industries.

TABLE 3. *Central government expenditure programmes.* £ million at
1977 survey prices

	1975–6	1976–7	1977–8 estimated	1978–9	1979–80
Defence	6,445	6,361	6,255	6,289	6,494
National health service	5,981	6,051	6,132	6,255	6,350
Social security	12,309	12,717	13,226	14,063	14,172
Other expenditure	15,544	14,109	12,620	15,048	14,964
Total	40,279	39,238	38,233	41,655	41,980

A further table (p. 8) shows the amounts spent through local
authorities; notably about £6,500m on education, and about
£1,100m on the personal social services, which are very closely
involved with the services provided by the NHS. By far the
largest part of these allocations is gained by the Department
in the continuous and unending battle for resources in Whitehall
and at Westminster. There is a different battle, or series of
battles, about the financing of local authority services; and
rather small sums are contributed by NHS contributions
(£600m in 1976/7) and by charges for services, for instance for
prescriptions (less than £250m in the same year). As can be
seen, these revenues are trivial in relation to the whole cost; a
Conservative government might try to increase their share, and
such changes might affect administration, in that some means
test would be necessary to keep the service available to the very
poor. But the main battle must continue to be that over the
continuing process of Treasury allocation.

In that battle, which is regularly fought up to the level of the
Cabinet, the Department and the Secretary of State himself
must 'play the hand'. But the cards he holds are dealt him by
the political process as a whole and are embodied in the army
which he leads. There is a parallel but distinct area of concern
for education, and also for defence. The NHS is strong both
because it concerns all of us, and also because its employees are
organized in many associations with many voices, and they

can shout very loudly. For much of the time they are shouting at the Department and apparently against it. But these protests can be used by an astute Secretary of State as arguments to strengthen his case for more resources.

The £ sterling is by far the most convenient measure of resources, but it is useless if it cannot be spent, especially in view of the Treasury rule that unspent balances are to be clawed back at the end of each financial year, so that services dependent on revenue from the national budget cannot stock-pile £s sterling as reserves for future contingencies (44). Underspending is most likely to happen if real resources (mainly manpower and buildings) fall short of expectations. Money cannot be spent on more nurses, if no nurses are available at the right place at the right time. Money cannot be spent on equipping and staffing a new hospital if the building has fallen behind the due completion date. Victories and defeats for the Department are signalled by the £ sterling as indicator; but the Department must budget also in terms of manpower and of other scarce resources, and here it is involved in a maze of uncertainties and intangibles. These are concerned particularly with time-lags, which are particularly important in regard to the availability of trained staff; there is also the problem of technological change, in that it takes at least ten years to plan, build, and equip a District General Hospital, and by that time the world has moved on, there are new users and new technologies.

There is in fact no national manpower budget. This was tried, not without some success, in the last years of the Second World War (45); but in the conditions of crisis then prevailing, time-lags were relatively short, and there were powers to direct labour such as could not be granted in time of peace.

Thus the process of planning in real terms is thrown back upon the Department, and becomes part of its internal process of allocation; the hierarchy of agencies is from this point of view a hierarchy of allocations. The Secretary of State must use his sovereign power of command to determine allocations. There is much talk of the market as making possible allocation by an 'invisible hand', in a way which diffuses power and eliminates personal human responsibility. It is true that in a sense the political world operates as a market of power and influence which can be measured simply by success—*Who Gets What, When How* (46). Nevertheless, in our polity, decisions must be publicly defended; the Department must say not only what it is allocating to whom but why.

From this follows much of its activity of the level of policy.

At the outset, in 1947, there was no policy except that of Beveridge, that an adequately financed health service would soon catch up with the back-log of untreated illness. But post-war euphoria lasted no longer than that of 1918. Brave dreams were chilled by the bitter winter of 1947 and were not thawed by the Festival of Britain in 1951. There ensued Harold Wilson's 'bonfire of controls' and Winston Churchill's campaign to 'set the people free'. At the same time there were funny stories of how 'they' exploited the NHS: free wigs, and false teeth, and endless prescriptions. Into this confusion there came the first steps in business management; the beginnings of work study and O and M, the beginnings of cost accounting and of comparative statistics; very elementary but essential (47). And it was lucky that the inevitable committee of enquiry was led by Mr C. W. Guillebaud, who 'kept his head when all around were losing theirs', and produced a report which settled that there could be no going back. The NHS was now part of the constitution, like the Throne and the TUC.

We now need a good history of what followed. There were at last beginning to be data about the working of the service, on which arguments could be based: there was a nucleus of inde-pendent academic observers, at least in London and in Man-chester; there was the 'planning mood' which came over the country in Harold Macmillan's time, by no means discredited by the doings of Christine Keeler and Captain Profumo, satirized by young Mr Frost in *That Was The Week That Was*; and there was Harold Wilson's phrase about 'the white-heat of technology'. Along with this there went a new mood at the Ministry of Health; various trends converged, and it is not possible, without serious historical research, to guess where the initiative lay. There was the Hospital Plan of 1962, a first attempt to work out the implications of new building to replace the Victoriana of the hospital service. There was a succession of 'good Ministers' (Powell, Kenneth Robinson, Crossman, Keith Joseph), three of them ambitious men eager for high office, who raised the status of the Department in the league table of Cabinet precedence. There was also a period of constructive thought about the social services among doctors and social workers, a period which opened up vistas for the future which would have seemed ridiculously Utopian in 1946; a new image of general practice; a proposed unification of the social work professions and a rapprochement with the profession of medicine; the rise of new ideologies about medicine and the community, especially in the fields of geriatrics, mental health, and mental deficiency; the build-up of a consensus that new administrative institutions were both necessary and possible in order to embody these ideas.

It seems in retrospect to have been a lively and creative period, though not a contented nor complacent one; it was, for instance, the first period of militancy among nurses, junior doctors, and ancillary workers. It also contained the seeds of our present discontents, in that projections of national growth rates had to be scaled down progressively; the rejection of Empire and the acceptance of EEC membership in 1973 produced no economic miracles; and there supervened the Egyptian attack on Sinai during Yom Kippur in 1973, and the consequent quadrupling of the price of oil. This may well have triggered world recession or even depression, but we had all been riding for a fall, swept up on a rising curve of growth; this was the period in which there was developed the concept of Limits of Growth, the logical necessity that a growth curve cannot climb for ever. There must in the end be an inflection.

My view would be that the England and Wales Act of 1973, the Scottish Act of 1972 represented the 1960s mood of faith in the future; their implementation followed in a period of pessimism and economic depression, to which we have not yet grown accustomed.

This history is presented only for debate, and as a challenge to serious research, based on far more material than is now available. It must serve in the present context as a basis for the hypothesis that in the mid-1970s a new situation emphasized new aspects of the Department's work and of the Minister's powers.

The Minister, whoever he may be, must be deemed, as a party politician, to have accepted the obligations of Cabinet membership: the Prime Minister and the Chancellor, if sufficiently resolute, can impose an economic policy on the Cabinet, even though it is very distasteful to Defence, Education, and Health and Social Services, the great spending departments. The little table on p. 167 shows what that has meant and will mean to health; the White Paper from which the table is drawn goes on to explain that in the bad years 1976 and 1977 there were real cuts in domestic spending by individuals, as well as virtual stagnation in industry.

This emphasized aspects of the Department's work which had hitherto grown quietly. To establish its position in debate with Treasury and Cabinet the Department has to sustain and document its reputation for economic rationality and managerial skill, in face of shrewd and sceptical observers.

As has appeared on earlier pages, I think poorly of the management theory embodied in the Grey Book; indeed, I thought it had been exterminated years ago. But it has the great merit that to inexperienced readers it seems lucid and tidy, orderly and even 'rational'. It requires some knowledge of the complexities of public institutions and a limited amount of academic training to see that its great platitudes are riddled with ambiguities and that the art of definition is not merely an academic game. One could give many examples of the use of terms not effectively defined, such as 'co-ordination', 'planning', 'decision-making', 'more uniform national standards', 'innovation', 'clear but flexible career structures'. But the most disastrous of all is the utterly unintelligible proposition that 'Delegation downwards should be matched with accountability upwards' (48).

It is easy for an academic to over-rate the harm done by semantic confusion; on the whole, people work things out for themselves; they 'negotiate an order' and the words are bent to fit it. But it does not make life easier if a new language has to be learnt and applied, and modified in the process.

There can be very much less doubt about the stress due to the inflection in the growth curve. There are four areas of stress which I can enumerate specifically; there is also the exasperatingly vague dimension expressed in terms of conditions hard to measure, such as 'mood', 'climate of opinion', 'complacency', 'exasperation', 'malaise', and 'morale'.

The first is that of salary negotiations. The hospital service emerged from the reorganization of 1947 with an elaborate structure of negotiation modelled on the Whitley Council system of the Civil Service which began during the First World War, and on a comparable system for local government which grew slowly between the wars and was consolidated in post-war years. The principle of orderly wage-bargaining in the public services is of course unimpeachable, but its practice is very difficult. The complex system of superimposed committee levels is of necessity slow; it is entangled with questions of competition between unions for membership and for representation on the staff side; it may be no more than a screen for decisions agreed elsewhere (49). Those with greatest influence, the GPs and the consultants, have been able to escape from Whitleyism and to create bargaining institutions of their own; these are equally difficult for the rank and file to understand, but at least they do permit explicit bargaining for a 'package', which includes many elements besides the cash question of basic payment. I have illustrated in Chapter 5 the way in which successive negotiations with the doctors have gradually modified their status in relation to each other and to the service, in ways which represent a sort of consensual drift.

One recurring difficulty for wage negotiations in the public services (now perhaps 30 per cent of the work force) is that on the employers' side a large front of lay members is in fact controlled by the representatives of the relevant Whitehall department or departments; and that these are in their turn controlled by 'the rats behind the arras', the Treasury men who are never seen but are the effective agents of national policy. This difficulty is built in to our situation; no one, Tory or Labour, civil servant or trade unionist, academic or participant, has made any plausible suggestion as to how 'free collective bargaining' can be applied to the situation of one employer and seven or eight million employees. In the last resort, the government makes policy, the electorate makes governments.

These frustrations are intensified when (as in 1977 and 1978) the government is forced to make wages policy as part of general economic policy in relation to the world situation. Very simple general rules, made with the idea of influencing world markets and world institutions, prevail over the very much more complex considerations involved in managing, comforting, developing the extraordinary work force who constitute the health service. As I write, in July 1978, the government proposes the crudest possible criterion, the 5 per cent maximum for the public services; it may not be backed by a majority in the House of Commons; it may not be backed by the support of the electorate. But whichever party wins, the dilemma will continue, and it will be eased only by renewed economic growth in the western world as a whole.

A second source of exasperation is also intensified by conditions of no growth, or of very slow growth. On the one hand, routine financial controls are tightened. The Treasury imposes a system of cash limits (50), intended to ensure that overspending is not possible; and the result obviously is to increase the probability of under-spending (51). That in turn adds an incentive (this is common in the defence services too) to spend up to the limit somehow, before the financial year ends, even though it would have been more prudent to carry forward a reserve to the following year. All this increases the power and prestige (and unpopularity) of the hierarchy of finance officers, the policemen of the system.

On the other side of the account there is an intensification in the pressure for cheapness under the slogan of 'effectiveness and efficiency'. This pressure has always been there, since it was first realized that the cost of the NHS was enormous and that it had a built-in tendency to grow; and it has forced the level of discussion up through the intellectual and social hierarchy of the service from work study, organization and methods, and comparative cost accounting, to operational research, to health economics, to the level of medical science and medical ethics. On the one hand, there are the questions raised by health economists about the public interest and the maximization of benefits in relation to resources. In the last resort this is a question of life and death. Surely the life of a young producer should count for more than that of a bed-ridden old lady in her eighties? But is there not a tacit compact with society that part of our reward in our working years is that we should not be put down like dogs when our working days are over? But, yet again, who wants to go on, 'sans eyes, sans ears, sans teeth, sans everything'? It is a relief to the observer of this analysis that at least one leader among the health economists feels logically compelled to revert to the old view, that the ultimate decisions are taken in unique situations, and there can be no general guidance other than the skill and conscience of the doctors at the point of decision (52).

But the doctors in their professional capacity are not exempt from critical analysis. Are treatments effective? Do they do any 'good'? Certain commonly used treatments have never been tested for effectiveness at all. Supposing they are 'effective', are they also 'efficient'? Could the same degree of effectiveness have been served at less 'cost'—and of course it is hard to define 'cost' so that it does not include ethical and affective elements (53). The medical profession, dedicated to the tradition of Hippocrates, is also dedicated to the maxim of his younger contemporary Socrates—'A way of life not critically examined is not one for a man to live' (Socrates put it better in Greek, in only six words). It is not a maxim which comes very easily to tired and hurried men and women, working under severe nervous strain. But there is no doubt that a movement goes on towards 'medical audit' in practice, 'critical science' in the laboratories. This is entailed by the acceptance of scientific authority, as distinct from reliance on placebos.

It can be argued that where there is no competition in terms of profitability spending cuts actually promote effectiveness and efficiency by enforcing self-examination. But this is a hard doctrine which no one likes if it is applied to himself or herself.

Constraints also enforce two other related measures; arguments about allocations, and about the definition of priorities. In a sense, these are two sides of one coin, but they seem to have developed rather separately in the government of the health service. It is characteristic of large non-commercial organizations that in principle the central authority allocates revenue afresh each year in terms of task to be performed; whereas in practice every department gets the same as last year plus some sort of percentage increment; a system which slowly but inescapably opens the gap between those who were for some reason lucky at some now forgotten time in the past, and those who were not. Some organizations (some universities for instance) modify the simple percentage principle by adding some other principle (for instance, that of success in the competition to attract students) which may boost percentages for those it favours. In times of generous expansion this can be done in such a way that some get more and none get less; the sense of grievance is blunted so long as the principle (for instance, that of teaching load) gains fairly general assent. But at a time of no growth (or apparent growth which is in fact a mirage due to monetary inflation), there is real deprivation; hence resentment, hence attempts to attack either the principle itself or the bias and corruption involved in its application.

This is what has happened to the hospital service in England in the sequel to the 1976 Report of the Resource Allocation Working Party—*Sharing Resources for Health in England*— RAWP (54). The Working Party (some 25 men and women drawn equally from 'court' and 'country', centre and periphery, Department and service) were charged in May 1975 to

> review the arrangements for distributing NHS capital and revenue to RHA, AHA and Districts respectively with a view to establishing a method of securing, as soon as practicable, a pattern of distribution responsive objectively, equitably and efficiently to relative need and to make recommendations.

Their report, submitted for publication in September 1976, is scrupulously exact in its attempt to operationalize the four agreed criteria; objectivity, equity, efficiency, and relative need—a marvel of manipulated consensus. It was accepted by the Secretary of State and went into action for the financial year 1977–8; and the predictable test of power and influence is now about to follow.

Ever since the comparable statistics became available, it has been known that there is a league table of health service regions in England, in terms of all readily available indicators. The four London Regions are at the top, the Trent and North Western Regions are generally at the bottom. There is no workable measure of quality of service; but there have been vigorous efforts to measure intensity of need, and on all the obvious indicators such as mortality, morbidity, age of population, and experience of child birth and child rearing, the worst-off regions have the greatest need. Equity and need appear to demand re-distribution; objectivity has been sought most conscientiously. The only effective London counter-attack has been in terms of efficiency, setting up against the doctrine of equity the doctrine that efficiency is best served by backing the leaders and let the rest follow. This is felt intensely by the great London hospitals and their influential public clients, and no one denies their relative excellence. But it may be that the best and the worst are both in the London regions, and that the average (how on earth could one measure it?) is no worse in the compact provincial regions than it is in the London regions as a whole.

The Secretary of State has absolute legal power to distribute money, by whatever formula he chooses to apply; the complex RAWP formula has been applied and (as I write) the first appeal is being made from legal power to political influence. The process of reallocation is to be a long one, staged over several years, but already one of the London Area Boards has begun to fight the Minister's allocation with threats of resigna-tion. Legally, they are not servants of the Department but of their own Regional Authorities, and thus another level of the hierarchy is automatically involved; and this makes it specially difficult to predict the next moves on the chess board of health service politics. Probably a general election will intervene be-fore the quarrel is forced to an issue; probably there will then be a new Secretary of State, a new set of troubles, and this issue will disappear from the columns of the Press. It will thus be difficult (as it has always been in England) to assess by the study of direct conflict where ultimate power lies. But there will be a learning process; future ministers will consider the political cost of proceeding with a policy of active reallocation.

This controversy has raised the issue of the Department's power in questions of geographical allocation, right down to the level of Districts. There are also delicate questions at each level about the allocating of resources between functions. I re-ferred earlier (55) to the public disclosures in the 1960s of intolerable conditions in provision for old people, for long-stay cases in mental hospitals, and for 'difficult' cases of mental deficiency. It is greatly to the credit of British administration in general, of the NHS in particular, that these cases were brought to light and given wide publicity, and it was never really disputed that there was below the surface an iceberg of lesser evils derived from the attempt to do an almost impossible job with inferior resources—inferior in numbers and quality of staff, in capital allocations for new buildings, in geographical location and in relationship to institutions with a warmer atmosphere and higher prestige.

Hence a variety of remedies, pursued though a whole series of publications, of which the climax was the policy document of September 1977, *Priorities in the Health and Social Services: The Way Forward* (56).

The new policy had at least four branches. A new Hospital Advisory Service (57) (in effect an inspectorate, however considerate its procedure) was set up in 1969; in 1978 its reports continue to be desperate in character, though most judiciously expressed. They confirm the impression given by the major public scandals, that one must fight very hard, for oneself and for those close to one, to avoid these institutions at all costs. Secondly, there was a recognition that the job imposed on doctors, nurses, and other staff in the custodial institutions was one that could not be done. Its isolation and its sheer sadness must be broken down by opening up the situation to community resources; volunteers coming into the hospitals, the patients, if there is any possibility at all, being released from 'custody' and transferred to 'community care'; a very loose phrase, which means in practice that responsibility should be transferred from the NHS budget to the budgets of local authority social service departments. There has always been an undertone of bargaining between the two services—'you take one of our old ladies into hospital and next time we'll take one of yours into "sheltered accommodation" '. The terms of trade are now to be shifted in favour of the NHS and away from the local authorities, and limited funds are available with which to buy their aid. The same Department is responsible for both services; but its authority is limited, and the national battle must be fought out in local skirmishes between Health Areas and Local Authorities.

Then (thirdly) there is the policy of bringing mental health wards and geriatric wards into district general hospitals (little is said about mental deficiency) (58). The move may well be beneficial to the existing staff of these wards and to the problem of finding additional staff for them. But they will still rank low in the pecking order of their profession, and it will be difficult to reconcile their role with that of the new general hospitals, concerned with clinical success, with bed occupancy rates, and with securing the highest possible turnover rates for acute cases and maternity cases. To 'block a bed' is perhaps as great a sin as ever it was.

And there are plenty of experimental expedients—day hospitals, five-day hospitals, and so on—which at least acknowledge that for every long-stay case in hospital there is at least one other case in the community kept out of hospital by devoted, even desperate, family care, contributed without reward and often at great personal sacrifice.

But in the last resort there is the question of shifting financial resources in accordance with policy, and in this instance the Department has no practicable legal power at its disposal. It cannot (even if it took direct control of administration) re-adjust budgets all the way down to the level of districts (171 of them) and of individual hospitals; and if it could do so, it could not supervise the spirit in which the allocations were used in practice. And indeed it is not certain how far public opinion would back any reallocation which was made clearly at the cost of remedial care in the acute wards for patients who still have their lives to lead. The policy is well-balanced and well-considered; concern for the old and helpless is quite genuine and quite strong. But is it in the last resort strong enough to support a strong policy?

My guess is that it is not, and that in this huge area of the health service the Department's rights are merely those of modern constitutional monarchy as defined by Walter Bagehot in 1867: 'to be consulted, to encourage, to warn' (59). The favoured official word is 'guidance'.

Retrospect

It is difficult, perhaps impossible, to re-state the conclusions of this chapter without over-simplification. One may simply tabulate as follows:

1. 'The Government' is a very big and complex assembly of men and women, each of whom doubles in two roles; in one role he or she plays a part set down in a formal list of duties,

in another role he or she is no more nor less than a citizen, a private person sharing the life experience of the other fifty million.

2. The Department of Health and Social Security, and its associated organizations, have grown enormously in size and complexity since the early days of 1947. Each step in growth has been adequately justified by the needs of the service; in terms of skill and personal devotion and openness to new ideas this is a 'good department'. It does not suffer noticeably, the disease which Professor Parkinson calls 'injelititis', a self-perpetuating mixture of inertia and mutual jealousy.

3. Nevertheless there is always the danger that as Departments grow bigger their officials may spend more and more of their time in talking to one another, and may lose touch with the outer world. This is a real danger for a Department which is almost wholly based in Greater London, and which does not have very much staff interchange at any level with other parts of England. One of the roles of political ministers is to make this gap good, and they are (or should be) activated in that way by their own experience in the constituencies, and by the pressure of parliamentary debate and of letters from MPs about individual cases. 'The Government' is not unresponsive—it does learn. Whether it learns fast enough is another question.

4. The Department does not go looking for trouble, but trouble is forced upon it, especially in times of financial stringency. It has to struggle with problems of allocation; on the one hand, allocation of cash rewards among its many grumbling servants; on the other hand, allocation between their patients on the basis of region, area, sector, and specialty. The Department and its ministers seem to stall, to prevaricate, to depend on the healing hand of time. But in the end, decisions are taken, legitimate authority is invoked.

5. There is a marked contrast between the sharp edges of financial authority and the rather relaxed consensual kind of authority which the Department is accustomed to exercise in other aspects of the service, and in particular in the guidance it gives about medical priorities. It is (collectively) well aware that stringency demands allocation, allocation demands argument, and argument demands reasoned propositions. What issues from the Department is a command expressed in financial

terms, and in its nature a command implies acceptance of responsibility—'my decision is that category A gets it, category B does not'. I am not certain that the Department is equally aware that these general propositions have to serve as the basis of individual actions. There is not, and there cannot be, the equivalent of a judicial system, in which judges of the lowest Courts relate the law to the facts, subject to appeal up the hierarchy of Courts of Law. The Department's allocations and its policies are in the last resort applied to individual cases by doctors, and indeed by nursing staff and other auxiliary staff.

One may get into trouble if one asserts bluntly that the caring relationship is built into all human beings, that it is both genetic and cultural. There is the disturbing definition of psychopathic disorder in the 1959 Mental Health Act:

> Clause 4–4. In the Act 'psychopathic disorder' means persistent disorder or disability of mind (whether or not including sub-normality of intelligence) which results in abnormally aggressive or seriously irresponsible conduct on the part of the patient, and requires or is susceptible to medical treatment (60).

There is the battle among geneticists (61) in which one side maintains that it is logically impossible that there should be a gene for self-sacrifice except within a close genetic community, because he or she who cares more for another than for self is endangering the survival of his or her own genetic heritage. There is the awkward assertion by the anthropologist Colin Turnbull (62) that he has observed a culture, that of small half-starved mountain people, the Ik, among whom the caring relationship is unknown. In these three respects the concept of 'caring relationship' is under radical attack; but the concept of health care is totally dependent on it. There is an interface at which one person accepts responsibility for the care of another.

CHAPTER 10 MYTHS AND
CONTRADICTIONS

> It is not only in the navy that there are two contradictory
> traditions of 'obedience to others' and 'turning the blind eye'.
> But one cannot provide rules in advance for the occasions
> when rules can and should be ignored. If management
> decisions on crucial issues of policy are to be effective, the
> fiction must be maintained that the rules are always obeyed.
> Only where there is such a fiction can one safely allow full
> play in practice to individual initiative and discretion . . .
> (p. 137)
>
> It seems to me that all social organization is full of contra-
> dictions of this kind. Myths, principles and ideals, as well as
> human weakness and fallibility and the demands made by the
> complexity and ever-changing variety of real life, all influence
> actual behaviour. If indeed there is a logic in social reality,
> it is a logic of inconsistency (p. 139).
>
> 'The role of the myth in politics' in ELY DEVONS, *Papers on
> Planning and Economic Management* (1970) (Manchester
> University Press).

As I was about to write this concluding chapter, the following headlines appeared in the centre page of the *Glasgow Herald* (31
October 1978), along with the usual sort of picture of masked
figures grouped around an operating table:

'You can take it we now have virtually no power
in hospitals'—surgeon

Who controls the health service?

Despite the settlement of the hospital dispute,
deep-rooted problems remain.
JOHN LINKLATER looks at the continuing
predicament of the hospital consultant—
responsibility without power.

The philosophers and theologians to whose books I referred
earlier would wish to say that this combination of words
is senseless because responsibility relates specifically to the

Notes and references for this chapter begin on page 208.

exercise of discretion. It is not logically possible that you should be called to answer for what it was outside your power to do. Responsibility entails free will and the exercise of choice; it is limited by the resources available for action.

Yet the surgeon in question is expressing a strong ethical emotion and does so effectively. Perhaps it can be re-stated as follows. The surgeon does indeed have both power and responsibility in his skilled hands as he stands over the patient on the operating table. But that situation arises out of an earlier situation, that of the decision to operate; that decision depends not only on the needs and priorities of patients as the surgeon sees them, but also on the availability of resources. These resources are partly physical—the condition of the theatre, the availability of sterilized equipment, of warmth and light; and partly human—the anaesthetist, the theatre sister, the porters, the unknown workers in the laundry, and so on. All this is outside the consultant's direct control; it entails money and people, and there never was a world in which there was no limit to these resources. But 'once upon a time' the hospital world was much more predictable; it was not one in which (as now) a leader in his profession may be told by a not very distinguished finance officer or general administrator—'I am sorry, Sir, the cash for this month is exhausted'—'I am sorry, Sir, there is a strike in CSSD.'

Not that the consultant is excluded from influence in such matters; but he can exercise it only through committees, hierarchically arranged, at the level of division, hospital, district and above, and committee-sitting (he will rightly say) is not his job. It is true that some consultants accept responsibility for 'politicking' on behalf of their patients and themselves, and become skilled at it. But most of them are not trained nor temperamentally suited for the politics of accountancy and of industrial relations.

'There are many contradictions in any major thing' wrote the late Chairman Mao in 1937 (1), and in his view of the world the adaptability of thought and of institutions depends on contradictions and their resolution. The NHS offers a particularly obdurate case.

On the one hand, there are the traditions and the organization of caring and curing. The guiding maxim and myth is that of personalized individual relations. The professional owes to the client (or patient) service without limit or qualification. The person whose need is in question is entitled to everything, to absolute finality. He or she may in his or her own interest be deceived; but must not be betrayed. There are many patients, their needs may conflict and compete, but each relationship is unique and demands infinite respect. We are in the presence of pain and death.

On the other hand the intervention of public management, the exclusion of bargaining in the market, implies that everyone is to count for one and no one for more than one. One can imagine a caste system of medical care in which (for instance) each Brahmin should count for five, each sweeper for one only. But there must be a rule, and a rule of inequality cannot be tolerated in a commonwealth of equals. Once it is realized that resources are not infinite, there must be a rule of allocation: and it must be a rule of equality, subject only to some informed, independent, and unbiased adjudication of need.

I have no doubt that we have here 'the principal contradiction' in which the NHS is involved during a period of 'no-growth'.

Hence the problems of hierarchy and allocation, expressed formally in terms of the prescription of budgets for capital investment and annual expenditure. In the words quoted at the head of this chapter, 'management decisions on crucial issues of policy' must 'be effective'. That is part of the constitutional bargain struck by the Secretary of State for Health and Social Services, with his colleagues in the Cabinet; the Secretary of State is transient but there are in a sense also continuing bargains between his Department and the Treasury. The Minister and his officials must battle in Cabinet and Whitehall to secure the largest slice of the 'national cake' that they can get; and their case is hopelessly weakened if it can fairly be argued either that money is being wasted or that it is not spent according to the agreed plan of allocation.

The constitutional formula is that of the individual responsibility of Ministers, the collective responsibility of the Cabinet; this is, as Devons says, a myth, in that a Minister cannot possibly carry moral responsibility for all the acts of a vast organization about which he knows very little.

As a matter of fact, our Ministers of Health, especially since the NHS was founded, have been people with a strong sense of moral responsibility, have made great efforts to understand and inspire the Service and have believed sincerely in decentralization. But their personal characters are slotted into the mythological structure of the Constitution: the officials are responsible to the Minister, the Minister is responsible to the Cabinet, both together are responsible to the House of Commons — which is in turn responsible to the sovereign electorate.

All this is necessary to our political life—and yet it proceeds on principles which contradict the principles of medical life. Devons suggests that such contradictions (which are common enough in large organizations, public and private) can be reconciled by the naval doctrine of 'the blind eye (the Nelson touch)'. The doctrine is indeed quietly accepted by good finance controllers, whether in military service, or in local authorities, or as university bursars: and Devons' central paradox is that the topic is by definition un-researchable. We all know that to sustain the rules we must sometimes bend the rules: but that principle is effective only if we don't talk about it too much. A good finance officer manoeuvres for himself and his constituency some space in which he and they have liberty of action, a refuge in time of trouble; and I am not sure that this is fully appreciated in what is still a very young service administratively (the changes made in 1973 were bigger than was appreciated at the time, and amounted almost to a new foundation of the Service); and difficulties have been increased by much mythological talk about 'cash-limits', a scarecrow device which amounts to little more than traditional Treasury practice (2). There is also the much more practical difficulty that reorganization coincided with financial crisis, and that redistribution of resources can no longer be floated off on the basis of giving everybody something, some people more than others.

Mao goes on to say, in his rather schoolmasterly way (3) that 'there are many contradictions in the process of development of a complex thing, and one of them is necessarily the principal contradiction whose existence and development determine or influence the existence and development of the other contradictions', and he explains that contradiction is the source of radical innovation through 'a series of struggles with many twists and

turns'. Surely this is much too bland? The essence of the contradiction between medicine and public finance is easy enough
to grasp intellectually, but it is not easy to reconcile, in particular
because each of the two groups of participants have great power
resources and also a strong sense of moral responsibility.
Doctors are apt to despise 'the bureaucrats'; the latter do not
despise doctors, and the best of them are well aware that their
own role is no more than that of men in the supply lines behind
the cutting edge of the organization. But the situation is not
one of a dialectical interpenetration and transformation of
opposites. On the contrary, it is one of total and continuing
interdependence.

These opposing parties are both in their moral characters
representatives of the public interest; a different kind of contradiction arises out of the representation of sectional interests
within the service. This has been dramatized recently by the
six-week strike of works supervisors, a dispute primarily about
relativities; 'who is worth more, him or me?'

> The trouble meant that more than 60,000 people had to
> be refused admission for treatment, and it took the hos-
> pital waiting list to record levels. The Department of
> Health said that six hospitals had been closed, more than
> 9,000 beds put out of use, and more than 300 hospitals
> reduced to emergency services. . . . 'The men involved in
> this dispute are very concerned about the service and about
> patient care, but have been frustrated in their ambitions
> for a very long time and we recognise that' said Mrs Kelly,
> chairman of the management negotiating team (4).

It is by no means certain that the NHS has a bad record of
industrial relations, in so far as that can be measured comparatively. But a strike or work-to-rule in the NHS is news, just as a
local bus strike is news, because it affects everybody to some extent. It is unthinkable that the Service should cease totally, that
there should be no more care or cure except what we patients
can puzzle out for ourselves. So even the threat of a little mini-
nuclear explosion in one part of the service is alarming to
everyone, including the strikers themselves as potential patients,
each with his own network of concern for potential patients.

So health service disputes generate a higher temperature than most industrial disputes, and that is likely to continue. But the management of industrial relations in the service has a bad reputation, and there is a conflict of myths; on the one hand it is seen as a caring service, on the other as a bad-tempered service; and no one, patient or participant, wants the latter story to prevail. There are three possible lines of defence.

Firstly, there is the improvement of personal relations at the level of small groups. Bit by bit the scope of involvement within the 'pale of the constitution', as recognized full members of a national service, has been broadened. Nurses, junior doctors, doctors from overseas, and the complementary professions have fought for and won recognition. But the ancillary workers and the maintenance workers have not been well integrated—much part-time and temporary employment, high turnover, and a poor level of pay. Individual doctors, individual administrators, and matrons have had the personal virtues of good employers: but as a whole the 'top people' in the service have been rather ignorant and not deeply concerned. That includes the Department as well as the local organizations. The DHSS has never thought of itself as an industrial ministry; concern for industrial relations and appropriate staff training has come in very late—perhaps too late, but it is agreed that much still can be done and must be done at the level of face-to-face personal contact.

But here is a quotation from a recent article by James Cameron (5), attributed by him to an anonymous (perhaps imaginary) surgeon.

> There are also (besides the fatal effects of 'bureaucracy') the divisive influences within the hospitals arising from the struggle to organize the largest single group of workers now outside the trade unions.
>
> It is of course enormously important to change the composition of our hospital workers from a transient, under-paid and unaligned collection into a stable group with a personal and social stake in the growth of the service. But this inter-union struggle for membership has just led to a display of populist activities that aren't at all helpful.

In other words, the ancillary staff of hospitals (some 200,000 people) are now entangled in a major struggle between very large trade unions, and face-to-face relations lose their effectiveness when faced by appeals for solidarity from such great organizations.

> There have been waves of amalgamation . . . which have greatly reduced the total number of unions but have done nothing to simplify the overall pattern. Instead they have strung together groups of members and areas of recognised bargaining rights [five unions were involved in the recent supervisors' dispute] in ever more incomprehensible confusion (6).

Hugh Clegg's study, from which this quotation is drawn, is a comparative one. British trade unions score high on some dimensions, but low on clarity of organization and low on factionalism, war between groups (often purely personal ones) within a single union.

Labour and Tory governments have in turn tried their hands at improving trade union organization by law, and both parties have retired hurt, grumbling about power without responsibility in the unions. It is unlikely that the DHSS will have better success than the industrial ministries; but it is at least clear that in future it must be very well briefed (Ministers and officials alike) about trade unions in the hospital service. From its earliest days the DHSS has been very expert and sensitive about the temperaments and rivalries of the professional organizations—an obvious necessity because these were all integrated into health service politics even before the days of the NHS. The new expertise will be more difficult to acquire because (this is the essence of the problem) only one big union (COHSE) is closely associated with the NHS. The others (for example, TGWU, MGWU, NUPE, ASTMS, NALGO) are spread over the whole industrial scene, public and private. But one is left with the feeling that the trouble over works supervisors had been dragging on and festering for years, and should have been forced up to top levels of decision-making much earlier.

Finally, at the third level of industrial relations, there is the problem of official machinery for negotiation. I have referred in passing earlier to the negotiating structure for medical and dental staff, who had escaped almost at the outset from the imposition of Whitley Council machinery on the NHS. 'Whit-leyism' had, in fact, worked rather well for the central Civil Service, not too badly for local authority staff; and it was an obvious step to introduce into the NHS, especially as the level of union membership was then low, and there were great varia-tions in practice in different parts of the country and different types of hospital authority. There is now a General Council and eight functional Councils, covering about a million people and 43 distinct staff organizations. In addition, there are some 'groups of craftsmen and semi-skilled operatives who negotiate directly with the Department of Health' (7) (I believe the works supervisors are among these), and some unusual or specialized grades not yet allocated to a Whitley Council.

Lord McCarthy's excellent *Review* of the system leaves the impression of an extremely complex and boring organization, masking some bitter rivalries under formal procedure; highly centralized and very slow-moving; showing little initiative and responding sluggishly to initiatives from outside. To put the matter less tactfully than does his *Review*, it gives the impression to outside observers that everything depends on a few not very brilliant civil servants in the Department, that behind them stands the Treasury, and that the general strategy of Whitehall is to play for time and to hope that problems will go away.

Lord McCarthy made 65 carefully-argued recommendations and Mr David Ennals, Secretary of State for Social Services, has recently recommended new NHS disputes procedures for the general Whitley Council, after a series of specially convened meetings (8).

These three levels together now perhaps constitute the most important political arena within the service, and one that can only be handled by a gifted and imaginative Secretary of State. The NHS is threatened by the myth of Them and Us, bosses and workers, exploiters and exploited; this may be in some circumstances a necessary myth, but it is not relevant to a fully-socialized health service, based on the principle (however hedged) of equal treatment for all, free at the point of service. The necessary myth is one of reciprocity, that we are all in turn sufferers and servants, carers and curers: to each according to his need, from each according to his capacity.

NOTES AND REFERENCES

CHAPTER 1

1. *Proceedings of the Aristotelian Society* (1956), **56,** p. 167. See also: MacIntyre, Alasdair (1974), 'The Essential Contestability of Some Social Concepts', *Ethics*, **84,** p. 1.

2. Alford, Robert R. (1975), sub-titled *Ideological and Internal Group Barriers to Reform* (Chicago University Press). There is valuable material also in Garceau, Oliver (1941), *The Political Life of the American Medical Association* (Harvard University Press), and in Amitai Etzioni's Epilogue to Greenfield, Harry I. (1975), *Accountability in Health Facilities* (New York: Praeger).

3. I think it was my colleague, Sir Andrew Watt Kay, who first suggested 'skins'.

4. Goffman, Erving (1963), *Stigma: Notes on the Management of Spoiled Identity* (Englewood Cliffs: Prentice-Hall).

5. Edinburgh (1956), Social Sciences Research Centre.

6. To simplify analysis, I have omitted discussion of dental, pharmaceutical, and ophthalmic services.

CHAPTER 2

1. Dicey, A. V. (1931), *The Law of the Constitution* (8th edition), p. 75, quoting Hume, David (1875 edition), *Essays*, **i,** pp. 109, 110.

2. Green, T. H. (1941 reprint), *Lectures on the Principles of Political Obligation*, p. 121.

3. *Management Arrangements for the Reorganized National Health Service* (1972) (London: HMSO).

4. Matthew 8:9. Moses applied the same principle to civil government: Exodus 18:24.

5. Compare the following sentence in: Pickering, Sir George (1978), *Quest for Excellence in Medical Education: A Personal Survey*, p. 28 (Oxford University Press for the Nuffield Provincial Hospitals Trust): 'What is learned when the trainee is to some extent responsible is far more than what is learned when he has no responsibility.'

6. Birch, A. H. (1962), *The Idea of Responsible Government* (Hull University Press); (1964), *Representative and Responsible Government: An Essay on the*

British Constitution (London: Allen & Unwin); and (1971), *Representation* (London: Macmillan).

7. GLOVER, JONATHAN (1970), *Responsibility* (London: Routledge & Kegan Paul) and (1977), *Causing Death and Saving Lives* (London: Penguin Books).

8. GUSTAFSON, JAMES M., and LANEY, JAMES T. (eds) (1969), *On Being Responsible: Issues in Personal Ethics* (London: SCM Press).

9. FRENCH, PETER A. (ed.) (1972), *Individual and Collective Responsibility: Massacre at My Lai* (Cambridge, Mass.: Schenkman).

10. Compare Esterson's distinction between Praxis and Process; see below, Chapter 3, p. 20 and reference 26.

11. The title of a very influential book: DEUTSCH, KARL (1963), subtitled *Models of Political Communication and Control* (New York: Free Press).

CHAPTER 3

1. *Report of the Committee of Enquiry into the Cost of the National Health Service* (Guillebaud) (1956), Cmnd. 9663, para. 96 (London: HMSO).

2. DEPARTMENT OF HEALTH AND SOCIAL SECURITY (1977), *Annual Report for 1976*, Cmnd. 6931, fig. 5, p. 31 (London: HMSO). Figures for England only.

3. Some interesting work has been done by Professor B. B. Schaffer about the function of queuing as a means of rationing 'free' services, see for instance: SCHAFFER, Professor B. B. (1973), *Easiness of Access: A Concept of Queues*, Institute of Development Studies, *Communication*, 104.

4. JUVENAL. *Satires*, x, l. 356.

5. E.g. FUCHS, V. R. (1973), 'The Output of the Health Industry', p. 135 in COOPER, M. H., and CULYER, A. J. (eds), *Health Economics, Selected Readings* (London: Penguin Books).

6. Quoted by: DUBOS, RENE (1959), *The Mirage of Health: Utopias, Progress and Biological Change*, p. 235 (New York: Harper).

7. *Nicomachean Ethics*, 1098a, translated by SMITH, J. A. (1911), p. 13 (London: Everyman, J. M. Dent).

8. In particular the comment in the *Iliad,* 'a good doctor is worth many fighting men' (Book II, 1.514); similarly in the heroic age of Gaelic Scotland: the MacBeths, physicians and surgeons at one time to the Lords of the Isles, who are described by a poet as:

> 'the clan MacBeth, accurate in their practice,
> carvers of bones and arteries'.

THOMSON, DERICK (1974), *An Introduction to Gaelic Poetry*, p. 34 (London: Gollancz).

9. This is the title of chapter V of: DUBOS, RENE (1959), reference 6 above.

10. *Measuring Social Well-Being: A Progress Report on the Development of Social Indicators* (1976), pp. 56–62 (Paris: OECD).

11. I know of no better short summary of the doctrine, for and against, than: WILLIAMSON, J. D., and DANAHER, KATE (1978), *Self Care in Health,*

pp. 60–61 (London: Croom Helm), basing themselves on PARSONS, TALCOTT (1951), *The Social System* (Chicago: Free Press).

12. COOPER, M. H., and CULYER, A. J. (eds) (1973), 'Is Medical Care Different?', p. 49 in *Health Economics* (London: Penguin Books).

13. FRANK, JOHANN VICTOR (1779), *Medizinische Polizei*, 9 vols.

14. BARNARD, CHESTER (1938). *The Functions of the Executive* (Cambridge, Mass.: Harvard University Press).

15. 'Ergo supervacua, aut sibi perniciosa petuntur?' JUVENAL, *Satires*, x l. 54.

16. 'Need as a Demand Concept', republished in CULYER, A. J. (1974), *Economic Policies and Social Goals*, pp. 67–68 (London: Robertson). Originally published in CULYER, A. J., LAVERS, R. J., and WILLIAMS, ALAN (1972), 'Health Indicators', in SHONFIELD, A., and SHAW, S. (eds) (1972), *Social Indicators and Social Policy* (London: Heinemann).

17. CULYER, A. J., LAVERS, R. J., and WILLIAMS, ALAN (1972), 'Health Indicators' in: SHONFIELD, A., and SHAW, S. (eds), *Social Indicators and Social Policy*, p. 67 (London: Heinemann).

18. CULYER, A. J. (1976), *Need and the National Health Service—Economics and Social Choice*, p. ix (London: Robertson).

19. Ibid., p. 19.
20. Ibid., p. 15.
21. Ibid., p. 16.
22. Ibid., p. 16.
23. Ibid., p. 17.
24. Ibid., p. 17.

25. But cf. CULYER, A. J. (1976), p. 17 on 'the duality of man'.

26. ESTERSON, A. (1970), *The Leaves of Spring: A Study in the Dialectics of Madness*, Introduction, p. 2, n. 5 (London: Tavistock Press), (Penguin edition, 1973).

27. ROBINSON, DAVID (1971), *The Process of Becoming Ill*, in the series WILLIAMSON, W. M. (ed), *Medicine, Illness and Society* (London: Routledge & Kegan Paul).

28. BOTT, ELIZABETH (1957, second edition 1971). *Family and Social Network* (London: Tavistock Press).

29. Compare COOPER, M. H. (1975), *Rationing Health Care*, p. 15 (London: Croom Helm).

30. Compare GOFFMAN, ERVING (1963), *Stigma: Notes on the Management of Spoiled Identity* (Englewood Cliffs: Prentice-Hall).

31. LOUDON, J. (ed.) (1976), 'Disease, Illness and Sickness: Social Aspects of the Choice of Healer in a Lusaka Suburb', in *Social Anthropology and Medicine*, A.S.A. Monograph no. 13 (London: Academic Press).

32. WILSON, BRYAN (1961), *Sects and Society: A Sociological Study of Three Religious Groups in Britain* (London: Heinemann), and WILSON, BRYAN (1971), *Religious Sects* (London: Weidenfeld & Nicolson).

33. WILLIAMSON, D. D., and DANAHER, KATE (1978), *Self Care in Health* (London: Croom Helm).

34. MILLER, JONATHAN (1978), *The Body in Question* (London: Jonathan Cape).

35. *New Society* (1977), 25 August, p. 388.

36. Parodied in a most depressing book about the American nursing home industry: MENDELSON, MARY A. (1975), *Tender Loving Greed* (New York: Vintage Books).

37. As reference 29 above, p. 105.

CHAPTER 4

1. LLOYD, G. E. R. (ed.) (1950), *Hippocratic Writings,* Introduction (new edition 1978) (London: Penguin Books).

2. All these five printed as Appendices to BLISS, BRIAN P., and JOHNSON, ALAN I. G. (1975), *Aims and Motives in Clinical Medicine: A Practical Approach to Medical Ethics* (London: Pitman Medical).

3. The last two printed as appendices to HADFIELD, STEPHEN J. (1958), *Law and Ethics for Doctors* (London: Eyre & Spottiswoode).

4. Translated in LLOYD, G. E. R. (ed.) (1950), *Hippocratic Writings,* p. 206.

5. ABEL-SMITH, BRIAN (1964), *The Hospitals 1800–1948: A Study in Social Administration in England and Wales,* chapter 8 (London: Heinemann).

6. The latest stage in a long debate is expressed in *Review of the Mental Health Act 1959* (1978), White Paper, Cmnd. 7320 (London: HMSO).

7. MARTIN, C. N. A. (1973), *Law in Relation to Medical Practice,* p. 523 (London: Pitman Medical).

8. I quote this from: MARSTON, MAURICE (1925), *Sir Edwin Chadwick (1800–1890),* p. 119 (London: Parsons).

9. FERRIS, PAUL (1965), *The Doctors* (London: Gollancz), chapter 8. The minor epidemic of September 1978 which cost the lives of Professor Henry Bedson of Birmingham University and of a medical photographer was particularly devastating in that WHO had just announced the virtual elimination of smallpox from the whole world. See also DHSS and the Welsh Office (1975), *Memorandum on the Control of Outbreaks of Smallpox* (London HMSO).

10. *Royal Commission on Medical Education* (1968) (Todd Report), Cmnd. 3569 (London: HMSO).

11. *Report of the Committee of Inquiry into the Regulation of the Medical Profession* (1975) (Merrison Report), Cmnd. 6018 (London: HMSO).

12. A remark quoted in: ROBINSON, D., and HENRY, STUART (1977), *Self-Help and Health: Mutual Aid for Modern Problems,* p. 116 (London: Martin Robertson).

13. See Chapter 3, reference 31.

14. Compare the reference in Ronald Eyre's article on 'Zulu Zion' in his TV series, 'The Long Search': 'All of the "healers" I met among the Zulus— of a variety of kinds, some herbalists, some diviners—were slender, fine-boned, volatile, even (and in no bad sense) haunted' (*The Listener,* 24 November 1977, p. 673).

15. INGLIS, BRIAN (1964), *Fringe Medicine* (London: Faber).

16. *A Report on the Treatment of Cancer at the Ringberg Clinic, Rottach-Egern, Bavaria* (1971) (London: HMSO).

17. ELLISON, NEIL, et al. (1978), 'Special report on Laetrile: the NCI Laetrile review, results of the National Cancer Institute's retrospective Laetrile analysis', *New England Journal of Medicine*, **299**, 549. Earlier in 1978 there was a short TV programme for the BBC followed by a long correspondence in *The Listener*.

18. See Chapter 3, reference 32.

19. *Committee of Enquiry into the Relationship of the Pharmaceutical Industry with the NHS, 1965–67* (1967) (Sainsbury Report), Cmnd. 3410 (London: HMSO); *Focus on Pharmaceuticals: A Report of the Pharmaceutical Working Party of the Chemicals Economic Development Council* (1972) (London: HMSO); and HEATH, J. B., et al. (1975), *A Study of the Evolution of Concentration in the Pharmaceutical Industry for the UK* (Brussels: EEC).

20. Beecham's Powders survive though Dr J. Collis Brown's is now 'The Mixture'. Although no survey of the non-ethical industry exists, there is much useful information in a Report by the Price Commission: *Prices, Costs and Margins in the Production and Distribution of Proprietary Non-ethical Medicines* (1978), HC 469.

21. The *Guardian* of 21 April 1978, reported that WHO had set up units for the study of traditional remedies in South Korea, Sri Lanka, Brazil, London, Chicago, and Hong Kong, and gave some further information about the Hong Kong Unit.

22. For discussion of Talcott Parsons' concept, see Chapter 3, reference 11.

23. As Chapter 4, reference 11. The General Medical Council deals also with 'professional' misconduct; see Chapter 5.

24. The Scots law of delict is thus summarized by: WALKER, DAVID (1955), *The Law of Damages in Scotland*, p. 87 (Edinburgh: Green). 'A medical practitioner owes a duty of care to his patient and is liable to him for lack of professional skill independently of the consideration of who employed him.'

25. SOMERS, Professor HERMAN M. (1977), 'The Malpractice Controversy and the Quality of Patient Care', *Milbank Memorial Fund Quarterly*, Spring, p. 200.

26. BUNBURY, SIR HENRY (ed.) (1957), *Lloyd George's Ambulance Wagon: The Memoirs of W. J. Braithwaite, CB* (London: Methuen), and KLEIN, RUDOLF (1973), *Complaints against Doctors: A Study in Professional Accountability* (London: Knight).

27. BRECKON, W. (ed.) (1978), *Your Everyday Drugs* (London: BBC Publications) and there are strong indications of DHSS policy in the Department's *Annual Reports*.

28. The 'Sans Everything' cases include the Committees of Enquiry concerning conditions at: *Ely Hospital* (1968), Cmnd. 3975 (London: HMSO); *Fairleigh Hospital* (1971), Cmnd. 4557 (London: HMSO); *Whittingham Hospital* (1972), Cmnd. 4861 (London: HMSO), and that at *Napsbury Hospital* (1973). We still have such headlines as 'Ill-treatment at mental hospital beyond belief' and 'jail sentences (suspended)'. *Guardian*, 1 November 1978.

29. *Report of the Committee on Hospital Complaints Procedure* (1973) (Davies Report) (London: HMSO). Their recommendations met with some

opposition from the organized professions and were accepted only in modified form (*Guardian*, 12 April 1978) and in May 1978, *Health Services Complaints Procedure: Consultative Document* (HC(78)39).

30. The statement of 22 February 1972 as quoted in: *Health Service Commissioner's First Annual Report, 1973–74* (1974), p. 4 (London: HMSO).

31. *Independent Review of Hospital Complaints Procedure in the NHS* (HC(78)45).

32. *Report of the Committee on Hospital Complaints Procedure* (1973) (Davies Report) (London: HMSO).

33. *Annual Report of the Health Service Commissioner, 1976–77* (1977) (HC(1977)322) (London: HMSO).

34. The source is DHSS *Annual Report for 1976*, Cmnd. 6931, table 12 (London: HMSO). This table does not give any general total.

35. WHITEHORN, KATHERINE (1972), *How to Survive in Hospital* (London: Eyre Methuen).

36. The attractions of 'Community Medicine' to the old MOHs were set out in the *Report of the Working Party on Medical Administrators* (1972) (Hunter Report) (London: HMSO); and the DHSS recommends that the appropriate Community Physician be appointed in a consultative capacity (with some executive powers) by the corresponding local authority as Medical Officer for Environmental Health. Certainly the local authority controls home helps and other social aids; it is not clear to me who now controls health visitors and domiciliary nurses—an officer in the nursing hierarchy?

37. KLEIN, RUDOLF, and LEWIS, JANET (1976), *The Politics of Consumer Representation: A Study of Community Health Councils* (London: Centre for Studies in Social Policy). A less ambitious study has been made in Glasgow: SHIVANANDA, S. (1978), 'Health Service Reorganization and the Public Interest: A Study of the Politics of Participation' (PhD thesis, Glasgow University).

38. —— —— (1976), p. 21, quoting DHSS, *Community Health Councils* (HRC(74)4).

39. See in particular Robinson and Henry (reference 12 above) and their bibliographical notes.

40. MACKENZIE, W. J. M. (1955), Pressure Groups: 'The conceptual framework', reprinted (1975) in *Explorations in Government* (London: Macmillan).

41. *The Directors of British Associations and Associations in Ireland* (1977/8), (Beckenham: CBD Research).

42. BEGBIE, HAROLD (1927), *Life-Changers (More Twice Born Men: Narratives of a Recent Movement in the Spirit of Personal Religion)* (London: Putnam).

43. The name of a magazine published in California. I draw primarily on the news-sheets published by the Alicia Patterson Foundation in New York, which include in 1977 two articles by Phil Weld, Jr, on various facets of the movement.

44. BERGER, P. L., and LUCKMAN, T. (1967), *The Social Construction of Reality: A Treatise in the Sociology of Knowledge* (London: Penguin); SCHUTZ,

ALFRED (1972), *The Phenomenology of the Social World* (London: Heinemann); and GOFFMAN, ERVING (1963), *Stigma: Notes on the Management of Spoiled Identity* (Englewood Cliffs: Prentice-Hall).

45. JOBLING, RAY (1977). 'Learning to Live With It: An Account of a Career of Chronic Dermatological Illness and Patienthood', chapter 5 in: DAVIS, ALAN, and HOROBIN, GORDON (eds), *Medical Encounters: The Experience of Illness and Treatment* (London: Croom Helm).

46. O'NEILL, JOHN (1972), *Sociology as Skin Trade: Essays towards a Reflective Sociology*, p. 6 (London, Heinemann).

47. See reference 5 above.

48. KLEIN, RUDOLF, and LEWIS, JANET (1976), *The Politics of Consumer Representation: A Study of Community Health Councils*, p. 132 (London: Centre for Studies in Social Policy).

CHAPTER 5

1. FERRIS, PAUL (1965), *The Doctors* (London: Gollancz) is balanced and witty: see also his sardonic novel *The Cure* (1974) (London: Weidenfeld & Nicolson) about the discovery of a cure for cancer.

2. STEVENS, ROSEMARY (1966), *Medical Practice in Modern England: The Impact of Specialization and State Medicine*, p. 128 (New Haven, Conn.: Yale University Press).

3. One of the earliest and best books on 'interest group politics' is: GARCEAU, OLIVER (1941), *The Political Life of the American Medical Association* (Cambridge, Mass.: Harvard University Press).

4. *Br. med. J.* (1935), **1,** 365 (quoted by Stevens, reference 2 above, p. 54).

5. PANTON, SIR PHILIP (1951), *Leaves from a Doctor's Life* (London: Heinemann).

6. FREIDSON, ELIOT (1970), *Professional Dominance: The Social Structure of Medical Care*, p. 96 (New York: Atherton).

7. Ibid., p. 105.

8. BERLANT, J. L. (1975), *Profession and Monopoly: A Study of Medicine in the U.S.A. and Great Britain* (Berkeley: California University Press).

9. GREGORY, JOHN (1772), *Lectures on the Duties and Qualifications of a Physician* (London: Strahan & Cadell).

10. Thomas Percival's work was reprinted in 1827 under the title *Medical Ethics*.

11. ALFORD, R. R. (1975), *Health Care Politics: Ideological and Interest Group Barriers to Reform* (Chicago University Press).

12. EHRENREICH, BARBARA, and EHRENREICH, JOHN (1971), *The American Health Empire: Power, Profits and Politics: A Report from the Health Policy Advisory Center* (New York: Random House).

13. INGLIS, BRIAN (1964), *Fringe Medicine* (London: Faber).

14. Cf. the protests against this form of words made by the BMA during the negotiations over the 1947 Act, in Stevens, reference 2 above, p. 87.

15. PICKERING, SIR GEORGE (1978), *Quest for Excellence in Medical Education: A Personal Survey* (Oxford University Press for the Nuffield Provincial Hospitals Trust).

16. Quoted by Stevens, reference 2 above, p. 169.

17. Ibid., p. 171.

18. Ibid., p. 176.

19. *Royal Commission on Medical Education* (1968) (Todd Report), Cmnd. 3569, pp. 324 and 363 (London: HMSO).

20. I recommend a very serious one by a Russian humorist; BULGAKOV, MIKHAIL, trans. GLENN, MICHAEL (1975), *A Country Doctor's Notebook* (Glasgow: Collins).

21. The figures are drawn from Appendix 19 of the Todd Report (19) above, and relate primarily to 1966. There have been changes during the last ten years, but not radical ones.

22. For this approach, see STANWORTH, P., and GIDDENS, A. (eds) (1974), *Elites and Power in British Society* (Cambridge University Press). Unfortunately, this does not include a chapter on doctors.

23. BURNS, TOM, and STALKER, G. M. (1961), *The Management of Innovation* (London: Tavistock Press).

24. WOODWARD, JOAN (1965), *Industrial Organization: Theory and Practice* (Oxford University Press).

25. PARETO, VILFREDO, trans. MIRFIN, DERICK (1966), *Sociological Writings: Selected and Introduced by S. E. Finer* (London: Pall Mall).

26. WORDSWORTH, *The Solitary Reaper*.

27. Quoted by Stevens, reference 2 above, p. 341.

28. The phrase originated early in the nineteenth century, writes: DONNISON, JEAN (1977), *Midwives and Medical Men: A History of Inter-Professional Rivalries and Women's Rights* (London: Heinemann). She quotes a reference from 1813.

29. PERCIVAL, THOMAS (1827 ed.), *Medical Ethics*, p. 1.

30. KUHN, T. S. (1962), *The Structure of Scientific Revolutions* (Chicago: University Press).

31. Hence I have a certain scepticism about the BSc in Human Biology as the main entrance to medical education.

32. ECKSTEIN, HARRY (1960), *Pressure Group Politics: The Case of the British Medical Association* (Stanford, California: Stanford University Press), and (1964) *The English Health Service: Its Origins, Structures and Achievements* (Cambridge, Mass.: Harvard University Press).

33. The reference is in particular to: BAILEY, F. G. (1969), *Stratagems and Spoils: A Social Anthropology of Politics* (Oxford: Blackwell).

34. 1955, reprinted in MACKENZIE, W. J. M. (1975), *Explorations in Government*, p. 272 (London: Macmillan).

35. WILLCOCKS, A. J. (1967), *The Creation of the National Health Service: A Study of Pressure Groups and a Major Social Policy Decision* (London: Routledge). There are many older books which I have not read; but I value in particular: BUNBURY, SIR HENRY, and TITMUSS, R. M. (eds) (1957), *Lloyd George's Ambulance Wagon: The Memoirs of W. J. Braithwaite, C.B.* (London: Methuen); and NEWMAN, SIR GEORGE (1939), *The Building of a Nation's Health* (London: Macmillan).

36. One of the medical heroes of that period (which was also the period of the first public health movement) was Thomas Wakley (1795–1862:

there is a good article in the *Dictionary of National Biography*) who founded the *Lancet* in 1823. See also: LITTLE, SIR ERNEST (1932), *History of the BMA 1832–1932* (London: BMA).

37. See reference 28 above.

38. There is a good description of the organization in: FOOT, MICHAEL (1973), *Aneurin Bevan: A Biography*, vol. ii, pp. 115–17 (London: Davis-Poynter).

39. This was largely because the creation of the war-time Emergency Medical Service enforced for the first time a general survey of hospital provision and its deficiencies; and because a good many GPs acquired war-time experience of specialties, without paper qualifications.

40. *Report of the Interdepartmental Committee on Medical Schools* (1968), (Goodenough Report) (London: HMSO); *Report of the Committee to Consider the Future Numbers of Medical Practitioners and the Appropriate Intake of Medical Students* (1957) (Willink Report) (London: HMSO); and the Todd Report, reference 19 above.

41. There are detailed figures in: *Report of the Committee of Enquiry into the Cost of the National Health Service* (1956) (Guillebaud Report) (London: HMSO) derived largely from the work of ABEL-SMITH, BRIAN, and TITMUSS, R. M. (1956), *The Cost of the National Health Service in England and Wales* (Cambridge University Press); but I hesitate to quote any of them out of context.

42. Affiliated to the Labour Party and influential out of all proportion to its numbers, which stand at about 1,800.

43. Descended from a line of associations concerned to be 'the champion of the ordinary medical man' (Donnison, reference 28 above, p. 126) and now affiliated through ASTMS to the TUC (about 5,000 members). I believe that the General Practitioners Association (about 4,000 members), founded with similar objects in the crisis of 1965/6, is now extinct.

44. *Report on Doctors' and Dentists' Remuneration 1957–60* (1960) (Pilkington Report), Cmnd. 939 (London: HMSO).

45. DEPARTMENT OF HEALTH AND SOCIAL SECURITY (1977), *Annual Report for 1976*, table 6, p. 20 (London: HMSO): 22,015 GPs in England at 1 October 1978, of whom 3,616 practised in 705 Health Centres.

46. MORLEY, JOHN (1903), *Life of Gladstone,* vol. ii, p. 126 (London: Macmillan).

47. See reference 2 above, p. 176.

48. The figures for foreign-born doctors are taken from: MAYNARD, A., and WALKER, A. (1978). *Doctor Manpower 1975–2000: Alternative Forecasts and their Resource Implications,* Royal Commission on the NHS Research Paper no. 4 (London: HMSO).

49. To reduce complications, I leave aside the rather different patterns of Scotland and the Irish Republic. Wales and Northern Ireland are in these respects subsumed under England.

50. 'One of the most elusive of all the concepts in hospital medicine', POWELL, J. ENOCH (1966), *A New Look at Medicine and Politics,* p. 48 (London: Pitman Medical).

51. A brutally vivid picture of old-style surgery is given in an unusual novel: GORDON, RICHARD (1975), *The Sleep of Life* (London: Heinemann).

52. See reference 2 above, p. 120.

53. FLETCHER SHAW, SIR WILLIAM (1954), *Twenty-Five Years: The Story of the Royal College of Obstetricians and Gynaecologists* (London: Churchill).

54. See reference 2 above in which Rosemary Stevens, on p. 117, quotes from the *Lancet*.

55. See reference 2 above, table 10, p. 198, 1963 (England and Wales): General Medicine 786; General Surgery 845; Anaesthetics 886; Pathology 758; Psychiatry 776; but this is for *all* consultants: among full-time consultants, psychiatry is dominant. (There are comparable figures for 1976 in the DHSS *Annual Report* for that year, table 28.)

56. MILLERSON, G. (1964), *The Qualifying Associations: A Study in Professionalization* (London: Routledge).

57. See table 28 in the DHSS *Annual Report for 1976*, as reference 45.

58. 'Clinical Professors' Pay', a letter in *The Times* of 5 April 1978.

59. See reference 19 above. The Todd Report devotes a whole chapter (chapter 9) to the special problems of London University and its Medical Schools.

CHAPTER 6

1. Hospital dentists are included, but the number is not large.

2. *Report of the Committee on Nursing* (1972) (Briggs Report), Cmnd. 5115, table 24 (London: HMSO), 29,018 out of 332,405; these are the figures for Great Britain, 1971.

3. This is a convenient point at which to list indispensable sources: ABEL-SMITH, BRIAN (1960), *A History of the Nursing Profession* (London: Heinemann); (1964), *The Hospitals 1800–1948: A Study in Social Administration in England and Wales* (London: Heinemann); DONNISON, JEAN (1977), *Midwives and Medical Men: A History of Inter-Professional Rivalries and Women's Rights* (London: Heinemann).

4. ABEL-SMITH, BRIAN (1960), *A History of the Nursing Profession*, p. 18 (London: Heinemann).

5. Ibid., p. 24.

6. Ibid., p. 22.

7.   Miss Beale and Miss Buss,
       They are not like Us,
       Miss Buss and Miss Beale
       Cupid's darts do not feel.

Cheltenham Ladies College was founded in 1854, and taken over by Miss Beale (aged 27) in 1858.

8. See reference 4 above, p. 28.

9. How this worked appears vividly in some of the stories in Bulgakov's book, trans. GLENN, MICHAEL (1975), *A Country Doctor's Notebook* (Glasgow: Collins) referred to in the previous chapter.

10. TITMUSS, R. M., *et al.* (1964), *The Health Services of Tanganyika* (London: Pitman).

11. In ancient Greece and Rome the goddesses Eilythuia and Lucina, respectively, were guardians of childbirth.

12. The opening chapters of CRONIN, A. J. (1937), *The Citadel* (London: Gollancz), illustrate such conditions.

13. Maternal mortality rate, 1900: 4·8 per thousand live births. Infantile mortality rate, 1900: 154 per thousand live births. Maternal mortality rate, 1976: 0·13 per thousand live births and stillbirths. Infantile mortality rate, 1976: 14·2 per thousand live births and stillbirths.

14. See for instance: TUCKETT, D. (ed.) (1976), *An Introduction to Medical Sociology*, p. 193 (London: Tavistock Press), on the 'routinization of care'; and the essays of HART, NICKY, and COMAROFF, JEAN (1977), in DAVIS, ALAN, and HOROBIN, GORDON (eds), *Medical Encounters: The Experience of Illness and Treatment* (London: Croom Helm).

15. TUCKETT, D. (1976), as reference 14, p. 377, quoting Professor A. L. Cochrane. A report in the *Guardian* of 12 May 1978 records that in 1974 in the UK there were 28,425 births ot home, 689,578 in hospital. Yet 82 per cent of women and 75 per cent of men think that facilities for home births should be available. This is very difficult to interpret.

16. JONES, KATHLEEN (1955), *Lunacy, Law and Conscience 1744–45* (London: Routledge); and (1960), *Mental Health and Social Policy 1845–1959* (London: Routledge).

17. *Review of the Mental Health Act 1959* (1978) (London: HMSO).

18. JONES, KATHLEEN (1960), reference 16 above refers the general reader to Charlotte Brontë's 'treatment' of the first Mrs Rochester in *Jane Eyre*.

19. Much has changed since the 1950s, but I still look back with interest to the work done by: GODDARD, H. A. (1955), *The Work of the Mental Nurse* (Manchester University Press) for the Manchester Mental Nursing Survey.

20. JONES, KATHLEEN (1960), reference 16 above, p. 14.

21. Ibid., p. 25.

22. Ibid., p. 123.

23. Probably a few others came forward, in general nursing, through experience as medical orderlies in the armed forces.

24. See reference 2 above, p. 22.

25. There is a useful account by: ELLIOTT, Dr ARNOLD (1978). 'District nurses: new training proposals', *Br. med. J.* **4**, 1316.

26. There is a figure of 103,679 for Great Britain at p. 44 (table 3.1) of: HARDIE, MELISSA, and HOCKEY, LISBETH (eds) (1978), *Nursing Auxiliaries in Health Care* (London: Croom Helm).

27. The Queen's Speech at the opening of Parliament (1 November 1978) announced that a Bill 'will be introduced on the regulation and training of the nursing, midwifery, and health visiting professions, on the lines recommended by the Briggs Committee on nursing' (*Guardian*, 2 November 1978).

28. ARNOLD, NANCY (1977), 'Briggs: The Lost Horizon?', *Nursing Times*, **73,** 1822.

29. WHEARE, K. C. (1955), *Government by Committee: An Essay on the British Constitution* (Oxford: Clarendon Press).

30. *Report of the Lancet Commission on Nursing* (1932). (London); ROYAL COLLEGE OF NURSING (1942), *Nurses' Reconstruction Committee* (Horder Committee) (London: RCN); MINISTRY OF HEALTH, DEPARTMENT OF HEALTH FOR SCOTLAND, AND MINISTRY OF LABOUR AND NATIONAL SERVICE (1947), *Report of the Working Party on the Recruitment and Training of Nurses* (London: HMSO); one should mention also *Report No. 60 of the National Board on Prices and Incomes* (1978) (London: HMSO).

31. TAYLOR, F. W. (1907), 'The Art of Cutting Metals', *Proc. Am. Soc. Mech. Eng.* **28**, 31–350. His book on *The Principles of Scientific Management* was published in 1911.

32. There is a very large literature; three books in contrasting styles may be helpful: MARCH, J. G., and SIMON, H. A. (1958), *Organizations* (New York: Wiley); STEWART, R. (1971), *The Reality of Organizations: A Guide for Managers* (London: Macmillan), and BAKER, R. J. S. (1972), *Administrative Theory and Public Administration* (London: Hutchinson).

33. DICKENS, MONICA (1942). *One Pair of Feet* (London: Michael Joseph) is particularly good on differences of 'management style' as between ward sisters.

34. CARLSON, SUNE (1951), *Executive Behaviour: A Study of Work Load and Working Methods of Managing Directors* (Stockholm: Stromberg).

35. See the following: DEPARTMENT OF HEALTH AND SOCIAL SECURITY AND WELSH OFFICE (1972), *Progress on Salmon* (London: DHSS); *Report of Working Party on Management Structure in the Local Authority Nursing Services* (1969) (Mayston Report) (London: Mimeo, DHSS and Welsh Office); and *Management Structure in the Local Authority Nursing Services: The Implementation of Mayston* (1973) (London: DHSS).

36. CARPENTER, MICHAEL (1976), *The New Managerialism in Nursing* (London: Mimeo, SSRC Industrial Relations Research Unit) notes that male nurses are less subject to these constraints, and foresees a relative preponderance of men in Grades 7 and above.

37. *The Oxford Dictionary of English Proverbs* (p. 575) says that the phrase became a by-word for insincerity. Not so here.

38. These last pages were written before I had read MILLER, HENRY (1973), *Medicine and Society* (Oxford University Press). His section on 'Nursing' (pp. 23–26) illustrates them exactly.

CHAPTER 7

1. 'People consume on average twice as many medications bought over the counter at a chemist's shop as they do drugs and medicine prescribed on GP's NHS prescription.' LEVITT, RUTH (1976), *The Re-organized National Health Service*, p. 189 (London: Croom Helm).

2. For the theme of 'folk-medicine' in the UK, see HELMAN, CECIL G. (1978), ' "Feed a cold, starve a fever"—folk models of infection in an English suburban community, and their relation to medical treatment', *Culture, Medicine and Psychiatry*, vol. 2, pp. 107–37.

3. Ashburton's motion in the Commons in 1780.

4. Swift, Jonathan (1726). *Gulliver's Travels,* chapter x: 'The Lugg-naggians commended. A particular description of the Struldbrugs, with many conversations between the Author and some eminent persons upon that subject.'

5. World Health Organization (1977), *Working Guide for the Primary Health Care Worker,* Experimental Edition (Geneva: WHO).

6. Pressman, Jeffrey, and Wildavsky, Aaron (1973), *Implementation; How Great Expectations in Washington are Dashed in Oakland* (Berkeley: California University Press). The following works point in the same direction: Hood, Christopher (1976), *The Limits of Administration* (London: Wiley); Norton, Alan (1978) *Implementation of Policies with Special Reference to the Field of Sociomedical Care in Britain* (Mimeo: prepared at the Birmingham University Institute of Local Government Studies for a conference of the European Consortium on Political Research, Grenoble, April 1978).

7. It will be obvious that this account depends very greatly on: Abel-Smith, Brian (1964), *The Hospitals, 1800–1948: A Study in Social Administration in England and Wales* (London: Heinemann).

8. Pickering, Sir George (1978), *Quest for Excellence in Medical Education: A Personal Survey,* chapter 6 (Oxford University Press for the Nuffield Provincial Hospitals Trust).

9. For instance, Cronin's hero in *The Citadel* (London: Gollancz, 1937), and Cronin himself (*Adventures in Two Worlds,* London: Gollancz, 1952).

10. Milton, John (1667), *Paradise Lost,* at the beginning of Book III.

11. See for instance the case of the Brownlow Hill Workhouse Infirmary at Liverpool, and the concerted operation to reform it, led by William Rathbone, Florence Nightingale, and the first matron, Agnes Jones. Abel-Smith, Brian (1960), *A History of the Nursing Profession,* pp. 38–40 (London: Heinemann) (Chapter 6, reference 3).

12. Department of Health and Social Security (1976), *Sharing Resources for Health in England: Report of the Resource Allocation Working Party* (London: HMSO).

13. Levitt, Ruth (1976), p. 156, reference 1.

14. Department of Health and Social Security (1977), *Annual Report of the Health Advisory Service for the year 1976* (London: HMSO).

15. Quoted in Williamson and Danaher (1978), *Self Care in Health,* p. 15 (London: Croom Helm) from the *Daily Telegraph,* 30 June 1973. The latest report of the National Development Group for the Mentally Handicapped (*Guardian* and *Glasgow Herald,* 17 October 1978) is equally explicit.

16. For instance: Etzioni, Amitai (1961), *A Comparative Analysis of Complex Organizations: On Power, Involvement and their Correlates* (New York: Free Press) and Stewart, Rosemary (1970), *The Reality of Organizations* (London: Macmillan).

17. See the *Professions Supplementary to Medicine Act, 1960* and the *Report of the Halsbury Committee on the Pay and Conditions of Service of the Professions Supplementary to Medicine, and Speech Therapists* (1975) (London: HMSO).

18. On the other hand, clinical psychologists might well be included, and new groups (such as play therapists and play leaders) are still emerging. For a review of the changing roles of the complementary professions see

STOCKING, BARBARA (1979). 'Confusion or Control', in MCLACHLAN, G. (ed.), *Patterns for Uncertainty?* (Oxford University Press for the Nuffield Provincial Hospitals Trust).

19. There is a very complex pattern, which only the patient experiences; see for instance references to nurses and physiotherapists in COMAROFF, JEAN (1977), 'Conflicting Paradigms of Pregnancy' in DAVIS, ALAN, and HOROBIN, GORDON (eds), Chapter 6, reference 14.

20. A point squarely faced by Harry Ewing, MP, Scottish Under-Secretary for Health (*Glasgow Herald*, 31 May 1978). There are comparable problems of staffing at haemophilia centres, *The Times*, 6 June 1978, quoting the *Br. med. J.* of 3 June 1978, and in relation to breast-scanning machines (the experience of the Lanarkshire Health Board; Jennifer Cunningham in the *Glasgow Herald*, 19 December 1978).

21. *Br. med. J.* (1974), **3**, pp. 71, 124, and 127.

22. DEPARTMENT OF HEALTH AND SOCIAL SECURITY (1977), *Health Services Board Annual Report*, HC 276 (London: HMSO).

23. HOMER, *Odyssey*, Book 9, ll. 112–15, as quoted by MAINE, SIR HENRY (1931), *Ancient Law*, p. 103 (Oxford University Press).

24. LAPONCE, JEAN A. (1978), 'Relating Biological, Physical and Political Phenomena: The Case of Up and Down', in *Social Science Information*, **17**, pp. 385–97 (London and Beverley Hills: SAGE).

25. LEVITT, RUTH (1976), p. 70, reference 1 above.

26. I am thinking in particular of BURNS, TOM, and STALKER, G. M. (1961), *The Management of Innovation* (London: Tavistock) which first established this line of thought.

27. I know of no history of TRE, but the atmosphere is there in the books of Sir Robert Watson-Watt and others.

28. A useful approach to the large literature is through BRAYBROOKE, DAVID, and LINDBLOM, CHARLES E. (1963), *A Strategy of Decision: Policy Evaluation as a Social Process* (Glencoe: Free Press) and LINDBLOM, CHARLES E. (1965), *The Intelligence of Democracy: Decision Making through Mutual Adjustment* (New York: Free Press).

29. There is a brief discussion of nucleus hospitals in OWEN, DAVID (1976), *In Sickness and in Health: The Politics of Medicine*, p. 46 (London: Quartet Books).

30. Much credit is due to grant-giving bodies, particularly the Medical Research Council, for their perceptive skill in choosing and backing winners outside the financial controls of hospitals and universities.

CHAPTER 8

1. VON NEUMANN, JOHN (1958), *The Computer and the Brain* (New Haven: Yale University Press).

2. CANNON, W. B. (1932). *The Wisdom of the Body* (New York), revised edition (1947) (London: Kegan Paul).

3. See for instance: WATSON, JAMES D. (1968), *The Double Helix* (London: Weidenfeld & Nicolson).

4. WIENER, NORBERT (1950), *The Human Use of Human Beings: Cybernetics and Society* (London: Eyre & Spottiswoode).

5. EASTON, DAVID (1953), *The Political System* (New York: Knopf).

6. DEUTSCH, KARL (1953), *Nationalism and Social Communication* (Cambridge, Mass.: MIT Press).

7. ―― (1963), *The Nerves of Government: Models of Political Communication and Control* (New York: Free Press). See also: (1970), *Politics and Government: How People Decide their Fate* (Boston: Houghton, Mifflin).

8. YOUNG, J. Z. (1966), *The Memory System of the Brain* (Oxford University Press). There is a more recent review by RITCHIE RUSSELL, G. W. (1975) (in association with A. J. Dewar of the MRC Brain Metabolism Unit, Edinburgh), *Explaining the Brain* (Oxford University Press).

9. For this general theme, see: McLACHLAN, GORDON (ed.) (1978), *By Guess or By What? Information Without Design in the NHS* (Oxford University Press for the Nuffield Provincial Hospitals Trust), in particular the essays by Peter Fox and by M. A. Heasman.

10. The Government Social Survey made a special study of sources of pharmaceutical information for the prescriber; (1967), *Report on the Pharmaceutical Industry* (Sainsbury Committee), Cmnd. 3410 (London: HMSO).

11. SIEGHART, PAUL (1976). *Privacy and Computers,* with a Foreword by Lord Justice Scarman (London: Latimer). Reviewed briefly in MACKENZIE, W. J. M. (1977), in *Town and Country Planning,* **45,** p. 413.

12. Government White Paper (1975), *Computers and Privacy,* Cmnd. 6353 (London: HMSO).

13. For discussion of the dispute between the BMA and DHSS see: 'Medical Confidentiality' (1978), *Br. med. J.* Supplement 3, p. 298.

14. *Guardian,* 28 October 1978.

15. The best account of this experience is in: DEVONS, ELY (1950), *Planning in Practice: Essays in Aircraft Planning in War Time* (Cambridge University Press).

16. There is an account by MACDOUGALL, SIR DONALD (a participant) in CHESTER, D. N. (ed.) (1951). *Lessons of the British War Economy* (Cambridge University Press).

17. BYRNE, PATRICK S., and LONG, BARRIE E. L. (1976), *Doctors Talking to Patients: A Study of the Verbal Behaviour of General Practitioners consulting in their Surgeries* (London: HMSO).

18. FLETCHER, C. M. (1973), *Communication in Medicine,* p. vii (London: Nuffield Provincial Hospitals Trust). Another excellent introduction is the report of a symposium for the Royal College of General Practitioners. TANNER, BERNICE (ed.) (1976), *Language and Communication in General Practice* (London: Hodder & Stoughton).

19. Work on language teaching for overseas doctors is now in progress, supported by the Nuffield Foundation and by the Nuffield Provincial Hospitals Trust.

20. Much of this work is reviewed in: BERNSTEIN, BASIL (1971), *Class, Codes and Control,* vol. i (London: Routledge & Kegan Paul). See also: CRYSTAL, DAVID (1976), 'The Diagnosis of Sociolinguistic Problems in Doctor/Patient Interaction', in TANNER, BERNICE (reference 18 above).

21. The saying is in fact very ancient; the Roman historian Tacitus attributes it to the Emperor Tiberius, a dogmatic and lonely man (*Annals*, vi, 46).

22. From an article: JONES, W. T. (the first Director-General of the Health Education Council) and GRAHAM, HELENE (a very experienced worker in this field) (1974), 'Research in Health Education', *Br. med. Bull.* **30** (September), p. 76.

23. FLETCHER, C. M., reference 18 above, p. 65.

24. Ibid., p. 62.

25. Health and Safety at Work etc. Act (1974).

26. Health and Safety Commission (1978), *Health and Safety Executive Accounts 1976/77*, Government White Paper, HC 270 (London: HMSO).

27. DEPARTMENT OF EDUCATION AND SCIENCE (1977), *Health Education in Schools* (London: HMSO).

28. WHITE, CYNTHIA L. (1977), *The Women's Periodical Press in Britain 1946–1978*. Working Paper no. 4 of the Royal Commission on the Press (London: HMSO).

29. FLETCHER, C. M., reference 18 above, p. 63.

30. One odd fact emerged from Mrs Mitchell's enquiry into 'skins'. Measured by visits to GPs the incidence of skin troubles associated with dirt, poverty, and overcrowding is much the same in Oxford as it is in Glasgow. But one cannot measure the hidden factor; the worse off you are, the less you are likely to seek help for 'minor' complaints.

31. CROSSMAN, RICHARD, *The Diaries of a Cabinet Minister,* vol. i (1975), vol. ii (1976), and vol. iii (1977) (London: Hamilton and Cape).

32. CROSSMAN, RICHARD, ibid., vol. iii, p. 321.

33. See Chapter 7, p. 109.

34. See: CROSSMAN, RICHARD (1972), Godkin lectures, *Inside View: Three Lectures on Prime Ministerial Government* (London: Cape), particularly Chapter 2.

35. STRAUSS, ANSELM (1963), 'The Hospital as Negotiated Order', in FREIDSON, ELIOT (ed.), *The Hospital in Modern Society* (New York: Free Press). I owe the reference to Miss Sue Pembrey, SRN, Area Nurse, Oxfordshire AHA(T).

36. STRAUSS, ANSELM, reference 35 above, p. 153.

37. Ibid., p. 159.

CHAPTER 9

1. AUSTIN, JOHN (1873), *The Province of Jurisprudence Determined* (4th edition) (London: John Murray), p. 226; italics as in that text.

2. The classical statement of this criticism of Austin is in: DICEY, A. V. (1931), *The Law of the Constitution* (8th edition) (London: Macmillan). But Dicey has in his turn been criticized and superseded.

3. MACPHERSON, C. B. (1966), *The Real World of Democracy* (Oxford: Clarendon Press).

4. Matthew 25:29.

5. Ministers concerned with the Health Service are rather exceptionally well-documented: BEVAN, ANEURIN (1952), *In Place of Fear* (London: Heinemann); FOOT, MICHAEL (1975), *Aneurin Bevan* (London: Paladin); POWELL, J. E. (1976), *Medicine and Politics: 1975 and After* (earlier edition, 1966) (London: Pitman Medical); ROBINSON, KENNETH (1967), *Partnership in Medical Care* (Glasgow University Press); CROSSMAN, RICHARD (1972), *A Politician's View of Health Service Planning* (Glasgow University Press); CROSSMAN, RICHARD (1977), *Diaries of a Cabinet Minister*, especially vol. iii (London: Hamilton and Cape); OWEN, DAVID (1976), *In Sickness and in Health: The Politics of Medicine* (London: Quartet Books).

6. This relates to a declaration of faith about the American electorate by KEY, V. O. (1966), *The Responsible Electorate; Rationality in Presidential Voting, 1936–1960* (Cambridge, Mass.: Bellknap).

7. This is self-criticism: I tried to do so and failed in my contributions to: HAGUE, D. C., MACKENZIE, W. J. M., and BARKER, A. (eds) (1975), *Public Policy and Private Interests: The Institutions of Compromise* (London: Macmillan).

8. The latest position is set out in the *Second Proposals of the Health Services Board* (HC 358 of May 1978).

9. The title of an essay by DEVONS, ELY (1970), 'Government on the Inner Circle', in *Papers on Planning and Economics Management* (Manchester University Press).

10. NEWMAN, SIR GEORGE (1939), *The Building of a Nation's Health* (London: Macmillan).

11. See in particular, FINER, S. E. (1952), *The Life of Sir Edwin Chadwick*, vol. ii (London: Methuen and Co. Ltd).

12. HAMMOND, JOHN, and BARBARA (1932). *James Stansfeld; A Victorian Champion of Sex Equality* (London: Longman).

13. McKEOWN, THOMAS (1976), *The Role of Medicine: Dream, Mirage or Nemesis?* (London: Nuffield Provincial Hospitals Trust); which should be read with Professor Colin Dollery's respectful criticism in (1978), *The End of an Age of Optimism: Medical Science in Retrospect and Prospect* (London: Nuffield Provincial Hospitals Trust).

14. The best of all accounts of how a civil servant works in relation to his Minister and his colleagues is in: BUNBURY, SIR HENRY, and TITMUSS, R. M. (eds) (1957), *Lloyd George's Ambulance Wagon: The Memoirs of W. J. Braithwaite, C.B.* (London: Methuen).

15. W. PEMBER REEVES was the author of *State Experiments in Australia and New Zealand* (1902) (London: Grant Richards).

16. BARNARD, CHESTER (1938), *The Functions of the Executive* (Cambridge, Mass.: Harvard University Press).

17. SIMON, H. A. (1945), *Administrative Behavior* (2nd edition, 1957) (New York: Macmillan).

18. I do not want to change much in the chapter 'The Structure of Central Administration', in MACKENZIE, W. J. M. (1950), contributed to *British Government since 1918* (London: Allen & Unwin, for the RIPA).

19. There is, however, an excellent memoir of Dr Addison by Maurice Schock in the *Dictionary of National Biography, 1951–1960*.

20. Dr David Owen was Minister of State in the combined Department of Health and Social Security, but was not in the Cabinet at that time. Walter Elliott was a medical graduate of Glasgow, and went through the First World War as a registered doctor; but apparently he never practised thereafter.

21. MINISTRY OF RECONSTRUCTION (1919), *Public Health: the Present Problem and the Ministry of Health* (Reconstruction Pamphlet no. 23) (London: HMSO).

22. NEWMAN, SIR GEORGE (1939), *The Building of a Nation's Health*, pp. 112, 114 (London: Macmillan).

23. CROSSMAN, RICHARD (1976), *Diaries of a Cabinet Minister*, vol. 11, p. 774, 10 April 1968. (London: Hamilton and Cape).

24. CIVIL SERVICE DEPARTMENT (1978). *Civil Service Year Book*, Col. 376 (London: HMSO).

25. We are in such a situation at the beginning of August 1978; four cases of botulism, the first in the UK since 1922. Tinned salmon is suspected; the first problem is to have it all withdrawn from *all* shops at once, in spite of vague organization, uncertain legal power, and the uncertainty of the provisions for compensation. *Guardian's* headline (2 August 1978) is 'World Alert'.

26. NEWMAN, SIR GEORGE (1939), reference 10 above, p. 111, para. 1.

27. *National Health Service Act, 1946*. First Schedule—Central Council and Advisory Committees (London: HMSO).

28. *The Hospital and Health Services Yearbook* (1978) (London: Institute of Health Service Administrators).

29. NEWMAN, SIR GEORGE (1939), reference 10 above, pp. 467, 468.

30. WHEARE, SIR KENNETH (1955), *Government by Committee: An Essay on the British Constitution* (Oxford: Clarendon Press).

31. DEVONS, ELY, reference 9 above.

32. See Chapter 5, p. 77.

33. There were to be 37 single district areas. Districts are the basic unit of service (Grey Book, para. 1.15), yet they are purely administrative entities, not safeguarded by statute.

34. DEPARTMENT OF HEALTH AND SOCIAL SECURITY (1972), *Management Arrangements for the Reorganized National Health Service* ('Grey Book') (London: HMSO).

35. STRAUSS, ANSELM (1963), 'The Hospital as Negotiated Order', in FREIDSON, ELIOT (ed.), *The Hospital in Modern Society* (New York: Free Press); and see Chapter 8, p. 141 above.

36. LEVITT, RUTH (1976), *The Reorganized National Health Service* (London: Croom Helm).

37. Ibid., p. 46.

38. DEPARTMENT OF HEALTH AND SOCIAL SECURITY (1963), *Report of the Committee of Inquiry into the Recruitment, Training and Promotion of Administrative and Clerical Staff in the Hospital Service* (Chairman: Sir Stephen Lycett Green) (London: HMSO).

The King's Fund Report of 1977 is scarcely more optimistic: SHEGOG, R. F. A. (ed.), *The Education and Training of Senior Managers in the NHS— A Contribution to Debate* (London: King's Fund).

39. It is difficult to think of any important published study except: WALKER, NIGEL (1961), *Morale in the Civil Service: A Study of the Desk Worker* (Edinburgh University Press). There is certainly nothing comparable to the careful and imaginative work of Michel Crozier and his associates in France.

40. More money was promised in the Queen's Speech of 1 November 1978; but there will be a General Election and further inflation before the cheque is due for payment.

41. The question posed wherever he went by the investigative journalist in his once famous book: GUNTHER, JOHN (1947), *Inside U.S.A.*, 'Who runs this place?' (Foreword, p. xv) (London: Hamilton).

42. DEPARTMENT OF HEALTH AND SOCIAL SECURITY (1978), *Report of the Supply Board Working Group*, Appendix 12 (London: DHSS).

43. Treasury (1978), *The Government's Expenditure Plans 1978/79 to 1981/82*, vol. 1, Cmnd. 7049-1, p. 6. See also vol. 2 of the same paper, Part 2, ch. 11 (London: HMSO). Note that these are figures for the whole UK, not for England only.

44. This rule, and the rule against virement between revenue and capital budgets, were somewhat relaxed for a time; there are now new restrictions but nevertheless the principle has at last been conceded.

45. PARKER, H. M. D. (1957), *Manpower, A Study of War-Time Policy and Administration* (London: HMSO and Longman).

46. LASSWELL, H. D. (1936), *Politics* (reprinted 1951) (Glencoe: Free Press).

47. I associate this period with H. A. Goddard, Lord Nuffield's work study man, and with Miss D. M. Livock, the cost accountant, unpretentious people for whom I had a great regard.

48. All these on p. 10 of the 'Grey Book', reference 34 above.

49. MCCARTHY, LORD (1976), *Making Whitley Work: Review of the NHS Whitley Council* (London: DHSS). There is much relevant material in BERRIDGE, JOHN (1976), *A Suitable Case for Treatment: A Case-study of Industrial Relations in the NHS* (Open University Press).

50. Perhaps the most useful official papers on cash limits are: *The Attack on Inflation* (1975), Cmnd. 6151 (London: HMSO). 'Cash Limit Control of Public Expenditure' (1975), *Twelfth Report of the Expenditure Committee*, HC 535 (London: HMSO). 'Supply Estimates and Cash Limits' (1978), *Fourth Report of the Committee of Public Accounts*, HC 299, HC 341-vi (London: HMSO). Some impression of what life is like 'at the coal face' can be gained from Royal Commission on the National Health Service (1978), Research Paper no. 2, *Management of Financial Resources in the NHS* (London: HMSO).

51. Treasury, reference 43 above, para. 21.

52. See my references to CULYER, A. J. in Chapter 3, and in particular to: JONES-LEE, MICHAEL (1976), *The Value of Human Life: An Economic*

Analysis (London: M. Robertson) which reviews critically the economic literature on this question.

53. The classical guide to these problems in: COCHRANE, A. L. (1973), *Effectiveness and Efficiency: Random Reflections on the Health Service* (London: Nuffield Provincial Hospitals Trust).

54. Hence the cant phrase—'we've been RAWPed'. The comparable Scottish document (Scottish Health Authorities Revenue Equalization—SHARE) has caused less turmoil. I have not seen similar documents for Wales and for Northern Ireland.

55. Chapter 4, p. 39, and reference 28.

56. Preceded by DEPARTMENT OF HEALTH AND SOCIAL SECURITY (1976), *Priorities for Health and Personal Social Services in England: A Consultative Document* (London: HMSO).

57. Since 1976 called the Health Advisory Service. For its origins, see CROSSMAN, RICHARD, as reference 5, vol. iii, pp. 410 and 599.

58. This was shown visually in *The Psychiatric Block,* one of the series of nine documentary films about the Bolton Area Health Authority: re-broadcast on BBC2, 24 July 1978. The problem of 'grouping' the mentally handicapped has been taken up in a research paper published by the Campaign for the Mentally Handicapped: *Guardian,* 11 December 1978.

59. BAGEHOT, WALTER (1867). *The English Constitution,* chapter iii, part II.

60. 'Paradoxically, the condition has been enshrined in English law before it has been effectively defined in medicine or psychiatry. The term *psychopath* is administrative and legal rather than medical, and the problem is one for society as a whole and transcends the boundaries and competence of medicine.' MILLER, HENRY (1953), *Medicine and Society,* pp. 70, 71 (Oxford University Press).

61. DAWKINS, RICHARD (1976), *The Selfish Gene* (Oxford University Press).

62. TURNBULL, COLIN (1973). *The Mountain People* (London: Cape). Peter Brook saw the destructive implications of this negative instance and reshaped the book into a stage performance.

CHAPTER 10

1. MAO, CHAIRMAN (1967), 'On Contradiction' in *Selected Works,* vol. i, p. 322 (Peking: Foreign Languages Press).

2. See Chapter 9, p. 173, especially reference 50.

3. See reference 1 above, p. 331.

4. Both quotations from a report by Julia Langdon on the back page of the *Guardian,* 28 October 1978.

5. Ibid., 30 October 1978.

6. CLEGG, H. A. (1976), *Trade Unions under Collective Bargaining. A Theory based on Comparisons of Six Countries,* p. 32 (Oxford: Blackwell).

7. McCARTHY, Lord (1976), *Making Whitley Work: A Review of the NHS Whitley Council System* (London: HMSO).

8. DEPARTMENT OF HEALTH AND SOCIAL SECURITY, Press release, 23 October 1978.

INDEX